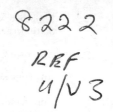
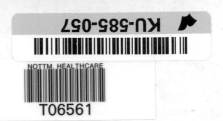

# The Mental Health Act Commission

## Eighth
Biennial Report
## 1997–1999

*Laid before Parliament by the
Secretary of State for Health
pursuant to Section 121 (10)
of the Mental Health Act 1983*

*London:* The Stationery Office

First published 1999

ISBN 0 11 322280 7




Mental Health Act Commission
Maid Marian House
56 Hounds Gate
Nottingham NG1 6BG

Tel: 0115 943 7100
Email: chief.executive@ms.mhac.trent.nhs.uk

Printed in the United Kingdom for The Stationery Office.
J0084102 C20 7/99 10170

# Contents

# Acknowledgments

The Commission wishes to thank the Trusts, social services departments, mental nursing homes, High Security Hospitals and health authorities, throughout England and Wales, for the assistance and courtesy shown to Commission Members during their visits.

This Report is based upon information supplied by the Commission's Visiting Teams through the Convenor of each team, plus contributions from individual Members of the Commission. Their invaluable assistance is gratefully acknowledged.

The main body of this Report was prepared by Jeffrey Cohen, the Commission's Policy Co-ordinator; Tony Wishart, Commission Member and Matt Kinton from the Commission's Secretariat.

# Chairman's Foreword

In her foreword to the last Biennial Report, Dame Ruth Runciman, Chairman of the Commission for most of the period covered by this Report, emphasised that the focus of the last few years on the provision of mental health care in the community should be matched by a commitment to provide a consistently high standard of in-patient care for the mentally ill, especially those detained under the Mental Health Act. In carrying out its statutory duties the Commission has been very conscious of its responsibility to contribute to this process.

During the period April 1997 to March 1999, the Commission has undertaken over 1,500 visits to mental health units, had private meetings with over 15,000 detained patients, made informal contact with 8,000 others and checked over 10,000 statutory documents. This marks a substantial increase over the previous reporting period. There has also been a substantial increase in the provision of second opinions, partly as a consequence of the rise in the detained patient population following the Court of Appeal judgment in December 1997 in the Bournewood case. As a result of these activities, the Commission has collected a substantial amount of quantitative and qualitative information on the care and treatment of detained patients.

It is a fundamental principle that those subject to compulsion by reason of mental disorder should be assured of an appropriate standard of care and treatment including the provision of a safe, calm and therapeutic environment and the proper observation of rights and entitlements. In the period under review the Commission has visited many services that more than adequately achieve these objectives, but a significant number do not and some fail to provide even an acceptable level of service. The challenge for the immediate future is effectively to address this significant variation in standards and the Commission looks forward to pursuing its remit and responsibilities within the context of the emerging NHS Quality Framework, including the new National Service Framework for Mental Health.

The proportion of in-patients detained under the Act continues to increase but the reasons for this upward trend are not fully understood. Of particular significance is the rise in the number of patients detained following informal admission. This may be a consequence of the professionals' desire to avoid compulsion at the point of admission and to treat patients in the least restrictive circumstances possible. It may also indicate that a number of patients are not prepared to stay on a voluntary basis because of the environmental conditions in some hospitals, the high level of disturbance on the wards and the lack of therapeutic activities. In addition, the Bournewood case highlighted the significant number of patients who lack capacity, are compliant with treatment but who, if they did attempt to leave, would be prevented from doing so. The distinction between patients who are formally detained and some informal patients who are de facto detained has always been blurred, with the latter being under duress but without the safeguards provided by the Act.

The high proportion of detained and de facto detained patients, and the increase in the pressure on beds in some areas, has resulted in a significantly changed patient population with a rising number of patients who are a serious risk to themselves or others. Concurrently there is a shortage of staff with the training and skills to deal appropriately with the increase in the number of patients presenting high levels of disturbance and management problems. The interests of staff and patients alike require that more attention is paid to these issues so that greater consistency, efficacy and fairness of treatment can be achieved. Consequently, the Commission welcomes the steps taken by the Chief Nursing Officers of England and Wales to improve practice guidance and training for staff in acute in-patient care settings.

The Code of Practice also provides those with responsibilities under the Act with authorative guidelines on its practical application. The third edition of the Code, which was published in March 1999, contains many detailed changes and frequent references to its guidance are made throughout this report. The Commission has also taken the opportunity presented by the publication of the revised Code to provide briefing sessions for those who deliver mental health services.

In July 1998 the Government announced a root and branch review of the Mental Health Act and in September appointed an expert group led by Professor Genevra Richardson to advise on the scope of the issues to be considered. The Committee is due to submit its proposals to Government at about the same time as this report is to be published. One of the main purposes of the Biennial Report is to comment on the operation of the Act. In describing the Commission's activities over the last two years, this report draws attention to some of the difficulties in interpreting and applying the current legislation in the hope that it will inform the debate when the Government consults on its proposals for legislative change.

In conclusion, I would like to pay tribute to the enormous contribution that Dame Ruth Runciman made during her period of chairmanship. Her energy, enthusiasm and dedication, combined with her strategic vision reinforced the impact the Commission has had in highlighting the needs of detained patients. The increase in the level of Commission activity over the last four years, particularly in the amount of direct contact Commissioners have had with detained patients, together with improvements in the Commission's ability to collect, interpret and disseminate information, is due in large measure to her leadership. Her commitment to the equalisation of opportunities has encouraged the Commission to develop policies and practices that seek to identify and address inequalities in the provision of mental health services. The principle that every patient should receive a non-discriminatory, high quality service continues to underpin every aspect of the Commission's work.

*Gordon Lakes*
*Acting Chairman*

# Rhagair Y Cadeirydd

Yn ei rhagair i'r Adroddiad Dwyflynyddol, fe bwysleisiodd y Fonesig Ruth Runciman, Cadeirydd y Comisiwn am y rhan fwyaf o'r cyfnod a gaiff ei gwmpasu yn yr adroddiad hwn, y dylai'r canolbwynt a roddwyd yn yr ychydig flynyddoedd diwethaf ar ddarpariaeth gofal iechyd meddwl yn y gymuned gael ei gyfateb gan ymrwymiad i ddarparu safon gyson uchel o ofal cleifion mewnol ar gyfer y rhai sydd ag afiechyd meddwl, yn enwedig y rhai dan orchymyn yn unol â'r Ddeddf Iechyd Meddwl. Wrth iddo gynnal ei ddyletswyddau statudol y mae'r Comisiwn wedi bod yn ymwybodol iawn o'i gyfrifoldeb i gyfrannu tuag at y broses hon.

Yn ystod y cyfnod Ebrill 1997 hyd at Fawrth 1999, y mae'r Comisiwn wedi ymgymryd â thros 1,500 o ymweliadau ag unedau iechyd meddwl, wedi cael cyfarfodydd preifat gyda thros 15,00 o gleifion dan orchymyn, wedi llunio cyswllt anffurfiol gydag 8,000 o rai eraill a gwirio dros 9,000 o ddogfennau statudol. Y mae hyn yn dangos cynnydd sylweddol dros y cyfnod adrodd yn ôl blaenorol. Fe fu cynnydd sylweddol yn ogystal mewn darpariaethau ail farn, yn rhannol o ganlyniad i'r twf yn y boblogaeth cleifion dan orchymyn yn dilyn dyfarniad y Llys Apêl yn Rhagfyr 1997 yn achos Bournewood. Y mae'r Comisiwn wedi casglu swmp sylweddol o wybodaeth feintiol ac ansoddol sy'n deillio o'r gweithgareddau hyn.

Y mae'n egwyddor sylfaenol bod y rhai hynny sy'n wrthrych gorfodaeth oherwydd anhwyldeb meddyliol yn cael sicrwydd o safon gofal a thriniaeth briodol yn cynnwys darpariaeth o amgylchedd diogel, tawel a therapiwtig a chadwraeth briodol o hawliau a breintiau. Yn y cyfnod dan arolwg y mae'r Comisiwn wedi ymweld â llawer o wasanaethau sy'n mwy na chyrraedd yr amcanion hyn yn foddhaol, ond y mae nifer arwyddocaol nad ydynt yn gwneud hyn ac y mae rhai sy'n methu â darparu hyd yn oed lefel gwasanaeth sy'n foddhaol. Yr her ar gyfer y dyfodol agos yw ymdrin yn effeithiol â'r amrywiaeth arwyddocaol mewn safonau ac y mae'r Comisiwn yn edrych ymlaen mewn dilyn ei gylch gwaith a'i gyfrifoldebau o fewn cyd-destun Fframwaith newydd Ansawdd GIG gan gynnwys y Fframwaith Gwasanaeth Cenedlaethol newydd ar gyfer iechyd meddwl.

Y mae cydran gynyddol o gleifion mewnol dan orchymyn yn unol â'r Ddeddf er nad yw'r rhesymau dros hyn wedi cael eu deall yn llawn. O arwyddocâd neilltuol, yw'r nifer o gleifion dan orchymyn yn dilyn derbyniadau anffurfiol. Fe all hyn fod o ganlyniad i awydd y bobl broffesiynol i osgoi gorfodaeth ar adeg y derbyn ac i drin y cleifion o dan yr amgylchiadau lleiaf cyfyngol ag sy'n bosibl. Fe all yn ogystal ddynodi nad yw llawer o'r cleifion yn barod i aros yn wirfoddol oherwydd yr amodau y maent yn eu canfod mewn rhai ysbytai, y lefel uchel o aflonyddwch ar y wardiau a'r diffyg gweithgareddau therapiwtig. Yn ychwanegol at hyn, fe amlygodd achos Bournewood y nifer arwyddocaol o gleifion sydd â diffyg cymhwyster, sy'n ufudd o ran derbyn triniaeth ond sydd, os ydynt yn gwneud ymgais i adael, yn cael eu hatal rhag gwneud hynny. Y mae'r gwahaniaeth rhwng cleifion dan orchymyn ffurfiol a rhai cleifion anffurfiol sydd mewn gwirionedd dan orchymyn, bob amser wedi bod yn annelwig gyda'r olaf o dan orchymyn ond heb y mesurau diogelwch a gynhwysir yn y Ddeddf.

Y mae'r gydran uchel o gleifion dan orchymyn a'r cleifion dan orchymyn mewn ffaith, a'r cynnydd yn y pwysau ar welyau mewn rhai ardaloedd, yn golygu newid arwyddocaol ym mhoblogaeth y cleifion gyda nifer cynyddol o gleifion sydd yn ddifrifol beryglus iddynt hwy eu hunain ac i eraill. Y mae prinder staff sydd â'r hyfforddant a'r sgiliau i ddelio'n briodol gyda'r cynnydd sydd yn nifer y cleifion sy'n cyflwyno lefelau uchel o aflonyddwch a phroblemau rheolaeth. Y mae buddiannau'r staff a'r cleifion fel ei gilydd yn gofyn am dalu mwy o sylw i'r materion hyn er mwyn cyrraedd mwy o gysondeb, effcithiolrwydd a thcgwch mewn triniaeth. O ganlyniad y mae'r Comisiwn yn croesawu'r camau a gymerwyd gan Brif Swyddogion Nyrsio Lloegr a Chymru i wella'r cyfarwyddyd ymarfer a'r hyfforddiant i staff sydd mewn cefndir gofal cleifion mewnol difrifol.

Y mae'r Côd Ymarfer yn erfyn hanfodol i'r holl rai sydd â chyfrifoldebau yn ôl y Ddeddf ar sut i fwrw 'mlaen pan fyddant yn ymgymryd â'u dyletswyddau. Y mae trydydd rhifyn o'r Côd, a gafodd ei gyhoeddi yn Chwefror 1999, yn cynnwys nifer o newidiadau manwl a fe wneir cyfeiriadau aml at y cyfarwyddyd sydd ynddo drwy gydol yr adroddiad hwn. Yn ychwanegol at hyn y mae'r Comisiwn wedi manteisio ar y cyfle a gyflwynwyd oherwydd cyhoeddi'r Côd diwygiedig i ddarparu sesiynau briffio ar gyfer darparwyr gwasanaethau iechyd meddwl.

Yng Ngorffennaf 1998 fe gyhoeddodd y Llywodraeth adolygiad cyflawn ar y Ddeddf Iechyd Meddwl ac ym Mis Medi fe benodwyd ganddynt grp arbenigol o dan arweiniad yr Athro Generva Richardson i gynghori ar gwmpas y materion a oedd i'w hystyried. Fe arfaethir i'r Pwyllgor gyflwyno ei gynigion i'r Llywodraeth ar o gwmpas yr un adeg ag y bydd yr adroddiad hwn yn cael ei gyhoeddi. Un prif bwrpas cyhoeddi'r Adroddiad Dwyflynyddol yw rhoi sylwadau ar weithrediad y Ddeddf. Wrth ddisgrifio gweithrediadau'r Comisiwn dros y ddwy flynedd diwethaf, y mae'r adroddiad hwn yn talu sylw arbennig i rai o'r anawsterau sydd mewn dehongli a chymhwyso'r ddeddfwriaeth bresennol yn y gobaith y bydd yn cyfrannu gwybodaeth at y ddadl pan fydd y Llywodraeth yn ymgynghori ar ei chynigion ar gyfer newidiadau deddfwriaethol.

Yn olaf, fe hoffwn i dalu teyrnged i'r cyfraniad aruthrol a wnaed gan y Fonesig Ruth Runciman yn ystod cyfnod ei chadeiryddiaeth. Fe fu ei hegni, ei brwdfrydedd a'i hymrwymiad, wedi'i gyfuno â'i harweinyddiaeth strategol gref yn fodd i atgyfnerthu'r effaith a gafodd y Comisiwn mewn amlygu anghenion cleifion dan orchymyn. Y mae'r cynnydd yn lefel gweithgarwch y Comisiwn dros y pedair blynedd olaf, yn enwedig ym maint y cyswllt uniongyrchol a gafodd y Comisiwn gyda chleifion dan orchymyn, ynghyd â'r gwelliannau yng ngallu'r Comisiwn i gasglu, dehongli a dosbarthu gwybodaeth, i'w dadogi i raddau helaeth i'w harweinyddiaeth hi. Y mae ei hymrwymiad i gyfartaleddu cyfleoedd wedi arwain at i'r Comisiwn ddatblygu polisïau ac ymarferion sy'n ceisio canfod ac ymdrin ag anghyfartaleddau yn narpariaeth gwasanaethau iechyd meddwl. Y mae'r Comisiwn yn parhau'n ymroddedig i'r egwyddor y dylai pob un claf dderbyn gwasanaeth o ansawdd, nad yw'n wahaniaethol.

*Gordon Lakes*
*Cadeirydd Dros Dro*

# Chapter 1

# Structure and Function of the Mental Health Act Commission

## Summary

*The Eighth Biennial Report covers the period April 1997 to March 1999.*

*An internal organisational review has recommended improvements in the Commission's visiting function, the refocusing of meetings with social services departments and the strengthening of the Commission's policy making arm*

*The Commission continues to take steps to ensure that there is good representation of women and black and ethnic minority groups in its membership, that they contribute to the work of the Commission at all levels and that all Commission members and staff have an awareness of the barriers which can prevent women and people from black and ethnic minorities from receiving a service which meets their needs, including from the Commission itself.*

*The Commission made a detailed submission to the Mental Health Legislation Scoping Study Review Team. It put forward the view that any successor body to the Commission should retain the function of meeting with patients subject to powers of compulsion both in hospital and community.*

*The Commission has run a programme of briefing sessions for local providers of mental health services to promote and enhance the use of the revised Code of Practice.*

*On May 11th, 1999, the Commission's second National Visit took place. The object of the Visit was to build up a picture of current policies and practice in the handling of race and culture issues.*

# Structure and Function of the

# Mental Health Act Commission

## General Role of the Commission

1.1   The main role of the Commission, which is a Special Health Authority, is to keep under review the operation of the Mental Health Act 1983 (the Act) as it relates to the detention of patients, or to patients liable to be detained, under the Act in England or Wales. In pursuit of that role the Commission:

- visits and meets detained patients in private; to this end all hospitals and registered nursing homes providing care and treatment for patients detained under the Act are visited on average twice each year;

- inspects the records relating to any patient who is or has been detained;

- meets with representatives of social services departments at least every two years to discuss their responsibilities under the Act;

- investigates complaints that fall within the Commission's complaints remit;

- monitors the operation of the consent to treatment safeguards set out in Part IV of the Act and appoints doctors to give second opinions;

- publishes a Biennial Report that is laid before Parliament; this is the eighth such Report which covers the period April 1997 to March 1999;

- monitors the operation of the Mental Health Act Code of Practice.

In addition the Commission is encouraged by the Secretary of State to advise on policy matters that fall within the Commission's remit.

1.2   The Commission's role is visitorial and only to a limited extent is it able to act as an 'inspectorate'. This was acknowledged in the Report of the Committee of Inquiry into the Personality Disorder Unit, Ashworth Special Hospital (Fallon, 1999), which stated that "at present it [the Commission] has neither the resources nor the statutory remit to undertake detailed inspections". The Commission does, however, comment on environmental standards and the extent to which the guidance in the Mental Health Act Code of Practice is observed. The Code is the Commission's primary source of standards.

1.3   The following extracts from the White Paper which preceded the Act outline some of the founding principles and expectations of the Commission.

*Extracts from Reform of Mental Health Legislation White Paper (1981)*

.....the proposed functions of the Commission will be separate to other inspectorial bodies; the Commission will not inspect and report on services in mental illness and mental handicap in hospitals and units in the way that the Health Advisory Service or the Development Team for the Mentally Handicapped do. The Commission's concern will be the particular problems which arise from detention of specific individuals in hospital rather than the general services which affect all mentally ill and mentally handicapped patients. The name "Mental Health Act Commission" has been chosen deliberately to emphasise its responsibilities for seeing that patients have full advantage of all the available legal safeguards under the Act... (para. 34).

[.....the Commission will appoint SOADs (Second Opinion Appointed Doctors).] This will ensure that the opinions are independent and will enable the Commission both to monitor the use of the power to impose treatment and to offer advice on professional and ethical complexities...the Commission will build up considerable expertise in the care and treatment of detained patients and particularly on consent to treatment. They will be able to include in the Code of Practice and in other publications advice about all aspects of the care and treatment of detained patients and guidance on the giving of treatment for mental disorder with or without the patient's consent. (para. 39)

.....the Mental Health Act Commission will therefore be given important responsibilities, on behalf of the Secretary of State, on consent to treatment as well as its more general protective function for detained patients. It will also be a forum for inter-professional discussion of issues concerning the law and ethics on the treatment of detained patients. The Commission will thus have a central role in the working of the revised Mental Health Act. (para. 40)

1.4    Although not formally part of its remit, the Commission responds to a substantial number of queries (up to 10 letters in any one week plus phone calls) about the detailed implementation of the Act. The Commission is not entitled to give formal legal advice (this should be provided by legal advisers), but is usually willing to offer a view on the matter of law or practice raised in the correspondence or phone call. The Commission has recommended that consideration is given in the context of the new mental health legislation to the advantages of the Commission or any successor body being properly equipped and authorised to provide advice, especially urgent advice about the implementation of compulsory mental health powers.

1.5    Further details about the various functions of the Commission can be found in its Policy on Openness, which can be found at Appendix 1. The policy has been updated, taking account of the Code of Practice on Access to Government Information issued in January 1997. The provisions of the Public Bodies (Admission to Meetings) Act 1960 have been extended to the Commission and notification of the dates of meetings of the Commission's Management Board, which take place approximately every 8 weeks, can be obtained from the Commission's office in Nottingham.

# Organisation of the Commission and Review of the Central Structure

1.6 The Commission has 150 members drawn from a range of disciplines in mental health and related fields and all having a knowledge of and interest in mental health and learning disability issues. They are recruited by national advertisement and after formal interview recommendations are made as to their suitability for appointment by the Secretary of State for Health or Secretary of State for Wales. Commission members fall into two categories: visiting Commission members whose primary duties include examining statutory documentation, meeting with detained patients and taking up immediate issues on their behalf, and Commission members who, in addition, lead the small groups which undertake the visits and write the visit reports. On average, members and visiting members commit two to three days a month to Commission activity. A list of all those who have been members/visiting members of the Commission in this reporting period and their professional backgrounds can be found at Appendix 2.

1.7 With the exception of the Chairman and Vice-Chairman and four Commissioners who undertake specialist tasks (i.e. the co-ordination of policy, complaints and advising on legal issues), members are attached to seven regionally-based Commission Visiting Teams (CVTs) or to one of the three High Security Hospital Panels. For each CVT or Panel, a Convenor is appointed for 3 or 4 days each month to take overall responsibility for management of the members and the organisation of visits.

1.8 The Commission has a duty under Section 121(2)(a) of the Act to appoint independent registered medical practitioners as Second Opinion Appointed Doctors (SOADs) to consider treatment plans for treatments falling within the provisions of Section 58, and also to appoint other persons to validate treatments falling within the provisions of Section 57. A list of SOADs and the Panel of Appointed Persons can be found at Appendix 3 (see 6.24 for further information about these appointments).

1.9 The Commission Secretariat has a staff of 34, who are Department of Health civil servants on secondment to the Commission. The staff are divided into teams to provide administrative support to the Board, the CVTs and Panels, the administration of SOAD referrals and other Commission activities; eg. the policy and complaints functions of the Commission.

1.10 The Commission has undertaken a review of its central organisational structure and associated costs. The purpose of the review was to consider how the Commission could make the most efficient use of its resources to enable it to undertake its statutory responsibilities as effectively as possible and reflect the developing needs of the Commission.

1.11 The Board has decided that it should step back from the executive management of the Commission to concentrate on strategic and directional issues, holding a strengthened Executive Management Team accountable for operational issues. It is accepted that there is a need to consolidate and reinforce the policy arm of the Commission to enable it to develop the guidance and information given out on the increasingly complex issues faced in mental health care and treatment. A strengthened policy team will also take over responsibility for the Commission's complaints remit.

1.12    In order to improve the management of the visiting function of the Commission, consideration is being given to the replacement of the 10 Convenor posts over the next two years with four area managers, who would be required to work for 8 to 12 days a month for the Commission. This change process would involve combining the High Security Hospital panels with teams visiting other psychiatric provision within the same geographical region, reflecting moves towards accountability of the High Security Hospitals to the respective NHS Executive Regional Offices and the regional commissioning of secure services.

## Implementation of Equal Opportunities Policy

1.13    The Commission cannot expect other agencies to provide services founded upon the principles of equality without demonstrating that it has incorporated such principles into its own practices. This requires steps to be taken to ensure that there is good representation of women and black and ethnic minority groups in the Commission's membership and that all Commission members and staff have an awareness and understanding of the barriers which can prevent women and people from black and ethnic minorities from receiving a service which meets their needs, including from the Commission itself.

1.14    The context for the Commission's strategy on equal opportunities is the Equal Opportunities Policy Statement adopted in 1996 and published in full in the last Biennial Report (p. 216/7). This states that:

*"All staff, Commission members and appointees will:*

- *provide an equal service to all regardless of their age, colour, culture, gender, health, status, mental ability, mental health, offending background, physical ability, political beliefs, race, religion, sexuality or other specific factors which result in discrimination.*

- *in the exercise of their duties be committed to the promotion of good practice and equal access to all service users by purchasers and providers of mental health services taking into account our diverse society."*

1.15    Women's issues, race and culture and disability have been the main areas on which the Commission has concentrated in its implementation of Equal Opportunities Policy during this reporting period.

### Women

1.16    Issues concerning the quality of care for detained women patients are considered in chapter 10 of this Report (see 10.57 et seq). However, the Commission has also been considering changes within its own organisation and culture which might enable it to address women's issues more effectively. Visit reports will normally comment on women's issues and use terminology which refers to patients as men and women rather than male and female. At least one woman member will be assigned to each visit team, unless exceptional circumstances dictate otherwise, and where possible women patients should be given the opportunity to meet with a woman Commission member.

1.17   Of 146 members who undertake Commission visits, 67 (46%) are women. However, there is a significant under-representation of women within the Commission's policy or special interest groups and within the Convenor group. The Commission has a number of talented women members who, for a variety of reasons, have not been able to take up opportunities to contribute to the work of the Commission at the highest level. The Board has a continuing commitment to create a climate conducive to the recruitment of women and which encourages them to contribute at every level within the Commission.

## Race and Culture

1.18   The Stephen Lawrence Inquiry Report (Macpherson, 1999) and its definition of "institutional racism" has had an impact on all government departments in that they are having to consider by what means such issues can be tackled within their own organisations. The Commission has long been conscious of the problems associated with institutional racism and had attached a high priority to tackling these issues well before the Stephen Lawrence Inquiry reported. A phased programme of action was begun in 1995 and for the first phase, three target areas were selected as a focus during visits, namely ethnic monitoring, racial harassment and the use of interpreters. Training and recruitment are two other components of the Commission's strategy to tackle race and culture issues.

1.19   During 1998/9, the Commission started a training programme to equip its members and staff to deal with the three target areas. The programme was evaluated by the participants and an independent analysis of the comments concluded that "Commissioners demonstrated that they would put the knowledge gained from the training into practice on visits and made many creative and useful suggestions concerning how they will do this" (Harris, J, 1999). The analysis also provides a resource to inform the Commission on the development of further training programmes.

1.20   The Commission intends to make the ethnic composition of its membership more representative of the community it serves. Black and ethnic minority patients may find it easier to talk to a Commission member from a similar ethnic background, particularly when discussing race and culture issues. An increased black and ethnic minority membership should instil more confidence in the Commission's sensitivity to race and culture issues, even if it may not always be practically possible for patients to meet with a Commission Member from a particular ethnic background.

1.21   The percentage of the current Commission membership from black and other ethnic minorities is 13%. Approximately 17% of detained patients are from black and ethnic minority groups (see table 18, para. 10.46), but the Commission has agreed with Ministers a higher target of at least 20% membership from such groups. Consequently, the Commission has decided to engage in a large scale project in 1999 with the threefold aims of:

- investigating mental health service provision issues for people from black and minority ethnic communities with particular reference to detained patients;

- raising the profile of the Mental Health Act Commission with black and minority ethnic communities; and

- identifying people from these communities with the potential to become members of the Commission.

1.22   The Ethnicity and Health Unit, University of Central Lancashire has been commissioned to arrange a series of consultation, advice and information giving sessions with purchasers, providers and user groups involved in mental health services for black and minority ethnic communities culminating in a series of seminars across the country.

### Disability

1.23   The Commission has produced internal guidance to ensure that its recruitment procedures comply with the Disability Discrimination Act 1995 (DDA). Commission members are Government appointments and as such, fall outside Part II of the DDA, but the Commission seeks to implement the spirit of the Act by adopting good practice procedures based on its requirements. Commission members may be assisted by accompanied visiting, special transport arrangements and communication aids. The Commission's office building has been extensively refurbished and is fully equipped with the essential requirements to assist people with a disability.

## Submission to the Mental Health Legislation Scoping Study Review Team

1.24   From the publication of its Fifth Biennial Report in 1993, the Commission has recommended that the Mental Health Act 1983 should be subject to a full review and therefore welcomes the decision by the Department of Health to commission 'a root and branch review' of the Act. The Commission made a detailed submission to the Mental Health Legislation Review Team and reference is made throughout this Biennial Report to deficiencies in the current Act's provisions as well as difficulties in its interpretation and application within the context of service delivery in the late 1990s.

1.25   One of the key themes identified in the Scoping Study was the role the Commission has to play in the provision of safeguards under the Act. Any future role would need to take account of the emerging quality and performance framework for health and social services. The National Service Framework for Mental Health will set standards to be monitored externally in different ways, including by the Commission for Health Improvement and the proposed Commissions for Care Standards. Nevertheless, detained psychiatric patients remain one of the most vulnerable groups in society and it is the Commission's view that any successor body to it should retain, as at least a part of its overall function, the particular activities of visiting detained patients, highlighting their concerns and focussing very specifically on the operation of the Mental Health Act. The enactment of new legislation would also provide an opportunity to address the Commission's past request that its remit should be extended to cover informal incapable patients subject to de facto detention and to patients subject to Guardianship, Supervised Discharge or their equivalents under new legislation. Indeed, should wider compulsory powers for community treatment be enacted, it is vital that the remit of any monitoring organisation such as the Commission is extended to those patients who are subject to such powers.

1.26   As noted above, the Commission acts primarily as a visitorial body rather than as an inspectorate. It does not have any statutory powers to direct that service providers should implement its recommendations. The Commission does have a Special Procedure, which allows it to brief Ministers on matters of serious and persistent concern that fall within its remit. It was envisaged that the procedure would be used rarely, as it is the Commission's experience that a high proportion of its recommendations are accepted and since the Special Procedure was introduced in October 1996, the Commission has not found it necessary to invoke it. However, if the Commission or its successor body were to take on an inspectorial role, one  way of providing it with sanctions against failing service providers could be through a role in the registration or accreditation of services (see 5.44 et seq).

## The Evaluation of Data Collected by the Commission

1.27   As part of the review of the Mental Health Act, the Department of Health has commissioned Nottingham University to review the information collected by the Commission from 1983 to 1998. The largest and most detailed part of the study is an analysis of information from some 20,000 second opinion visits that have taken place since 1995 and of files containing reports and correspondence about the visiting programme since records were centralised in 1990. Archival material reflecting the activity of the Commission over the years between 1983 and 1995 will also be reviewed to provide less detailed information about historical trends in consent to treatment and the development of institutions treating detained patients. The research team will report in the year 2000 and its findings may be expected to influence consideration of how the Commission or any successor body could contribute to future developments in mental health legislation.

## The Revised Code of Practice

1.28   A revised Code of Practice came into force on April 1st 1999, replacing the second edition of the Code which had been operational from November 1993. While the Code of Practice is prepared by the Department of Health and the Welsh Office, the Commission has a responsibility for submitting proposals to Ministers for changes it considers necessary and for monitoring its implementation. A draft revision of the code was circulated for comments in 1996 by the Department of Health. Following a delay while the Bournewood case was being considered by the House of Lords, it was eventually laid before Parliament in December 1998. An outline of the changes is given in Chapter 2 and reference is made to some of the detailed changes throughout the rest of this Report.

1.29 In order to enhance knowledge about the revised Code and promote its use, the Commission offered to run briefing sessions for local providers of mental health services. The briefing takes a day and is led by two or three Commission members. It includes a general overview of the main changes and a series of workshop sessions covering particular topics and chapters in the Code in more detail. It gives managers and practitioners the opportunity to explore with the Commission how any problems in implementing the Code might be overcome in particular localities. There was a substantial take-up of this offer (with approximately 100 sessions run) and an enthusiastic response to the Commission's initiative of carrying out its remit of promoting the Code in this way. The following, for example, is a comment received from the Chairman of Sussex Weald and Downs NHS Trust on behalf of the Mental Health Act managers, who attended the briefing session.

*"I can say with certainty, that the non executive directors and associate hospital managers found it extremely useful to be led through the Code of Practice in such an authoritative way. It was also helpful to focus on this aspect of the Trust's responsibilities with a wide cross-section of practitioners from both health and social services. Thus, the workshop discussion time was equally useful and stimulating."*

At the end of the day, participants are asked to evaluate each part of the programme on a scale of 1 (poor) to 5 (excellent); an average score of 3.9 has been achieved.

1.30 To monitor compliance with the Code of Practice, the Commission may check during a visit that:

- wards have a copy of the Code of Practice (March 1999 edition);
- there are arrangements to ensure that patients have access to the Code;
- there are regular training sessions on the Code of Practice for doctors, nurses, ASWs and other mental health practioners and managers; and
- there is a programme of audit of specific policies and procedures which appear in the Code.

The Commission has copied to provider units a list of local policies and procedures which the Code of Practice specifies should be drawn up in a range of circumstances. Commission members may seek to ascertain whether providers have been able to implement selected policies and procedures.

## The Bournewood Case

1.31 The case of L v Bournewood Community & Mental Health NHS Trust cast a long shadow over the reporting period (see 2.12 et seq for details and discussion of the case). The Court of Appeal held on 2nd December 1997 that patients who lack capacity to consent to hospital admission cannot receive treatment for mental disorder as informal patients even though they have not expressed dissent. The position was reversed by the House of Lords on 25th June 1998, but in the intervening period of 6 months there was considerable uncertainty about what steps Mental Health Act managers and others with responsibilities under the Act needed to take to ensure compliance with the Court of Appeal judgment. The Commission issued an interim Guidance Note on the implications of the case, giving its opinion on how those providing medical treatment for mental disorder should ensure that those who fell within the Court of Appeal's judgment should be detained in accordance with the provisions of the Act.

1.32    Such was the significance of the case that the Commission took the unusual step of submitting to the House of Lords a petition for leave to intervene. This was granted and the Commission's written submission sought to provide information about the beneficial consequences of the judgment of the Court of Appeal in the extension of the safeguards of the Act to the compliant incapacitated patient, but also to highlight some of the resource implications and the uncertainties which arose in the implementation of the judgment.

## The Commission's National Visits

1.33    The Commission's first National Visit took place in 1996, when 309 acute admission and intensive care wards in 118 NHS Trusts were visited in one day. The aim of the Visit was to obtain a picture across England and Wales of specific aspects of mental health provision of central importance to the care and treatment of detained patients. The matters investigated were the number, qualifications and deployment of nursing staff, the adequacy and understanding of policy and procedures about leave for detained patients and the safety and privacy of women patients. The findings have had a significant impact at national level, providing an additional impetus to improving the quality of care and safety in psychiatric inpatient units.

1.34    The Commission's second National Visit took place on 11th May 1999 and was conducted in collaboration with the Sainsbury Centre for Mental Health and the Ethnicity and Health Unit, University of Central Lancashire. The object of this Visit was to look at the care and treatment of detained patients from black and ethnic minorities with a particular focus on the three target areas within the Commission's programme of action; i.e. ethnic monitoring, racial harassment and the use of interpreters. The provision of training in race equality and anti-discriminatory practice were also investigated as well as certain aspects of the care received.

1.35    A stratified sample of 117 units was selected from both the NHS and independent sectors, taking account of the size of the black and ethnic minority population for which a service was provided. The sample included acute admission wards, medium and high secure units and hospitals for people with learning disabilities. The intention was to build up a representative nationwide picture of current policies and practice in the handling of race and culture issues at a single point in time. The information obtained has not been attributed to any individual unit visited, although examples of good practice will be published with the permission of the provider involved.

## Commission Publications

1.36    The Commission publishes Guidance Notes (formerly called Practice Notes) which give advice on particular issues drawn to its attention. The Guidance Notes will generally refer to matters not included in the Mental Health Act Code of Practice. Occasionally they will provide amplification or explanation by the Commission of the Code. The Commission will, from time to time, also publish Position Papers and Discussion Papers containing its views on particular issues.

1.37    During this reporting period the Commission has published an interim Guidance Note on the Bournewood case following the Court of Appeal judgment and Guidance Notes on the treatment of anorexia nervosa under the Mental Health Act and the scrutiny and rectification of statutory forms. It has reviewed and substantially changed Practice Notes 3 and 4, replacing them with a new Guidance Note on issues surrounding Sections 17, 18 and 19 of the Act, which now includes a sample Section 17 leave form. At the time of going to press Practice Note 5, which provides guidance to mental nursing homes on the administration of the Act, is being revised to take account of changes in practice and legislation and to assist in the clarification of some potential areas of confusion.

1.38    All the Practice and Guidance Notes have been updated to accord with the 1999 edition of the Code of Practice. The Commission also issued in June 1998 a Discussion Paper, 'The Threshold for Admission and the Deteriorating Patient'. This offers a way forward for the compulsory re-admission of patients who are non-compliant with medication and are at risk of relapse (see 4.13 et seq).

## Contact with Governmental and other National Organisations

1.39    An annual meeting is held with the Minister of State for Health during which the Commission reviews its annual work programme. The Commission identifies a number of key issues to draw to the attention of the Minister. A similar meeting is a held with officials in the Welsh Office. The NHS Executive Regional Offices are kept informed of the Commission's observations on the implementation of the Act and standards of care for detained patients.

1.40    Annual meetings are held with the Chief Nursing Officers in England and Wales and with national bodies, including the Royal Colleges of Psychiatry and Nursing, the Association of Directors of Social Services, the Social Services Inspectorate, the Mental Health Unit in the Home Office, the NHS Confederation and the Independent Health Care Association. Such meetings provide an opportunity for the Commission to highlight some of the key themes arising from the Biennial Report and its visiting programme. In particular, they have served to focus attention on the key findings of the first National Visit; i.e the low level of contact between staff and patients, staff vacancies and the facilities for the privacy, safety and dignity of women.

## Examples of Good and Bad Practice

1.41    Examples used to illustrate practice points appear throughout this Report. Most are taken from visit reports and it continues to be the Commission policy to name the Trusts and mental nursing homes to which they refer. The exception to this policy is where it may be possible from the information given in the example to identify an individual patient. The examples are chosen to illustrate good or bad practice and the comments made often apply equally to many other providers. Where particular events or circumstances are cited, it must not be taken necessarily to imply that they are typical of the overall practices of the Trust or home in question.

1.42    Visit reports commend good practice as well as criticising bad. If the examples in this Report seem to relate more often to bad practice that is because they have been selected to point up matters causing concern. Where relevant, follow-up action which has been taken to improve practice and about which the Commission has been notified is reported.

# Chapter 2

# Changes in Law and the Code of Practice

## Summary

*A number of legislative changes have introduced greater controls over mentally disordered offenders, where serious offences have been committed, and brought about new distinctions between patients detained under Part II and Part III of the Act.*

*The Bournewood case has drawn attention to a group of patients who are unprotected by law. The Commission suggests a limited extension to its remit, which would enable it to monitor policies and procedures which have been developed in accordance with Health Service Circular 'L v Bournewood Community and Mental Health NHS Trust' (HSC 1998/122).*

*A selection of other cases occurring during the reporting period, including some heard by the European Court of Human Rights, is outlined in this chapter.*

*The Code of Practice has been substantially updated and amended to take account of the changes in law, policy and practice. Reference to some detailed changes is made in this chapter and also throughout the rest of this Report.*

# 2 Changes in Law and the Code of Practice

## Introduction

2.1 During the past two years there have been a number of changes in both legislation and case law that have had a particular impact on powers of detention and the care and treatment of patients subject to the provisions of the Mental Health Act. In addition, the Code of Practice has been substantially updated and amended to take account of the changes in law, policy and practice.

2.2 Concerns about public safety have been the driving force behind the legislative changes. A small number of highly publicised tragic incidents and related inquiries have prompted the Government to introduce measures to bring about greater controls over those with a history of mental disorder, particularly those at risk of offending. Case law has developed through patients and/or their representatives seeking redress from the courts when they believe that their rights have been infringed or that those with responsibilities under the Act have exceeded their powers. Two such cases, the Bournewood case and a case involving search powers at Broadmoor Hospital, were of such significance that the publication of the third edition of the Code of Practice was delayed so that any implications for the guidance offered in the Code could be considered.

2.3 Some of the main changes in legislation which affect detained patients, significant developments in case law and the key revisions in the Code of Practice are summarised in this chapter.

## Legislative Changes[1]

### New Powers under the Crime (Sentences) Act 1997

2.4 Section 46 of the Crime (Sentences) Act 1997 introduced new Sections, 45A and 45B, to the Mental Health Act 1983. Section 45A creates a power for the Crown Court to attach a hospital direction (and a limitation direction) when imposing a sentence of imprisonment on mentally disordered offenders who are assessed as suffering from psychopathic disorder. The

---

[1] A more comprehensive summary can be found in the Institute of Mental Health Law website: Mental Disordered Offenders and Sex Offenders: Developments since 1997 (http://www.imhl.com/mdo&sexoff.htm).

requirements for making a hospital direction (i.e. the procedures for giving medical evidence) are the same for making a restricted hospital order, but the Court is given the new option of directing to hospital when it considers that a custodial sentence is appropriate. If the offender is not benefiting from treatment, he or she can be transferred to prison at any time during the sentence by warrant of the Home Secretary under Section 50(1) of the Mental Health Act (see also Code of Practice, 3.16).

2.5     The new power has not been used to date as it can only be applied in cases where the crime was committed after 1st October 1997. In its submission to the Mental Health Legislation Review, the Commission has reiterated its reservations about this 'hybrid' order. The continued threat of transfer to prison may be anti-therapeutic in that it could sour relations between patients and staff and could even enable patients to avoid confronting their problems by engineering a retreat to prison. On the other hand, it can be argued that management problems may occur where patients cease to co-operate with their treatment and rehabilitation programmes, but are allowed to remain in hospital rather than being transferred back to prison.

2.6     Section 2 of the Crime (Sentences) Act requires the Court to impose an automatic life sentence on a person convicted of a second serious violent or sexual offence, unless there are exceptional circumstances. The Commission expressed concern in the Seventh Biennial Report (p. 185) about mentally disordered offenders, who might otherwise have been given a Hospital Order at the time of the court hearing, being committed to prison and adding to the backlog requiring transfer to hospital.

2.7     Other changes in the Crime (Sentences) Act include:

- an extension of the power of the courts or the Home Secretary to specify a particular hospital unit when making a hospital order with restrictions; the purpose of this power is to allow the courts or the Home Secretary to specify an appropriate level of security if there is a high risk of serious harm to others should the offender abscond;

- a provision for enabling the transfer of responsibility for supervising conditionally discharged patients between the separate jurisdictions of the British Islands (defined as the United Kingdom, the Channel Islands and the Isle of Man);

- the extension of interim hospital orders from six to twelve months duration; and

- removal of the ban on the transfer of prisoners by warrant of the Home Secretary under Sections 47 or 48 of the Mental Health Act 1983 to mental nursing homes.

## Police Powers to Register Mentally Disordered Offenders

### The Criminal Evidence (Amendment) Act 1997

2.8     This Act empowers police officers to take non-intimate samples (for example non-pubic hair, nail samples and mouth swabs) without consent, for DNA profiling purposes, from prisoners and patients detained under Part III of the Mental Health Act who were convicted of a relevant offence (or acquitted on the grounds of insanity or unfitness to plead) before 10th April 1995, when the national DNA database came into operation. Broadly speaking, relevant offences are sexual and violent offences and burglary. It was estimated that there were about 2,000 mentally disordered offenders in psychiatric hospitals to whom the new power applied, when it became operational on March 19th, 1997. The power to take a non-intimate sample applies only so long as the person is detained in hospital under the Act. Once a person is discharged, the power to take a sample lapses. The RMO may advise that the taking of sample should be deferred if the patient's mental condition makes it counter-therapeutic to subject the patient to the procedure.

**The Sex Offenders Act 1997**

2.9   This Act, which came into force on 1st September 1997, imposes requirements on sex offenders to notify the police of their name and address and any subsequent changes. The Act applies to people who are liable to be detained in hospital or subject to a Guardianship Order following conviction or cautioning for a relevant offence. Offenders must register within 14 days of release from detention, including leave of absence if the leave of absence is expected to last for 14 days or more (including aggregated days during any twelve month period).

2.10   Hospital managers are expected to support effective implementation of the Sex Offenders Act. Health Service Guidelines (HSG(97)37) advise that when a patient who has been convicted or cautioned for a relevant offence is discharged, managers should give serious consideration to notifying the local police. This may involve overriding the patient's consent to disclosure. Managers were also expected to ensure that patients already detained under Part III of the Mental Health Act when the Sex Offenders Act came into force were notified of the requirements to register.

2.11   Clinicians have only limited discretion over their compliance with these expectations to assist the police and some have raised concerns about how the therapeutic relationship may be compromised and how the role of psychiatrists, albeit in subtle and small ways, is increasingly becoming merged with the coercive powers of the criminal justice system. The requirements also introduce new distinctions between patients detained under Part II and Part III of the Act. They undermine the principle that once a mentally disordered offender is admitted to hospital under the Act without restriction on discharge, his or her position should be regarded as being almost exactly the same as a civil patient and that, in effect, he or she passes out of the penal system into the hospital regime (*R v Birch [1989]*, cited in Jones (1996) p168).

## The Bournewood Case

2.12   The case of *R v Bournewood Community and Mental Health Trust ex parte L [1998] 3 AER* concerned Mr L, a 48 year old autistic man who was unable to speak and was incapable of consenting either to admission or medical treatment. After almost thirty years in

Bournewood Hospital, he had been discharged into the hands of paid carers. In July 1997, however, he became extremely agitated and, in accordance with what were considered to be his best interests, was returned to Bournewood Hospital where he appeared to be fully compliant and did not resist admission. Although Mr L was considered to be an informal patient, his consultant psychiatrist stated that if he had resisted admission she would have sought to arrange for him to be detained under the Mental Health Act. The carers asked for the return of Mr L to them, but this was refused. Mr L, through his carers, then sought judicial review of the decision to detain him, a writ of *habeas corpus* to secure his release, and damages for false imprisonment and assault.

2.13 Refusing all the applications, the judge at first instance held that Mr L had not in fact been detained; he had been informally admitted under Section 131 of the Act and his consent was not required as long as he did not dissent from the admission. Whilst in hospital he was being lawfully treated under the common law doctrine of necessity.

2.14 Upon appeal, the Court of Appeal took a different view. It held that Mr L had in fact been detained because those with control over the premises intended that he should not leave and had the ability to prevent him from doing so. They further concluded that the Mental Health Act created a complete regime, which excluded the application of the common law doctrine of necessity. The right to detain a patient for treatment for mental disorder was contained only in the Act. Moreover, informal admission could only take place with the consent of the patient. The Court of Appeal was satisfied that Mr L had not been informally admitted, as he had not positively consented to admission. Nor was he detained under the Act. Therefore, it concluded, his detention was unlawful.

2.15 The implications of the Court of Appeal's decision were far-reaching. Whilst it was envisaged that many more patients would be afforded the statutory protection of the Mental Health Act, there was a fear that there would be a substantial increase in the demands placed on the mental health services. Bournewood Community and Mental Health NHS Trust subsequently appealed to the House of Lords which received written representations from the Mental Health Act Commission (see 1.31), particularly on the matter of the protection to be gained from admission under the Act. The Trust's appeal was upheld and the decision of the Court of Appeal reversed.

2.16 Giving the leading judgment, Lord Goff noted that Section 131 of the 1983 Act was drafted in identical terms to Section 5(1) of the Mental Health Act 1959. The origins of both could be traced directly back to the Percy Commission of 1954-57, which first recommended the creation of informal admission for those who were 'not unwilling' to receive care and treatment (Percy 1957). The Percy Commission particularly had in mind patients who were incapable of expressing a positive desire for treatment and who were until then required to be 'certified'. In the light of the statutory history, Lord Goff considered that the decision of the House of Lords must be that Section 131 applied both to patients who had positively consented to admission, and to those who, like Mr L, had not dissented.

2.17   On the matter of detention, there was division as to whether Mr L had in fact been detained. Lord Steyn memorably remarked, "The suggestion that 'L' was free to go is a fairy tale". There was, however, unanimity that any detention and treatment undertaken was justified by the doctrine of necessity and therefore lawful. Summarising the position, Lord Steyn said, "On orthodox principles of statutory interpretation the conclusion cannot be avoided that Section 131(1) permits the admission of compliant incapacitated patients where the requirements of the principle of necessity are satisfied". Going on to express concern as to an 'indefensible gap in our mental health law' created by the absence of statutory safeguards under the Act for this group of patients, he added that his only comfort was that the Secretary of State had, through his counsel, given an assurance that reform of mental health law was 'under active consideration'.

2.18   Whilst this case might appear to have changed little, it has drawn attention to a group of patients who are unprotected in law. In recognition of the need to ensure good practice, Health Service Circular 'L v Bournewood Community and Mental Health NHS Trust' (HSC 1998/122) was issued immediately following the House of Lords decision. This states that it is important to take account of the patient's ascertainable wishes and feelings and the views of relatives or carers on what would be in the patient's best interests – advice which has now been incorporated in the Code of Practice (2.8). The Circular additionally advises that it is good practice for the clinical team to arrange for incapacitated patients to be visited periodically by the hospital managers or by an independent advocate, if no-one from outside the hospital would otherwise take a continuing interest in their care. Bournewood makes it clear that, where informal admission and/or treatment relies on the doctrine of necessity, the principle to be applied is that outlined in the case of *Re F (Mental Patient: Sterilisation) [1990] 2 AC 1* namely " ... there must be necessity to act when it is not practicable to communicate with the patient", and "the action taken must be such as a reasonable person would in all the circumstances take, acting in the best interests of the patient".

2.19   The Commission has repeatedly made the request for its remit to be extended to cover the visiting of de facto detained patients. This would require a significant increase in the Commission's resources, given the number of such patients (see 4.6), but it is suggested that a more limited extension to enable it to monitor what policies and procedures have been developed in accordance with the Health Service Circular would go some way to plug the gap in the provision of independent oversight of the interests of incapable patients.

## Other Significant Cases

### The 'Broadmoor' Case

2.20   Among other cases of major significance was that of *R v Broadmoor Special Hospital Authority and Another, ex parte S [1998] 142 SJLB 76*. Three patients at the hospital sought judicial review of the policy of random and routine searches. The Court of Appeal held that there was a general power to authorise random searches of patients without their consent and without cause, overriding, if necessary, medical opinion against its exercise.

2.21   The significance of this judgment is that the justification for the hospital's exercise of its power of control and discipline was not, as has always been the case previously, in terms of the patient's treatment, but because of the need to maintain order for the safety of all. A safe therapeutic environment was needed for patients and staff, and it was obvious that the express power of detention carried with it a power of control and discipline. Medical objection should not be permitted to prevent the power to search, as this would be 'a recipe for disaster'.

2.22   However, the judgment has been interpreted narrowly as it relied heavily on the fact that the High Security Hospitals cater for patients who require "treatment in conditions of special security on account of their dangerous, violent or criminal propensities". For this reason what could have been viewed as a test-case is not necessarily universally applicable (see 10.7 et seq. for further discussion of this case).

## Complaints and the Commission's Remit

2.23   In *R v Mental Health Act Commission, ex parte Smith [1998] 43 BMLR 174*, the Commission's complaints remit came under scrutiny. The applicant was the sister of a patient who had committed suicide whilst detained under Section 3 of the Act. She complained that:

i.     his detention had been neither appropriate nor legal

ii.    his detention in a secure unit had been inappropriate

iii.   he had been given drugs in such quantities that it was unlikely that he could have given consent and the level of dosage had been inappropriate; and

iv.    he had been inadequately cared for during his detention, and there had not been an adequate assessment of risk.

2.24   The Commission accepted jurisdiction to entertain complaints (i) and, to a limited extent, (iii). The question was whether it might also act in respect of (ii) and (iv). The central issue was the construction of Section 120(1)(b)(ii) of the Act, the sub-section which gives the Commission jurisdiction to investigate complaints other than those made by patients themselves. The Commission's jurisdiction is limited to investigation of complaints concerning "the exercise of the powers or the discharge of the duties conferred or imposed" by the Act. This case wrestled with the meaning of 'powers and duties'; were they only those expressly contained in the Act or could other powers and duties be implied?

2.25   Complaints (i) and part of (iii) clearly concern express powers and duties, involving the legality of detention and consent to treatment. However, the Act contains no express power as to the management and control of patients, and no express duty to treat. Expanding upon the earlier *Broadmoor* case, it was held that the power to detain for treatment implied the power to manage and control, and the duty to treat. Additional powers and duties concerning care and treatment could therefore be implied into Section 120(1)(b)(ii), thus dramatically broadening the investigatory powers of the Commission. In finding that the Commission did have jurisdiction to investigate complaints (ii) and (iv) Latham J said:

"...management, control and treatment are all part of a package of compulsion which is the essence of Section 3 detention, which it is the duty of the Secretary of State to keep under review under Section 120(1) of the Act".

2.26    By the inclusion of care and treatment within the scope of Section 120(1)(b)(ii) the Commission's duties are potentially substantially increased, although the duty to investigate is tempered by Section 120(2) giving the Commission discretion as to whether in any particular case it considers to be inappropriate to undertake or to continue any investigation (see 7.10 et seq for further discussion of implications for the Commission).

## Refusal of Medical Treatment

2.27    The Commission has previously reflected upon the developing line of cases concerning the right of patients to refuse medical treatment (see, for example, Sixth Biennial Report p22-23). During this reporting period two cases were heard that are of importance, in that they lay down certain principles to determine a person's capacity to consent to treatment.

2.28    In *Re MB [1997] 2 FLR 426*, due to complications with MB's pregnancy, it was considered necessary for the baby to be delivered by caesarian section. However MB was frightened of needles and refused to consent to the operation. The Court of Appeal granted a declaration allowing the operation to proceed without MB's consent and subsequently gave detailed reasons for its decision. In particular the Court considered the test for capacity:

*"A person lacks capacity if some impairment or disturbance of mental functioning renders the person unable to make a decision whether to consent to or refuse treatment. That inability to make a decision will occur when:*

*a) the patient is unable to comprehend and retain the information which is material to the decision, especially as to the likely consequences of having or not having the treatment in question.*

*b) the patient is unable to use the information and weigh it in the balance as part of the process of arriving at the decision. If, as Thorpe J observed in Re C, a compulsive disorder or phobia from which the patient suffers stifles belief in the information presented to her, then the decision may not be a true one."*

2.29    The Court of Appeal found that MB had consented to the caesarian, but was refusing to allow the use of the anaesthetist's needle because of a fear of needles. The Court concluded:

*"On that evidence she was incapable of making a decision at all. She was at that moment suffering an impairment of her mental functioning which disabled her. She was temporarily incompetent. In an emergency the doctors would be free to administer the anaesthetic if that were in her best interests."*

2.30    In *St George's Healthcare NHS Trust v S (no 2) (Re S) [1998] 3 All ER[1]* a pregnant woman, suffering from severe pre-eclampsia, was advised that unless she underwent an urgent induced delivery, her own health and that of the baby would be at risk. Fully understanding that risk, but wishing her child to be born naturally, she rejected this advice. She was therefore admitted to a psychiatric hospital for assessment under Section 2 of the Act. Against her will she was transferred to a maternity unit where an application was made to dispense with her consent to treatment. That application, made ex parte, was granted and she was delivered of a baby girl by caesarian section.

2.31    The Court of Appeal held that the social worker and doctors involved in the admission under Section 2 had been entitled to conclude from the material available to them that S was suffering from depression. However, detention under the Act must be linked with mental disorder of a nature or degree to warrant detention. They had failed to distinguish between S's urgent need of treatment arising from her pregnancy, and the separate question whether her mental disorder warranted detention, which in this case it did not. The application was therefore unlawful.

2.32    The declaration to dispense with S's consent was similarly rejected. An unborn child was not a separate person from that of its mother. Its need for medical assistance did not prevail over her rights. An adult of sound mind was entitled to refuse treatment, and the declaration in this case involved an infringement of the mother's autonomy.

2.33    The Court of Appeal issued guidelines (superseding the draft guidelines set out in the original judgment) intended to apply to any case involving capacity where surgical or invasive treatment may be needed by a patient. The first principle made in the guidelines is that they have no application where the patient has capacity, adding that a patient may remain competent notwithstanding detention under the Act. The third principle (referred to in the revised Code of Practice) is as follows:

*"If the patient is incapable of giving consent or refusing consent, either in the long term or temporarily (e.g. due to unconsciousness), the patient must be cared for according to the authority's judgment of the patient's best interests. Where the patient has given an advance directive, before becoming incapable, treatment and care should normally be subject to the advance directive. However, if there is reason to doubt the reliability of the advance directive (for example it may sensibly be thought not to apply to the circumstances which have arisen) then an application for a declaration may be made".*

## A Duty of Care?

2.34    The case of *Clunis v Camden & Islington Health Authority [1998] 2 W.L.R. 902* arose out of the killing of Jonathan Zito by Christopher Clunis at Finsbury Park tube station. Mr Clunis had been discharged from hospital less than three months previously and had killed in a sudden, unprovoked attack. He brought a claim of negligence against the local health

[1] Also referred to as *R v Collins and Others, ex parte S (no 2) [1998] 1 FLR*

authority, contending that they had breached a duty at common law to treat him with reasonable care and skill, and that as a result he had suffered injury loss and damage. In particular he alleged that there was a failure to conduct a mental health assessment of him prior to the killing.

2.35   Although Mr. Clunis had been charged with murder, he pleaded guilty to manslaughter on the basis of diminished responsibility. The Court of Appeal accepted that his mental responsibility was substantially impaired but did not accept that this removed liability for his criminal act. His mental state had not justified a verdict of not guilty by reason of insanity. As a matter of public policy a court should not enforce any obligations allegedly arising out of a criminal act, and there was therefore no cause of action in this case.

## Restricted Patients

2.36   At least two cases during the reporting period are of considerable interest in relation to patients detained under Part III of the Mental Health Act.

2.37   In *R v Secretary of State for the Home Department, ex parte Harry [1998] 3 All ER 360*, it was held that the Secretary of State was not obliged to implement the recommendations of a Mental Health Review Tribunal when deciding whether to consent to the transfer of a mentally disordered patient who was the subject of a Restriction Order to a less secure hospital. It was the Secretary of State and not the Tribunal who was entrusted with the task of deciding where the patient should be detained.

2.38   The patient concerned was held in conditions of maximum security at Broadmoor  Hospital when a Mental Health Review Tribunal recommended a transfer to the lesser security of a Regional Secure Unit. The Home Secretary refused consent to the transfer. This decision was upheld. It was also held that he was entitled, as he did, to refer the case to the Advisory Board on Restricted Patients to obtain further information, but that he should have given the patient the gist of any new information arising from that reference, and given him an opportunity to make written representations both to the Board and to the Secretary of State. Thus, there was a failure to comply with the requirements of procedural fairness, and to that extent the appeal was successful.

2.39   *R v North West London NHS Trust, ex parte Stewart [1997] 4 AER 871* concerned an application by a patient for judicial review of a decision to detain him under Section 3 of the Act when he was a conditionally discharged restricted patient. It was held that the powers granted by Part II and Part III of the Act could co-exist and operate independently of each other. Therefore, there was power to detain under Section 3 a restricted patient, who had been conditionally discharged.

## Mental Health Review Tribunals (MHRTs)

2.40    In *R v South Thames MHRT, ex parte M (QBD, 3 September1998 unreported)* M was admitted to hospital under Section 2 of the Act and applied for a Tribunal hearing. Three days before the hearing she was reassessed and made subject to Section 3. The President of the Tribunal decided that this could be her only application while detained under Section 3. M decided not to proceed with the hearing but sought judicial review. Allowing her application, it was held that the decision of the Tribunal was clearly wrong. There was nothing in the Act taking away the right of appeal under Section 2 if the patient happened to be made subject to Section 3 detention after a valid application for a Tribunal hearing had been lodged. The guidance contained in the Code of Practice (5.3)[1] was correct in law.

2.41    *R v Merseyside MHRT, ex parte Kelly [1998] 39 BMLR 114* concerned the procedure at a Tribunal hearing. Mr Kelly had been detained at Ashworth Hospital under Sections 37 and 41 of the Act before he was conditionally discharged. Following his arrest on suspicion of assault and criminal damage he was recalled to hospital and his case came before a Tribunal. Despite the discontinuance of criminal proceedings the Tribunal placed considerable emphasis on Mr Kelly's alleged criminal conduct and on the medical reports which assumed that the alleged conduct had taken place, yet no cross examination was permitted on the allegations. Allowing the appeal by Mr Kelly and quashing the decision of the Tribunal, it was held that the actions of the Tribunal had been procedurally unfair, contrary to the rules of natural justice and that its decision was *ultra vires*.

2.42    It is as yet unclear how, if at all, the case of *R V MHRT ex parte Smith; The Times 9 December,1998* will affect the decision making of MHRTs. Upon judicial review of a Tribunal's decision, the Court considered the interpretation of the words *'nature or degree'* in Section 72(1)(b) of the Act. The section reads:

*"the tribunal shall direct the discharge of a patient liable to be detained otherwise than under Section 2 above if they are satisfied- (i) that he is not then suffering from mental illness, psychopathic disorder, severe mental impairment, or mental impairment or from any of those forms of disorder of a nature or degree which makes it appropriate for him to be liable to be detained in a hospital for medical treatment..."*

2.43    The Court was asked to indicate whether *'nature or degree'* should be read conjunctively or disjunctively. No previous cases had examined this question. Expressing his view that this was rather an academic exercise the judge said, "It seems to me that in very many cases the nature and degree will be inevitably bound so that it matters not whether it is dealt with under nature or degree".

2.44    Mr Smith was suffering from paranoid schizophrenia and at the time of the Tribunal he was presenting with neither positive nor negative symptoms. His condition was described as chronic, stable and static. It was accepted that 'degree' in this case was not relevant. The

---

[1] Reference to the Code of Practice have been updated to correspond with the paragraph numbers of the revised edition of the Code.

question was whether detention could be justified on the basis of 'nature' alone. The court held that it could be because the 'nature' of Mr Smith's condition was such that it might cease to be static. The judge said, "If one had simply to look at the degree it would have been right for the discharge to take place, but the nature of the condition was such that it was clear that he should not be discharged". The significance of this case lies in its endorsement of detention, on the basis of 'nature' of disorder only, for the chronic asymptomatic patient where a fluctuating history indicates that there may be deterioration in the near future. (see discussion of this issue at 4.13 et seq.).

## Hospital Managers

2.45   The case of *R v Riverside Mental Health Trust, ex parte Huzzey [1998] 43 BMLR 167* clarified the factors to be taken into account by hospital managers when reviewing a patient's detention following a Nearest Relative's application for discharge. Mr Huzzey was detained under Section 3 of the Act when his Nearest Relative made an application for his discharge under Section 23. Seeking to bar discharge, the Responsible Medical Officer (RMO) made a report under Section 25(1), stating that if he were to be discharged he was likely to act in manner dangerous to other persons or himself. The managers, on reviewing Mr Huzzey's detention, appropriately considered all the Section 3 factors, but they did not consider that procedurally there was a need to examine the question of dangerousness, as raised by the RMO.  It was held that, in these circumstances, managers had to consider not only the Section 3 factors but also whether or not the patient, if discharged, would be likely to act in a manner dangerous to other persons or himself. If they were not so persuaded then the Nearest Relative would be entitled to a discharge.

## Section 3 as a Community Treatment Order?

2.46   For many years the case of *R v Hallstrom, ex p W, R v Gardner, ex p L [1986] 2 WLR 883* has been authority for the proposition that a Section 3 detention cannot be renewed while a patient is on Section 17 leave. Whilst not strictly overturning *Hallstrom* the important case of *Barker v Barking, Havering & Brentwood Community Healthcare NHS Trust [1999] 1 FLR 106* re-defines inpatient treatment in such a way that Section 3 may, under some circumstances, now be renewable whilst a patient is on Section 17 leave. Miss Barker was consenting to treatment and living in the community for all but two nights of every week when she stayed in hospital for assessment of her mental state. The Court of Appeal interpreted 'treatment' and 'detention' broadly and held that her detention could be renewed. Lord Woolf MR considered the position where much of a patient's treatment takes place outside of hospital:

*"...for the treatment as a whole to be successful there will often need to be an inpatient element to the treatment which means it is in fact "appropriate for him to receive medical treatment in a hospital" and "that it cannot be provided unless he is detained"*

*"...the detention does not have to be continuous, as Section 17 makes clear, but even when on leave the patient still has a hospital at which he is detained when not on leave. Equally he*

*will for the purpose of Section 20(4) continue to be detained whether when the report is furnished he is in hospital or liable to be required to return to hospital...*"

"*...The fact that assessment by itself cannot amount to treatment for Section 3 does not mean that assessment cannot be a legitimate treatment under sections 3 and 20. Often assessment and monitoring of progress will be an important part of the treatment.*"

2.47    This case may yet reach the House of Lords for further clarification of a complicated judgment which could have far reaching consequences.

## Public Authorities

2.48    The case of *R v Liverpool City Council, ex parte F (unreported)* examined the question of the Nearest Relative under the Act and the 'ordinary residence' test. J, who was 18 years old, had lived with his grandmother for several years when he was young. Prior to his admission to hospital he had lived with his mother, Mrs F, but spent several nights at the home of his grandmother. Upon application under Section 3 of the Act and applying the 'ordinary residence' test in Section 26(4) of the Act, the Approved Social Worker considered that the grandmother was the Nearest Relative and consulted with her. The grandmother did not object and admission under Section 3 proceeded. It was held that the determination of the identity of the Nearest Relative had not been in accordance with the law. Neither in relation to J's 'ordinary residence', nor in relation to whether there had been a change in the person 'caring' for him, did the ASW address all the questions which should have been considered before concluding that the identity of J's Nearest Relative had changed. The case gives guidance on the matters to be taken into account. Duration, continuity, quality of care and intention will all be relevant as to whether a person is displaced as the Nearest Relative under Section 26(4).

2.49    *Re Whitbread, sub nom Whitbread v Kingston & District NHS Trust [1998] 39 BMLR 94* concerned the process of consultation with the Nearest Relative upon admission under the Act. The patient, Peter Whitbread, had applied for a writ of habeas corpus on the ground that his detention was unlawful because the social worker's consultation with the Nearest Relative had taken place *after* seeing the patient and making the application. It was asserted that this was contrary to Section 11(4) of the Act, which states that no application shall be made by a social worker 'except after consultation with the person......appearing to be the Nearest Relative'. Failing in his application, it was held that the Act contained no express provision as to when the consultation must take place, but a nexus must exist between the consultation and the application. If the intention of the Act had been to provide a strong safeguard against an application being made contrary to the wishes of the Nearest Relative, it would have made this quite clear. That it did not might reflect a deliberate decision to strike a balance between the viewpoint of a relative who may be emotive and irrational, and the desirability of treatment. In an Act where some of the requirements were so precise, it was right to be cautious about implying a need for precision where that was not expressed.

2.50    In the case of *R v Central London County Court and another ex parte London; The Times
23 March 1999* the power to displace a patient's relative was considered by the Court of
Appeal. It was held that hospital managers had acted lawfully when they compulsorily
admitted a patient for treatment under Section 3 of the Act whilst an application under
Section 29 to displace the Nearest Relative had still not been finally determined. The patient
had first been admitted under Section 4, which was converted to a Section 2. The County
Court made an interim order displacing the applicant's mother as the Nearest Relative,
adjourning the matter for further consideration. This was done on an *ex parte* basis, that is,
without hearing from the mother. It was argued that the procedure of obtaining an order
under Section 29 had to be completed and the Nearest Relative displaced by the final order,
before an application for admission under Section 3 could be made. The Court of Appeal
held that the County Court had the power to make an *ex parte* or interim order and there
was nothing unlawful about the Section 3 detention. However, the Court of Appeal also
expressed the view that unless there were cogent reasons to the contrary, questions under
Section 29(3)(c) should be finally determined before an application was made under Section
3, if necessary using the extension of detention to Section 2 provided by Section 29(4).

2.51    In the case of *R v Kent County Council, ex parte Marston [1997] unreported*, the Court of
Appeal considered the scope of a local authority's discretion when acting as Guardian under
Section 7 of the Act. The applicant D was the foster-brother of J, who has severe learning
disabilities. Until 1990 D played a significant part in J's care but following an incident the
Social Services Department and his psychiatrist considered that he should no longer do so. J
was made the subject of Guardianship under Section 7 of the Act. D complained that the
local authority refused to disclose J's whereabouts, that he had been refused all contact with
J, that J was not permitted to live with him and that J had not been sufficiently informed so
that he could make his own decision as to these matters. D's application for judicial review
was refused. Having heard details of J's disabilities and his failure to respond to any letters
from or photographs of D, it was concluded that the Guardian had behaved with the utmost
propriety. Refusing leave to appeal, the Court of Appeal nevertheless considered that 'there
may in future be a need for litigation to clarify certain outstanding doubts as to the proper
scope of an authority's discretion when acting as a Guardian under this legislation'.

## European Cases

2.52    Recent cases from the European Court of Human Rights have gained added importance
from the passing of the Human Rights Act 1998 which, while it does not incorporate the
European Convention on Human Rights, will give effect to its central provisions. The
revised Code of Practice also refers to the European Convention in its chapter on guiding
principles.

2.53    The 1997 case of *Pauline Lines v United Kingdom* concerned a patient, PL, who had been
detained by warrant under the 1959 Mental Health Act, and who, following the
introduction of the 1983 Act, was subject to a restriction order without limit of time.

Between 1970 and 1995 PL was conditionally discharged and recalled to hospital a number of times, eventually being discharged by the Home Secretary to a group home.

2.54    During 1993 PL had also been admitted twice under Section 3 of the Act in order to gain control of her treatment in a way which formal recall would not allow. She complained that on the first occasion it had taken too long for the Mental Health Review Tribunal to arrange a hearing of her case, and that she had been refused permission to apply to the Tribunal on the second occasion. This, she claimed, was a violation of Article 5(4) of the European Convention on Human Rights, which states:

*"Everyone who is deprived of his liberty by arrest or detention shall be entitled to take proceedings by which the lawfulness of his detention shall be decided speedily by a court and his release ordered if the detention is not lawful".*

2.55    It was accepted that PL could not appeal to a Tribunal against her hospital admission under Section 3 because of the ability to recall her in any event, but the European Commission held that the complaint raised serious issues under Article 5(4). Although this case was subsequently settled on amicable terms it serves as a warning that cases should be brought speedily before a Tribunal.

2.56    Where a person has engaged in physical, emotional or sexual abuse it may seem inappropriate for them to remain as the Nearest Relative under the Mental Health Act, but at present those circumstances do not constitute sufficient grounds for removing such a person from their role (see 4.46 et seq). From the case of *J.T.v United Kingdom [1997] EHRLR 437* it would now seem that this deficiency may constitute a breach of the European Convention. The applicant had made allegations of sexual abuse against her step-father. She feared there would be disclosure of personal information to her mother with whom she had a very difficult relationship, and to her step-father. She therefore wished to replace her mother with a new Nearest Relative. The fact that the domestic law did not permit her to do this amounted to a violation of Article 8, the 'right to respect for private and family life', in the view of the European Commission. This case highlights a weakness in our domestic law, although the matter has not, at the time of writing, proceeded further to the European Court.

2.57    The final Strasbourg case is that of *Stanley Johnson v United Kingdom [1996] EHRLR 89; [1997]EHRLR 105-8; [1998] HRCD Vol IX, No 1, 41.* In 1984 Mr Johnson was admitted to hospital under Sections 37 and 41 of the Act. Between 1989 and 1993 his continued detention was considered by several Mental Health Review Tribunals, each concluding that, whilst Mr Johnson was no longer suffering from mental illness, his illness might recur if he was released without rehabilitation. No suitable rehabilitation accommodation could be found and he remained in hospital. At his final Tribunal hearing in 1993 his RMO conceded that Mr Johnson had not suffered mental illness since 1987. Following his release several days later Mr Johnson alleged a breach of Article 5(1) of the Convention, which states, inter alia:

*"Everyone has the right to liberty and security of person. No one shall be deprived of his liberty save in the following cases.........(a) the lawful detention of a person after conviction by a competent court;....(b) the lawful detention of....persons of unsound mind...."*

The European Commission decided there had been such a breach from the date of the first MHRT decision. It stated:

*"...a release cannot be indefinitely deferred....a deferral of discharge of a person who has been found to have recovered from mental illness must be ....limited and must be subject to strict procedural safeguards to ensure the discharge of the person at the earliest opportunity." [1996] EHRLR 89.*

The European Court concurred with the European Commission and awarded Mr Johnson damages of £10,000 together with costs of £25,000.

## The Revised Code of Practice

2.58   The Code provides guidance to doctors, managers and staff of hospitals and mental nursing homes and Approved Social Workers on how to proceed when undertaking duties under the Act. It is also aimed at others working in health and social services (including the independent and voluntary sectors) and the police. It is hoped that it will be helpful to patients, their families, friends and others who support them and it was drafted with this aim in mind.

2.59   The Code has been prepared in accordance with Section 118 of the Act. The introduction to the Code notes in the first paragraph that: "The Act does not impose a legal duty to comply with the Code but as it is a statutory document, failure to follow it could be referred to in evidence in legal proceedings."

### The Main Changes from the Previous Version of the Code

2.60   The changes in the 1999 edition of the Code are based on comments on the draft, recent case law, and changes in practice and terminology. Some factual material from the previous Code is now in the revised version of the Memorandum which was published in 1998.

2.61   The Code has been updated but its structure has not changed substantially from the previous editions. However, the content of Chapter 1 has changed significantly. There is an expanded section on 'guiding principles', including reference to the European Convention on Human Rights. It places the implementation of the Act within the framework of the Care Programme Approach, the Welsh Office Mental Illness Strategy and care management. It also brings together and expands on the principles of communicating with patients, confidentiality (including reference to victims of mentally disordered offenders) and the provision and recording of information, including ethnic monitoring of patients admitted under the Act. Chapter 1 should therefore be read before and as background to the advice in each of the subsequent chapters.

2.62    The guiding principles include statements that people to whom the Act applies should:

*"receive recognition of their basic human rights under the European Convention on Human Rights...be given respect for their qualities, abilities and diverse backgrounds as individuals...be given any necessary treatment or care in the least controlled and segregated facilities compatible with ensuring their own health or safety or the safety of other people; and be discharged from detention or other powers provided by the Act as soon as it is clear that their application is no longer justified." (1.1)*

2.63    The importance of clear communication with patients is emphasised. It notes that barriers might exist where the patient's first language is not English or where there are hearing or visual impairments and advises that when the need arises, staff should make every attempt to identify interpreters who match the patient in gender, religion, dialect, and as closely as possible in age. The patient's relatives or friends should not normally be used as an intermediary or interpreter (1.6). Approved Social Workers are advised that it may be appropriate for a deaf or hearing impaired patient who is being assessed under the Act to have a friend or advocate present who is also deaf or hearing impaired (2.13)

2.64    The definition of an informal patient was an important feature of the Bournewood case. The various references to informal patients in the new Code reflect the Law Lords' judgment. For example, paragraph 2.8 states:

*"If at the time of admission, the patient is mentally incapable of consent, but does not object to entering hospital and receiving care or treatment, admission should be informal... The decision to admit a mentally incapacitated patient informally should be made by the doctor in charge of the patient's treatment in accordance with what is in the patient's best interests and is justified on the basis of the common law doctrine of necessity ... If a patient lacks capacity at the time of an assessment or review, it is particularly important that both clinical and social care requirements are considered, and that account is taken of the patient's ascertainable wishes and feelings and the views of their immediate relatives and carers on what would be in the patient's best interests."*

## Medical Treatment

2.65    In considering medical treatment in Chapter 15, the Code notes that under the common law valid consent is required before medical treatment can be given, except where common law or statute provide authority to give treatment without consent. A presumption is made that an individual has capacity to make a treatment decision. A person suffering from mental disorder is not necessarily incapable of giving consent. The guidance on the circumstances where the individual might be assessed as not having the capacity to make treatment decisions has been changed to reflect the principles outlined in *Re MB* (see 2.28 above) and *Re C (Refusal of Treatment) [1994] 1FLR 31* (Code of Practice, 15.10). The Code also contains guidance on advance directives and refers to guidelines in St George's Healthcare NHS Trust v S case (see 2.30 et seq).

2.66   The chapter on children and young people has been revised and links with the issues of capacity and valid consent. Similarly, the chapter on Guardianship contains new advice on mental incapacity regarding recognition of the authority of the Guardian. It can be seen that mental incapacity is a common thread running through the Code. The law concerning mental incapacity is being considered as part of the current review of the mental health legislation.

## Other changes

2.67   There is an emphasis on the need for the ASW to persist in seeking to contact the Nearest Relative to inform them of their powers to discharge the patient.

2.68   With regard to police powers under Section 136, the Code (10.5) states that, as a general rule, it is preferable for a person thought to be suffering from mental disorder to be detained in a hospital rather than a police station (see 4.78).

2.69   The situations when leave is required are clarified and the Code gives advice on the application of Section 117 and custody during leave. There is guidance on action needed if someone goes absent without leave.

2.70   There is more detailed guidance on the exercise of the hospital managers' power of discharge, especially with regard to the composition of review panels, criteria for reviews and the conduct of reviews.

2.71   Chapter 25 includes the implications for personal searches of the Broadmoor case (see 2.20). Finally, after-care under supervision is now included in a new chapter but this does not replace the 1996 supplement to the Code.

2.72   There are many detailed changes to the Code of Practice to which attention is drawn throughout this Report. It is suggested that readers may wish to check the index under 'Code of Practice' to locate the references. To avoid confusion, all references to the Code relate to the paragraph numbers in the 1999 edition, even where they are used in examples of Commission visits which took place before the Code was published.

# Chapter 3
# Commission Visits

## Summary

*During the previous reporting period the Commission revised its visiting format and procedures to enable it to increase the frequency and quality of Members' contact with detained patients, and to make more effective use of the information and material collected during visits. These objectives have been realised. However, the Commission is concerned that the distinctions between different types of visits to Trusts and mental nursing homes, and the objectives of visits to social services departments, have become obscured over time. In future, visits to Trusts and mental nursing homes will be reduced from four to three visits every two years and visits to social services departments will concentrate on the functions and discharge of duties in respect of patients detained or liable to be detained, focusing particularly on the practices of ASWs.*

*Commission Members have held private meetings with substantial numbers of detained patients and collected information on the issues that have concerned them. The most frequent issues of concern for patients are about detention and deprivation of liberty, medical care, and living arrangements and privacy. The Commission has achieved its target of contacting, each year, all detained patients in the High Security Hospitals and interviewing those who wish to be seen. Concerns about leave, parole and transfer delays are the most frequently raised issues when Commissioners meet with these patients.*

*During the current reporting period, eleven complaints have been made against the Commission or its Members and eleven complaints have been made against Second Opinion Appointed Doctors.*

# 3 Commission Visits

## Visiting Organisation and Policy

### The Commissions' Visiting Remit

3.1 The principal function of the Commission is to visit psychiatric units or nursing homes where patients could be detained and, where there are detained patients, to offer private meetings to as many of them as wish to be seen. During these visits, the Commission also monitors the unit's compliance with the Mental Health Act and the Code of Practice. The Commission undertakes this task on behalf of the Secretary of State, the remit for which is set out in Section 120 of the Act as follows:

- to keep under review the exercise of the powers and the discharge of the duties in the Act which relate to the detention of patients or to patients liable to be detained; and

- to visit and interview in private patients detained under the Act in hospitals and mental nursing homes.

3.2 Meetings with patients may be with individuals or groups of patients and may also include Patients' Councils. The Commission's Visiting Policy also requires Commissioners to offer, where necessary, advice and guidance on the implementation of the Act and the Code of Practice and to observe the general conditions under which patients are detained. The highest priority is always given to meeting patients and scrutinising the detention documents.

### Visiting Format

3.3 During the previous reporting period the Commission revised its visiting format and procedures in order to:

- increase the frequency and quality of contact between members of the Commission and detained patients;

- improve the Commission's communication with detained patients;

- ensure more effective monitoring of the quality of the Commission's work; and

- make more effective use of the information and material collected during visits.

3.4 The Commission is able to confirm that during the current reporting period these objectives have been realised. Each hospital / mental nursing home has received a **Full Visit** at least once every two years, which contrasts with the previous practice of annual visits. Full Visits terminate with a formal meeting at which hospital staff and representatives from relevant outside agencies are normally present. The reduction in the frequency of Full Visits has enabled the Commission to concentrate its resources on a programme of **Patient Focused Visits**, where the emphasis is on meeting detained patients rather than reviewing the full range of services and facilities provided. Hospitals and mental nursing homes have received at least three Patient Focused Visits during the two year period. Regional/Medium Secure Units have received at least one Patient Focused Visit and one Full Visit each year.

3.5 In addition, the Commission has undertaken **Targeted Visits** to examine specific issues which have been of particular concern in certain units or localities. These issues have included bed pressures, the authorisation and recording of Section 17 leave and after-care arrangements under Section 117. Both Targeted and Patient Focused Visits can be **Unannounced** or at **Short Notice**, allowing the Commission to investigate matters while normal routines of care were in progress.

3.6 The three High Security Hospitals have continued to be visited more frequently than other hospitals, with a greater number of Unannounced Visits, which in some instances have taken place during the evenings and at weekends. Patients in these hospitals are generally long-stay patients, and the Commission has sought to have a meeting, or some form of meaningful contact, with every patient who wishes it, at least once a year. Twice yearly meetings have also taken place with the Patients' Councils in the High Security Hospitals. The Visiting Panels have also periodically examined particular issues, such as seclusion, the implementation of the Care Programme Approach and access to fresh air, and provided reports to the hospital managers. Written reports are also given to each clinical director on matters within their particular area of responsibility.

3.7 Every patient interviewed by a member of the Commission is provided with a personal letter summarising the issues raised and outlining any further agreed action which, with the patient's agreement, is to be taken by themselves or by the Commission. With the patient's agreement, a copy of the letter may also be given to the ward manager.

3.8 The Commission has also continued to meet, on a two-yearly cycle, with representatives from social services departments (SSDs) in order to encourage a co-ordinated approach to the operation of the Act. During these meetings the Commission has continued to pay particular attention to:

- SSDs' responses to the Act and the Code of Practice;
- the process of assessment, compulsory admission and detention under the Act, including the availability of Approved Social Workers, communication with general practitioners, hospitals, Section 12 doctors and the emergency service;

- the planning and delivery of appropriate residential places, alternatives to detention and aftercare procedures and facilities; and

- the extent to which hospital and community services are able to integrate all aspects of a patient's detention from the initial assessment to the termination of aftercare.

3.9 During Full Visits, Commissioners have met with representatives of the relevant commissioning authorities to ensure that the contractual and commissioning arrangements meet the needs of the detained patients and to help to encourage the purchasers to engage in the routine monitoring of service delivery.

3.10 Commission reports sent to hospitals and SSDs follow a specified format, highlighting examples of good practice and identifying issues which require attention. The Commission may request specific responses to identified areas of concern and, where appropriate, details of a timed programme of remedial action. Although the Commission does not have specific legal powers to direct that its recommendations are implemented, in most cases they are accepted. Copies of the reports are also sent to the relevant health authorities, which may make use of them when monitoring the provider's compliance with the Act and the Code of Practice and the general provision of services for detained patients.

## New Visiting Arrangements

3.11 The Commission's existing Visiting Policy has now been in operation for over five years and during this time has been subject to regular scrutiny in order to ensure that the visiting cycle, and the different types of visit, are an effective way for the Commission to fulfill its statutory responsibilities. During 1997/8, the Commission conducted a small survey to measure satisfaction of the Commission's performance with regard to visiting, feedback meetings, visit reports and SOAD arrangements. Chief Executives from seven Trusts were contacted for this exercise, one from each CVT area. The respondents were generally satisfied with the performance of the Commission, although one Trust was dissatisfied with visit reports not giving sufficient emphasis to positive aspects of the service. The Commission was widely viewed as being helpful in raising standards. At the time of writing, a larger scale exercise is being undertaken by the Audit Commission to obtain the views of a sample of Chief Executives about the Commission's performance.

3.12 The Commission is concerned that the distinction between Full and Patient-Focused Visits to Trusts has become obscured over time. The result is that neither Commissioners' activity during the visits nor the content of the final reports to Trusts or other providers reflect the Commissioners' remit; i.e. to *either* concentrate on interviews with detained patients and to scrutinise the legal documents *or* to systematically review the development and provision of the service overall. Similarly, the Commission is also concerned that visits to SSDs are increasingly becoming concerned with broad ranging reviews of mental health service delivery, often involving meetings with many interested professional and non-professional groups, rather than concentrating on issues relating directly to the process of patients' assessment and detention under the Act. As a result of these concerns, the Commission has completed a review of its Visiting Policy and will be introducing a revised visiting cycle and format for visits to Trusts, mental nursing homes and SSDs.

## Trusts and Nursing Homes

3.13    The number of Commission visits to Trusts and mental nursing homes will be reduced from four to three visits every two years. This will include two Patient-Focused Visits and one Full Visit. This reduction in the visiting cycle will allow the Commission to utilise its limited resources more effectively and will permit the complement of Commissioners to be strengthened during both types of Visit. A revised visit report format will also be introduced for Patient-Focused Visits in order to give greater emphasis to issues relating directly to currently detained patients. Patient-Focused Visits will be closely tied in with the format of Full Visits to develop a comprehensive system of visiting and reporting. An important objective of this system will be the development of a clear audit trail which, at the end of each two-year visiting cycle, should demonstrate whether or not a Trust is consistently achieving a satisfactory standard. Where this is not the case or where there is a failure to respond adequately, the series of reports should provide the Commission with sufficient written evidence to further pursue its remit.

## Social Services Departments (SSDs)

3.14    It is the policy of the Commission to make joint visits to Trusts and SSDs wherever possible. However, recent changes in the public sector have resulted in an increased number of local authorities and reductions in the number of Trusts, to the extent that it is no longer practicable for the Commission's Full Visits to take place jointly with SSDs in many instances. Nevertheless, where it is practicable, the Commission will continue to visit jointly where a Trust and SSD share boundaries or where either is contained entirely within the boundaries of the other. All SSDs will continue to be visited, whether jointly with a Trust, or separately, once every two years.

3.15    Visits to SSDs will reflect the central function of the Commission, which is to keep under review the exercise of functions and discharge of duties conferred or imposed by the Act in respect of patients who are detained or liable to be detained. The Commission will therefore concentrate on those agencies and professionals concerned with the process of assessing people with a view to detention under the Act and their subsequent conveyance, compulsory admission and detention in hospital or a place of safety. A primary focus of the Commission's attention will be on the service provided by Approved Social Workers (ASWs). In order to develop an understanding of the extent to which hospital and community services are able to integrate all aspects of patients' detention, from initial assessment through to discharge from detention, the Commission will also hold discussions with other relevant professionals and agencies, including:

- the police;
- the ambulance service; and

- other groups providing a **direct** service to detained patients.

The latter may include in-patient advocacy groups, GPs, residential establishments that accommodate patients on Section 17 leave of absence, and the Probation Service where it provides social supervision for restricted patients subject to conditional discharge arrangements.

3.16   In order to focus more closely on the work and practice of ASWs, visiting Commissioners will spend more time in discussion with ASWs and they will also pay particular attention to ASWs' recorded details of their assessments. Such reports are usually copied to the admitting psychiatric unit, an element of practice reinforced by the Code of Practice (11.13). A random selection of reports will be scrutinised against a checklist covering important aspects of the implementation of the Act and the Code of Practice. This will include observations on the ASWs' recording of:

- the patient's spoken language and ethnic group;
- the interview with the patient;
- discussions with other relevant non-professionals;
- discussions with recommending doctor(s) and other professionals;
- the reasons for deciding to make an application, including an assessment of risks to the patient or other people, and consideration of alternatives to detention;
- the full details of the person appearing to be the Nearest Relative, and whether he or she has received notification of the application and their rights under the Act;
- any comments on avoidable delays in the assessment and admission process; and
- other key information for hospital staff, including the details of a local authority contact person.

The Commissioners' findings in respect of this scrutiny will form the basis of the feedback to senior managers, along with any issues that have arisen during discussions with ASWs and the other groups mentioned above.

## Information

3.17   The Commission's visit reports provide qualitative, detailed information about the operation of Act and the treatment and care of detained patients throughout England and Wales. A summary of these reports is compiled every six months in order that instances of good and bad practice can be monitored and matters identified which may need attention at a local or national level. These summaries provide the main body of information for the Commission's Biennial Report.

3.18   In addition, the Commission collects statistical data concerning:

- the number of Commission visits undertaken;
- the number of visit reports dispatched to the provider units within target time limits;

- the age, gender, ethnic group and category of disorder of patients seen; and
- the issues raised by the patients seen in private meetings.

## Analysis of the Information

3.19 The Commission made 1,245 visits to mental health units (excluding the High Security Hospitals) between 1.4.97 and 10.3.99 (see table 1). This included a total of 11,669 private meetings with detained patients and 6,328 informal meetings. Compared to the final year of the previous reporting period, this represents an increase of 28% in the total number of patient meetings and contacts by Commission Members.

**Table 1. Commission Visiting Activity\*: 1 July 1995 to 10 March 1999**

| Activity | 1995/6 | 1996/7 | Current reporting period 1997/8 | 1998/9 |
|---|---|---|---|---|
| Visits | 474 | 748 | 638 | 607 |
| Private meetings | Not collected | 4,714 | 6,302 | 5,367 |
| Informal contacts | Not collected | 2,301 | 3,005 | 3,323 |
| Patients' statutory documents checked | Not collected | Not collected | Not collected | 10,003 |

\* Not including activity relating to the High Security Hospitals

3.20 To achieve maximum impact the visit report needs to be prepared and dispatched to the unit concerned and the relevant purchaser as soon as possible. The Commission has set a performance target of 5 weeks for this process and has been able to achieve this for 76% of reports in 1998/9, an increase of 2% on the previous year. The Commission recognises that there is room for improvement in meeting the target.

## Contact with Patients

3.21 During the process of a Commission visit all patients who are detained are offered the opportunity of a *private meeting* with a Commissioner. Whilst visiting the wards Commission members may also have the opportunity for *informal contacts* both with individual patients and with patients wishing to meet with a Commissioner as part of a group.

3.22 Figure 1 shows the age and gender of patients with whom private meetings were held during the current reporting period. Sixty per cent of the patients interviewed were men. The distributions of both the gender and age group of these patients are strikingly similar to those reported in the period 1995-1997 (Seventh Biennial Report, p. 32).

3.23 Although this data refers to meetings, rather than patients, excluding those patients seen in the High Security Hospitals very few detained patients are interviewed on more than one occasion in a given reporting period, and therefore the figures can be taken as an approximation of the number of individuals who have had contact with Commissioners.

Precise data regarding the numbers and details of *individual* patients would require relatively sophisticated information systems, on the part of both the Commission and the Trusts, that would be capable of supporting a unique identifier for each patient (e.g. the new NHS number).

**Figure 1. Patient meetings\* by age and gender**

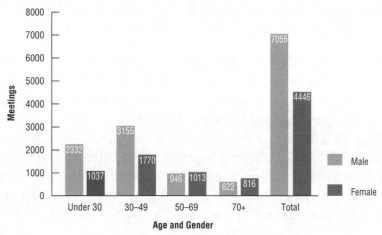

\* Excluding meetings in the High Security Hospitals. Figures cover the period 1.4.97 to 10.3.98

3.24   Information regarding the patients' ethnicity is extracted by Commissioners from the hospital case file. The Commission's records are, therefore, dependent upon the completeness and reliability of the patients' records. The census categories used by The Office of National Statistics for monitoring ethnicity permit patients to decline to give their ethnic group. During the current reporting period 1.4% (172) of the patients interviewed were in this category. In 12.8% of meetings, Commissioners found no record of the patients' ethnicity in the hospital case files. However, the total of 14.2% not allocated to an ethnic group does represent a substantial improvement on that noted in the previous Biennial Report, when a fifth of the cases were unallocated (p. 33).

**Figure 2: Meetings\* by ethnic category (n=11,979)**

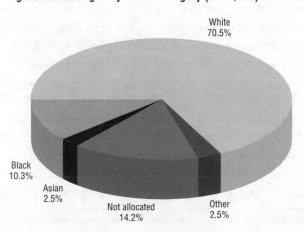

3.25    The above data excludes the activity of Commission teams visiting the High Security Hospitals. In March 1999 there were 1,307 patients resident in these hospitals. During 1997-1999 a total of 307 visits were undertaken. The Commission continues to adhere to its target of providing every patient with the opportunity of meeting with a Commissioner at least once a year, although not all patients may wish to be seen and others have a meeting on more than one occasion. During this period, Commissioners held 1,390 first time meetings with patients, 1,622 repeat meetings, and had 2,081 informal contacts.

3.26    In the High Security Hospitals, Commission Members only record the patients' ethnic group during the initial meeting to avoid duplicating information. This data therefore relates to individual patients rather than individual meetings. In these hospitals, Commissioners could not find any ethnic group recorded in the patients' notes in 40.4% of cases; although this figure varied significantly across the three sites (Rampton, 32.8%; Broadmoor, 39%; Ashworth, 52.8%). It is also of interest to note that 22.8% of the patients interviewed in the High Security Hospitals had declined to give their ethnic group, compared to only 1.4% of detained patients interviewed in units elsewhere. This figure also varied significantly across the three hospitals (Rampton, 33.3%; Broadmoor, 6.8%; Ashworth, 22.1%).

## Issues raised by patients

3.27    Meetings are held in private, with the understanding that the discussion will be treated with the strictest confidence if the patient so wishes. However, most patients are anxious that those providing their care should be made aware of any concerns they may have. With the patients' consent, these issues are then brought to the attention of the hospital staff. In the majority of cases, Commissioners find that most issues can be resolved by discussion on the ward, while others may require to be brought to the attention of hospital managers during the feedback meeting at the end of the visit. In only 2.4% of meetings, during the current reporting period, have Commissioners felt it necessary to advise patients to use the hospital's formal complaints procedure.

3.28    The Commission's observations on most of the issues concerning the care and treatment of detained patients appear later in this report (see Chapter 5), but it is worth noting the areas of concern that the patients themselves bring to the attention of Commissioners during the meetings. Table 2 shows the frequency with which certain issues are raised with Commissioners. Coding of these issues is completed by Commissioners following the meeting. Most patients' concerns are about their medical care or the curtailment of their liberty. Concerns about the latter may also include the conditions of their leave or parole, or the opportunities for transfer to another ward or hospital. Another major issue concerns the domestic living arrangements and the degree of privacy on the wards. The table also illustrates differences between men and women in the frequency of issues raised, and between patients from white and ethnic minority groups. Although the differences may appear to be marginal, an analysis of this data suggests that women are significantly[1] more

---

[1] Statistically significant. Chi-squared test; $p < 0.05$. Full details of these results are available from the Commission upon request.

likely than men to raise issues relating to offences against the person, patients rights, medical, nursing or other professional care, living arrangements and privacy, finances and benefits, and those categorised as 'other'. On the other hand, they are less likely to raise concerns relating to leave, parole or transfer, social and educational matters, or Mental Health Act issues.

3.29 Patients from an ethnic minority background appear significantly more likely than white patients to raise concerns about their medical care, but less likely to raise concerns about nursing or other professional care. Issues relating to ethnicity or cultural and religious matters are raised more frequently by patients from black and ethnic minorities, but the number is relatively small. It is uncertain whether this proportion is an accurate reflection of the patients' concerns, whether it is an indication of a lack of confidence in the Commission to respond sensitively to race and culture issues or a matter of how concerns are recorded, (i.e. the race and culture dimension of the patient's concern may be missed by the Commission member). The Commission intends to refine the data it collects on issues raised by patients, which should enable them to be monitored more closely.

**Table 2. Issues raised by detained patients during private meetings (excluding the High Security Hospitals) by gender and ethnic group.**

| | Gender | | Ethnicity | | All meetings* |
|---|---|---|---|---|---|
| | Men | Women | White | Minority Groups | |
| Issue category | (n=7,175) % | (n=4,722) % | (n=8,450) % | (n=1,825) % | (n=11,979) % |
| Offences against the person | 1.8 | 3.2 | 2.4 | 2.6 | 2.4 |
| Patients' rights | 8.2 | 10.2 | 9.1 | 9.7 | 9.0 |
| Medical care | 17.1 | 19.8 | 18.7 | 20.9 | 18.5 |
| Nursing care | 10.8 | 14.5 | 13.0 | 10.0 | 12.3 |
| Other professional care | 5.1 | 6.1 | 6.0 | 4.7 | 5.5 |
| Living arrangements, privacy | 14.1 | 15.8 | 14.9 | 14.2 | 14.8 |
| Finance, benefits, property | 3.9 | 4.2 | 4.4 | 3.6 | 4.0 |
| Deprivation of liberty | 18.2 | 18.8 | 19.4 | 18.3 | 18.4 |
| Leave, parole, transfer | 18.7 | 16.9 | 18.1 | 19.7 | 18.0 |
| MHRT matters | 14.9 | 13.7 | 14.7 | 15.1 | 14.4 |
| Family matters | 4.6 | 5.2 | 5.0 | 4.1 | 4.8 |
| Aftercare | 5.3 | 4.8 | 5.2 | 5.8 | 5.1 |
| Local authority services | 2.0 | 2.5 | 2.2 | 2.5 | 2.2 |
| Social, educational | 5.0 | 4.0 | 4.8 | 4.5 | 4.6 |

| | | | | | |
|---|---|---|---|---|---|
| **Cultural, religious, ethnic** | 1.2 | 0.9 | 0.9 | 1.8 | 1.1 |
| **DoH & Home Office matters** | 0.5 | 0.6 | 0.6 | 0.3 | 0.6 |
| **Mental Health Act** | 4.1 | 2.8 | 3.3 | 3.9 | 3.5 |
| **Others** | 5.7 | 4.7 | 5.1 | 6.7 | 5.3 |

Note: Column percentages may add up to more than 100% as patients may raise more than one issue during a meeting.
* Excluding 310 meetings where data processing was incomplete at the time of writing.

3.30 Many patients express concerns that their condition does not warrant detention and wish to be discharged from hospital and are often disappointed to learn, despite having being forewarned, that the Commission has no power to authorise this. They may also object to the restrictions imposed upon them, such as confinement to the ward or the necessity for nurse escorts when they visit a local shop or take a walk in the grounds. Shortages of nursing staff for escort duties are, understandably, a major source of concern for them under such circumstances. Some patients may also complain that their family and friends are unable to visit them as often as they might wish because the hospital is some distance from their home area, as can often be the case in medium secure units, and transfer to a unit nearer their area of origin has been delayed. Delays in being transferred to a ward or unit more suitable to their needs, often as part of a progressive programme of rehabilitation, can also be relayed to Commissioners as a source of anxiety. Some patients, who have appealed against their detention and are awaiting a date for a Tribunal hearing may sometimes complain of delays.

3.31 Patients' concerns about their medical care often include worries about the side effects of their medication, or limited opportunities to discuss their treatment plan with their Responsible Medical Officer. Patients may also not fully understand, or be aware of the details of, their treatment plan under the Care Programme Approach (CPA). Sometimes they complain that they have found large CPA review meetings very intimidating or that they do not feel that their views have been fully taken into account. Patients sometimes express dissatisfaction with the inadequate opportunities for therapeutic and activity-based programmes of care on the wards, that all they receive is medication and complain of boredom. As noted in the Seventh Biennial Report, nurses being so busy that they have little time to spend with patients also continues to rank highly on the list of issues raised with Commissioners.

3.32 Domestic living arrangements on the wards can also be a major source of concern to patients. These might include routine, but nevertheless important, matters such as the provision of a monotonous diet or cold servings, failure to cater for vegetarian or ethnic dietary requirements, or simply not being permitted to make a hot drink when they would wish. More serious issues raised include those of lack of privacy, and concerns about the security of personal belongings or the aggressive or offensive behaviour of other patients.

3.33 As Table 3 demonstrates, the major issues for the patients interviewed in the High Security Hospitals are those relating to i) leave, parole and transfers, ii) nursing care, and iii) domestic living arrangements and privacy. For example, patients often raise concerns about delays in implementing Tribunal decisions. Acute shortages of nursing staff can affect patients' access to therapeutic, recreational and social activities, and the lack of privacy and the unsuitability of some living arrangements are regularly raised as issues by women patients. These issues are also matters of considerable concern for the Commissioners visiting the High Security Hospitals and are discussed in more detail in Chapter 5 of this Report.

3.34    All of these three areas of concern were significantly[1] more likely to be raised during meetings with patients in Broadmoor Hospital than in either Ashworth or Rampton Hospitals. Patients at Broadmoor Hospital were also significantly more likely to raise concerns in relation to offences against the person, patients' rights, medical care, other professional care, family matters and social and educational issues. On the one hand, these findings may reflect a greater openness on behalf of these patients, who may be actively encouraged to raise their concerns with Commissioners by the hospital staff. On the other hand, these concerns may be a function of some the problems that predominate in this Hospital. For example, Broadmoor has suffered serious shortages of nursing staff that has resulted in severe restrictions to patients' access to therapeutic and social activities, and fresh air (see 5.138). Similarly, the recreational facilities at Broadmoor are the poorest of the three High Security Hospitals (see 5.136).

3.35    A greater proportion of patient meetings in the High Security Hospitals resulted in Commissioners advising patients to use the hospital complaints procedure, compared to meetings in other units. This proportion was considerably higher in Broadmoor Hospital (13.4%) than Ashworth (5.9%) or Rampton (3.1%). This might be a reflection of differing practices between the Commission visiting teams, or an indicator of the strength of the patients' and Commissioners' concerns. Where patients at Broadmoor had been advised to use the complaints procedure, the principal issues raised related to leave, parole and transfers (55.5%), patients rights (21.2%) and nursing care (18.2%).

**Table 3. Issues raised during private meetings by patients detained in High Security Hospitals**

| Issue category | Ashworth (n=1,085) % | Broadmoor (n=1,021) % | Rampton (n=941) % | All meetings (n=3,047) % |
|---|---|---|---|---|
| Offences against the person | 2.3 | 6.7 | 3.6 | 4.2 |
| Patients' rights | 10.4 | 21.1 | 5.2 | 12.4 |
| Medical care | 8.9 | 18.8 | 10.4 | 12.7 |
| Nursing care | 6.6 | 26.3 | 15.3 | 15.9 |
| Other professional care | 7.7 | 8.6 | 5.5 | 7.4 |
| Living arrangements, privacy | 7.6 | 21.5 | 11.1 | 13.4 |
| Finance, benefits, property | 4.9 | 4.8 | 4.4 | 4.7 |

[1] Statistically significant. Chi-squared test; $p < 0.05$. Full details of these results are available from the Commission upon request.

| | | | | |
|---|---|---|---|---|
| Deprivation of liberty | 4.8 | 6.3 | 4.0 | 5.1 |
| Leave, parole, transfers | 22.6 | 30.4 | 19.9 | 24.4 |
| MHRT matters | 6.5 | 8.0 | 10.2 | 8.1 |
| Family matters | 2.0 | 10.4 | 3.3 | 5.2 |
| Aftercare | 1.8 | 0.9 | 0.3 | 1.1 |
| Local authority services | 0.7 | 1.1 | 0.6 | 0.8 |
| Social, educational | 2.6 | 21.7 | 6.4 | 10.2 |
| Ethnic, cultural, religious matters | 1.5 | 2.0 | 0.9 | 1.4 |
| DoH, Home Office matters | 1.4 | 2.3 | 2.1 | 1.9 |
| Mental Health Act | 1.9 | 5.2 | 6.4 | 4.4 |
| Others | 5.0 | 3.6 | 11.8 | 6.6 |

Note: Column percentages may add up to more than 100% as patients may raise more than one issue during a meeting.

## Additional Information Collected by the Commission

### Matters Requiring Particular Attention

3.36  As part of a Patient Focused Visit, Commission members collect information in a standardised format on "Matters Requiring Particular Attention". The procedure was introduced in 1998 and has been successful in focusing attention on a number of specific concerns about the implementation of the Act and the care and treatment of detained patients. The matters examined were: Forms 38 (Certificate of Consent to Treatment), seclusion, the physical examination of patients, women's care and ethnic monitoring. The Commission's observations on these matters are reported in the relevant sections of this Report.

3.37  A pro forma was completed for every ward visited from April 1998 until the end of the visiting cycle the following December. A total of 1311 forms were completed, 1176 for NHS units, 62 for mental nursing homes and 73 for High Security Hospitals.

3.38  The data collection was found to be more time consuming than anticipated, as it required Commission members to access several sources of information including a number of patient files, ward policies and records and records held centrally in the unit. The procedure has been streamlined for 1999/2000 and reliability enhanced by identifying topics where most of the information can be obtained by examining one patient file or visiting one part of the unit. The topics selected are:

- Statutory information given to patients;

- Contact with the Responsible Medical Officer;

- The operation of a 'named' nurse or equivalent system; and

- ECT facilities.

Each Trust and mental nursing home has been notified of these matters in advance so that they have an opportunity to enhance standards, where necessary, before the Commission begins to collect the information in the Autumn 1999.

### Hospital Profile Data

3.39 The Commission has collected data on an annual basis from each hospital and mental nursing home visited in England and Wales on the use of the Act and other matters concerning detained patients. The primary purpose of this exercise is to provide information for the visiting team about the pattern and level of use of the Act in each individual unit. The Commission also does some simple analysis of the data to identify regional and national trends. To avoid duplication of effort, arrangements have been made with the statistical branch of the Department of Health and the Welsh Office to have early access (pre-publication) to the data which is collected via annual returns on the use of the Act. Consequently, the Commission has been able to reduce its own request for information to a small number of supplementary items. These are:

- the ethnicity of patients detained under the Act;
- the number, and outcomes, of applications to Mental Health Review Tribunals;
- the number, and outcomes, of applications to a Managers' Review;
- the number of treatments authorised under Section 62 of the Act; and
- the use of seclusion.

3.40 The Commission has in previous Biennial Reports drawn attention to inadequacies in the collection of data about the uses of the Act. It included in its submission to the Mental Health Legislation Review Team a proposal that the Commission or any successor body should receive (probably through electronic transmission) and scrutinise all the statutory documentation related to the detention and treatment of patients subject to compulsion. This is a function currently undertaken in Scotland by the Scottish Mental Welfare Commission. There would be considerable resource implications, but it would enable the collation of more detailed and reliable information on statistical trends, including demographic, geographic and ethnic variables which would be useful for both national and local audit purposes.

## Complaints Against Commissioners

3.41 During the current reporting period, six Trusts and one patient have made a total of eleven complaints against the Commission or its members. These complaints have, in general, been about the manner and style of individual Commissioners during visits or concerns that Commissioners have failed to pay due attention to the security of patients' records following their scrutiny of the statutory documents. Each complaint was investigated in detail by a senior member of the Commission's Management Board and copies of the final adjudication were provided to the complainant and the Commissioner concerned. Six of the eleven complaints were upheld and letters of apology from the Commission were duly sent to each complainant.

3.42 The Commission takes the issue of the security of patients' records extremely seriously and has since reviewed and amended its Visiting Policy to provide clear guidance to Commissioners regarding their responsibilities in this area. Commissioners have also been reminded that their position demands that at all times they behave in a courteous and respectful manner towards Trust staff.

## Complaints against SOADs

3.43 Although there has been a considerable rise in the number of Second Opinions undertaken in this two-year period (see 6.36), eleven complaints against Second Opinion Appointed Doctors (SOADs) have been received in this time, one more than in the previous reporting period. Five complaints were made by patients or their legal representatives, two were made by patients' Responsible Medical Officers (RMOs), two by hospital administrators and two by persons who acted as non-medical consultees for the purposes of Section 58(4). Two complaints have not been concluded at the time of writing. These complaints are outlined below in more detail than those made against Commissioners, because of their direct relevance to the treatment of individual detained patients.

3.44 The Commission's role in appointing SOADs to undertake Second Opinions under Part IV of the Act does not extend to its being able to consider appeals against those doctors' decisions. The Commission is, however, entitled to withdraw Forms 39, which record the second opinion, under Section 61(3) and would consider doing so for any SOAD authorisation that it felt was seriously compromised by the subject of a complaint. No Forms were withdrawn in this period.

3.45 Most of the complaints against SOADs alleged failures or shortcomings in the procedure of Second Opinion consultations. One non-medical consultee complained that her views had not been considered with sufficient gravity by the SOAD. This complaint was not upheld upon investigation, although the SOAD did apologise for any inadvertent impression given on the visit. Two complaints – from a non-medical consultee and an RMO respectively – stated that the SOAD had not met with the RMO face to face before issuing the Form 39. Both were upheld. A hospital administrator complained about the legibility of Forms 39 issued by a SOAD; this complaint was upheld and legible copies were supplied. One Mental Health Act Administrator complained of the time taken to issue a Form 39 following a SOAD visit. The Commission found that the delay had been caused by difficulties in contacting a non-medical consultee, the availability of whom is the responsibility of hospital managers. This complaint was not upheld.

3.46 Three of the five complaints made from patients were made via their solicitors. All three alleged that SOADs had made insufficient contact with the patient or had misled the patient as to what they intended to authorise. In two cases, independent witnesses confirmed that the allegations were unfounded and in the other, it was clear from the SOAD's records that proper procedures were carried out. None of these complaints was upheld. The Commission also received a complaint from a patient that the SOAD who authorised his treatment had previously sat on a Mental Health Review Tribunal considering his detention and that this amounted to a conflict of interest. Upon investigation it was discovered that this was a case of mistaken identity and that the SOAD had had no previous dealings with the patient.

3.47    The Commission is revising its policy on complaints against SOADs in the light of its experience over the last two years and will continue to monitor closely any complaints received. In many cases it appears that misunderstandings caused by lack of effective communication are the root cause of complainants' grievances and, even when complaints are not upheld, the Commission continues to draw any lessons that may be learnt from its investigations to the attention of all SOADs.

# Chapter 4

# Mental Health Act Issues

## Summary

A high proportion of patients (nearly one third in psychiatric acute units) are detained. While the increase in the use of compulsion at the point of admission to hospital appears to be levelling off, the number of patients admitted informally and then made subject to the Act continues to increase. The Bournewood case has highlighted the high number of patients who are 'de facto' detained.

It is suggested that the four categories of mental disorder defined in Section 1 of the Act could be replaced by a single category of mental disorder in new legislation. Such a broadly drawn definition of mental disorder should be combined with a range of limiting provisions relating to health or safety and the lack of an alternative to the use of compulsory powers, which would ensure that the Act was used only in a narrowly defined set of circumstances.

In the case of patients who are not actively psychotic but are refusing treatment in the community, the opinion of the

*Commission is that early intervention under the Act may be appropriate, provided that, among certain other conditions, there are clear signs of relapse.*

*About one in every three detentions involve the use of holding powers under Section 5. The Commission continues to recommend that where there is high usage, audits should be undertaken.*

*There is a general difficulty in obtaining reliable and speedy attendance of Section 12 doctors and/or doctors with previous acquaintance.*

*The problems in finding a bed in some areas is causing particular difficulties for ASWs in the implementation of a compulsory admission.*

*The requirement for the ASW to consult with the Nearest Relative can, in a small minority of cases, cause difficulties in that it allows an abusing or potentially abusing person to regain contact with the patient in the most vulnerable of circumstances.*

*The Commission issued the Guidance Note, "Scrutinising and Rectifying Statutory Forms for Admission under the Mental Health Act" in November 1998 and re-issued a Guidance Note on "Issues Surrounding Section 17, 18 and 19 of the Mental Health Act 1983".*

*Concerns have been raised with the Commission about considerable delays in effecting a transfer from prison to hospital under Section 47 of the Act.*

*The Commission has decided to monitor the giving of statutory information (Section 132 of the Act) more closely by selecting it as an issue for its 'Matters Requiring Particular Attention' procedure for 1999/2000.*

*There is still no standard format for recording the use of Section 136 and so there is no reliable information about its use.*

*There is a backlog of cases waiting to be heard by Mental Health Review Tribunals. The MHRT Secretariat and the NHS Executive are introducing improvements to speed up the process.*

*General hospitals without a psychiatric unit are making use of the Act for a relatively small but not insignificant number of patients. The Commission intends to issue a Guidance Note on the use of the Act in general hospitals.*

*There has been a rapid growth of providers of health care in the independent sector. It is vital that the Commission receive notification from registering authorities when such homes are registered.*

*The Commission has taken the opportunity of reiterating in its submission to the Mental Health Legislation Review Team its view that the remit of any monitoring organisation such as the Commission should be extended to those patients subject to any new powers of compulsion in the community.*

# 4 Mental Health Act Issues

## Trends in the Use of the Act

4.1 Until the 1990s there had been a downward trend in the use of compulsory admission. This reflects the intention of the 1959 and 1983 Mental Health Acts that patients should normally be admitted to hospital for mental disorder without special formalities in the same way as they are for physical disorder and that statutory procedures should only be used for a minority of patients in limited and well defined circumstances. The Code of Practice also underlined the principle that people should be given treatment and care in the least restrictive setting possible, thus placing an emphasis on the need for mental health professionals actively to explore alternative arrangements to compulsory admission. Consequently there had been a steady fall in the proportion of detained patients from the 1950s to the late 1980s. In 1989, compulsory admissions amounted to 7% of the total number of psychiatric hospital admissions compared to 15% in 1973 and 27% in 1955.

4.2 However, hospitals are now reverting to the position where a sizeable proportion of patients are detained. The heavy pressure on beds combined with the introduction of new approaches to treating acute mental illness in the community has led to a higher threshold for admission to hospital. There is an increasing level of disturbance among in-patients and they are more likely to be detained under the Act.

4.3 The number of compulsory admissions increased dramatically in the first half of the 1990s, rising, in England, from about 18,000 in 1990/1 to 25,600 in 1994/5 (Dept. of Health, 1998a and 1998b) – about 10% of all admissions (see 9.15 for Mental Health Act data in Wales). Since then they have begun to fall off again, although the Department of Health warn that this may be due to more accurate recording of admission data. The fall is also only apparent at the point of admission, as an increasing number of patients are being admitted informally and then subsequently being detained.

**Table 4. Mental Health Act Admissions for England (Dept. of Health, 1998a and 1998b)**

|  | 1987/88 | 1990/1 | 1994/5 | 1996/7 | 1997/8* |
|---|---|---|---|---|---|
| **Admissions under Part 11** | | | | | |
| Section 2 | 8,868 | 10,309 | 13,175 | 11,406 | 12,405 |
| Section 3 | 2,564 | 4,201 | 8,647 | 8,89 | 19,200 |
| Section 4 | 1,878 | 1,275 | 1,438 | 1,521 | 1,561 |
| **Total** | 14,510 | 16,021 | 23,278 | 21,818 | 23,166 |
| **From informal to:** | | | | | |
| Section 5 (2) | 5,372 | 6,507 | 8,053 | 9,238 | 9,706 |
| Section 5 (4) | 770 | 954 | 1,316 | 1,505 | 1,616 |
| Section 2 | 1,837 | 2,546 | 2,446 | 2,266 | 2,354 |
| Section 3 | 1,737 | 2,275 | 3,460 | 4,107 | 4,432 |
| **Total** | 9,716 | 12,282 | 15,275 | 17,116 | 18,108 |
| **Court and Prison Disposals** | | | | | |
| Sections 35-38 and other Acts | 1,302 | 1,523 | 1,466 | 1,259 | 1,159 |
| Sections 47 and 48 | 171 | 317 | 645 | 614 | 705 |
| **Total** | 1,473 | 1,840 | 2,111 | 1,873 | 1,864 |

* The Court of Appeal judgment in L v Bournewood could have resulted in more detentions in the last quarter of 1997/8 and may account for some of the increase between 96/7 and 97/8.

4.4 The trends during the 1990s in the use of Part II (civil admissions) and Part III (court and prison disposals) at the point of admission to hospital and changes in legal status following admission can be more clearly seen in the following line graph.

**Figure 3: Mental Health Act Trends**

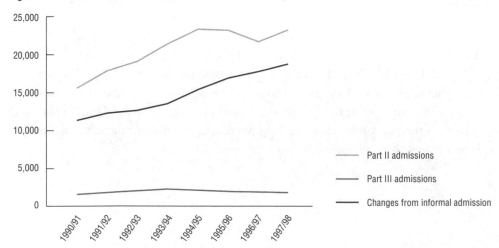

4.5   There is considerable geographical variation between urban and rural areas and between inner London and elsewhere - the frequency of formal admissions is four times greater in inner London than the rest of the country (Johnson et al, 1997). Detained patients may also be more likely to have longer lengths of stay in hospital than those admitted informally, resulting in the current position where a substantial proportion of patients at any one time are detained. The first National Visit of the Commission in 1996 revealed that nearly one third of the patients in acute units were detained, although in some areas the proportion reached over 90%.

4.6   These statistics conceal the fact that there is a large number of patients who, to all intent and purposes, are detained in hospital. These are the patients who lack capacity but are compliant and are treated in hospital under common law in their own best interests. The Bournewood case focused attention on the position of these patients who, as Lord Steyn observed, are detained because they are subject to the control of health care professionals to such a degree as to amount to complete deprivation of liberty. In its written submission to the House of Lords for the Bournewood case (see 1.32), the Commission estimated that there are 48,000 admissions a year which fall into this group. On any one day in England and Wales there are an estimated 22,000 informal incapable patients resident in hospital compared to approximately 13,000 patients detained under the Act. These vulnerable mentally incapacitated patients lack the safeguards of the Mental Health Act and arguments are emerging for more people to be brought under the protection of law and subject to statutory safeguards, rather than fewer.

4.7   The policy of diverting mentally disordered offenders from the criminal justice system is also increasing the pressures on the health service to provide more secure beds for the detention of patients as an alternative to prison. However, this policy has not yet been reflected in any significant increase in the number of Part III admissions, apart from the number of transfers from prison to hospital under Sections 47 and 48. The number of such transfers has doubled from the beginning of the decade to 700 a year and evidence suggests that the number would be greater still if more secure beds were available. Research studies indicate that 19% of sentenced prisoners and 25% of remand prisoners have problems of mental disturbance and if substance dependency or abuse is included the percentages increase to 39% and 63% respectively. Prison conditions with restricted regimes in which mentally disordered prisoners may be locked in their cells for much of the day are likely to exacerbate these mental health problems (Penal Affairs Consortium, 1998).

4.8   In the Seventh Biennial Report, the Commission identified a need for further research concerning demographic, geographic and ethnic factors underlying these statistical trends. It welcomes the fact that the Department of Health has commissioned the Royal College of Psychiatrists' Research Unit to co-ordinate a programme of research with the objective of gathering 'data on the way that the Act is used in the context of wider provision of mental health services and what factors affect its use' (Marriott et al, 1998).

# Section 1 – The Coverage of the Act

4.9    The Act defines mental disorder as "mental illness, arrested or incomplete development of mind, psychopathic disorder and any other disorder or disability of mind". Provided that the other statutory conditions are satisfied, a diagnosis of mental disorder is sufficient for short term admissions, including admission for assessment for up to 28 days under Section 2. For longer term sections, a diagnosis of one of the four specific categories of mental disorder - mental illness, mental impairment, severe mental impairment or psychopathy - is required. Nearly all admissions to NHS facilities are categorised as mental illness - 98% in 1997/8 (Dept of Health, 1998b). Out of every 1000 compulsory admissions, only about 14 are categorised as mental impairment, 9 as psychopathic disorder and 2 as severe mental impairment. Only the High Security Hospitals have a significant number with a psychopathic disorder; 22% of the 103 admissions in 1997/8 fell into this category.

4.10   How useful are these categories in distinguishing those who should be included within the scope of the longer term Sections of the Act? It has been argued that they are neither legally nor clinically appropriate and that the opportunity should be taken in the review of the mental health legislation to abandon the categories of 'mental impairment' and 'psychopathic disorder'. If the safeguards of the Mental Incapacity Bill were effected, it might be that the need for the formal detention of patients with learning disability would no longer be justified by the disability as such, but would only be authorised on the grounds of mental illness (or possibly the behaviour disorder) associated with the learning disability. Similarly, the Government's proposals to introduce a new form of reviewable detention for severe anti-social personality disorders may obviate the need for the inclusion of psychopathic disorder as a specific legal category. Nevertheless, it is important that the possibility of treatment for personality disorder is not forgotten in the current climate. As the Report of the Committee of Inquiry into the Personality Disorder Unit, Ashworth Special Hospital (Fallon, 1999) concluded, personality disorder incorporates a wide range of conditions, its association with other mental disorders is common and hospital management and treatment is appropriate for compliant patients. It is a matter for careful assessment in each case. People diagnosed as suffering from personality disorders and their families can be made extremely vulnerable by the fact that mental health care agencies are sometimes unwilling to take on the responsibility of providing any care or treatment.

> **Visit to Worthing Priority Care NHS Trust and West Sussex SSD; 19 May 1998**
>
> Some Social Services staff were concerned that people with certain conditions, such as personality disorder, who could fall within the admission criteria of the Act as defined in Section 1, may find it difficult to get access to mental health services provided by the Trust because of the health authority's criteria for entry to them. Commissioners were told that the policy is not to offer a service to patients with personality disorder but to refer them to a specialist service such as one of those provided by the Henderson Hospital.

4.11    It is important to arrive at a definition of mental disorder that neither excludes those who should be included, nor includes those who should be excluded. One particular problem within the treatment sections of the current Act, for example, is that it excludes patients suffering from an acquired brain injury, unless there is an associated mental illness. The category of mental impairment is not applicable, as it is defined as " .. a state of arrested or incomplete development of mind..", implying onset in childhood. A single category of mental disorder could be one way to describe persons falling within the scope of future mental health legislation. The concept of mental disability proposed in 'Who Decides' (The Lord Chancellor's Department, 1998) could be applied as part of the test to decide whether a person should be compulsorily admitted for psychiatric treatment in the same way as for other decisions about personal welfare, physical health care and financial matters (Hoggett, 1996). This concept would cover "any disability of the mind or brain, whether permanent or temporary, which results in an impairment or disturbance of mental functioning". Alternatively or additionally, further consideration could be given to the proposal to define those falling within the ambit of mental health legislation by reference to an incapacity test. The use of such a test as a reason to deprive persons of their liberty would be a radical departure from previous legislative models. Amongst the issues to be addressed would be defining what is meant by incapacity, what to do about fluctuating capacity and what would happen to the presumption that a person can be capable in relation to one area of decision making but not in others. Any incapacity-based legislation would need to be able to address effectively the temptation to regard all that appears as unreasonable refusal of care and treatment as indicative of incapacity.

4.12    The wide discretion afforded to doctors in broadly drawn definitions of mental disorder or incapacity could be limited by keeping existing or similar criteria relating to health or safety and the lack of an alternative to the use of compulsory powers so as to prevent unnecessary or arbitrary detention. The combination of a broad definition with a range of such limiting provisions should ensure that mental health professionals use their powers in an appropriately narrow way in what Fulford (1998) refers to as the 'broad definition - narrow use' solution.

## Section 2, Section 3 and the Threshold of Admission

4.13    A patient may be admitted under Part II of the Act if he or she is suffering from a mental disorder of a nature or degree which, in the case of Section 2, warrants detention in a hospital for assessment (or for assessment followed by medical treatment) or, in the case of Section 3, makes it appropriate for him or her to receive medical treatment in a hospital where it is necessary in the interests of his or her health or safety or for the protection of other people. What is meant by the term 'nature or degree' is open to interpretation (see 2.42 et seq, *R V MHRT ex parte Smith*). Neither the Act nor the Code of Practice offers guidance on how severely disordered a person must be before the statutory grounds for detention are satisfied. There is confusion amongst mental health practitioners whether compulsory admission is only possible where there is overt evidence of mental illness or whether earlier intervention can be justified in the case of an asymptomatic patient refusing medication, on the grounds that the patient's medical history suggests that he or she will relapse in the future. The issue was raised in the Falling Shadow, an official report of a homicide inquiry commissioned by the South Devon Health Care Trust (Blom-Cooper, 1995) and has been further discussed in a Commission Discussion Paper, 'The Threshold for Admission and the Relapsing Patient'.

4.14   The opinion of the Commission is that early intervention under the Mental Health Act may be appropriate even if the patient is not actively psychotic, provided that, among certain other conditions, there are signs of relapse, i.e. it is clear that the disorder is beginning to manifest itself in a recognisable way. While the *degree* of mental disorder may be negligible, the fact that there are not necessarily any symptoms is not proof that the underlying disorder is not of a severe *nature*. This is not to say, as the Discussion Paper points out, that there is a duty to make a medical recommendation in these circumstances or that it would be negligent not to do so. Mental health professionals have a considerable discretion in terms of how best to help the patient and how best to manage the situation. However, if compulsory admission is to be recommended, the Commission's opinion is that a Section 2 recommendation is to be preferred to Section 3. This is because the latter requires that admission is *necessary* for the patient's health or safety and is a stronger test than that which applies under Section 2, indicating that nothing short of in-patient treatment will adequately safeguard the patient's health. Consequently it was suggested that where a patient is being detained on the grounds of the nature but not the degree of mental illness, detentions for a short defined period of assessment would usually be more appropriate.

4.15   It should be emphasised that this is a point of view and not definitive legal advice. However, this interpretation of the Act allows earlier intervention when there are definite signs of deterioration in the patient's mental health. The treatment regime can be re-commenced without waiting for the patient to become so unwell that treatment then becomes difficult. Such admissions to hospital may also reduce the risk of tragic events which have occasionally occurred when patients refuse to receive psychiatric treatment in the community.

4.16   The Discussion Paper has been widely circulated and discussed among mental health practitioners and over 30 written responses were received. Although one respondent was alarmed at what he saw as a backdoor attempt to introduce community treatment orders, nearly all the other respondents agreed with the view that a wider threshold for the compulsory admission of a relapsing patient should be, and is, allowed under the Act. One Trust is considering a review of the format of its aftercare plans so that there will be an opportunity not only to record indicators of relapse but also what action should be taken if relapse is indicated. While welcoming the Discussion Paper, another respondent cautioned that using the power to admit under Section 2 should not pre-empt assertive outreach work and other efforts to engage the patient in treatment without resorting to compulsion. Indeed, the need for coercive measures to improve compliance is likely to be minimal if the quality of services is improved, in particular by the provision of information to patients and families about medication and side effects and by mental health professionals maintaining regular contact.

4.17   While supporting the main thrust of the Discussion Paper about earlier intervention, many of the respondents disagreed with the view that Section 2 should be used rather than Section 3. It was argued that if the form of mental disorder is known (i.e. is known to be mental illness, mental impairment or personality disorder), the warning signs of relapse are clearly documented and the object of admission is for treatment (i.e. to reinstate a pre-existing treatment plan and not to do a complete re-assessment) then Section 3 should be preferred. Section 2 may also be a less effective tool because it gives less time to establish a pattern of compliance with treatment and it may be difficult to convert to a Section 3 when there is only a modest manifestation of the illness, which may in fact subside very quickly with treatment.

4.18   A further disadvantage is the less extensive powers granted to a Nearest Relative under Section 2. There appears to be a paradox in the Nearest Relative's having the right to block admission for a relapsing patient who is actively psychotic and admitted under Section 3 and not having the same safeguard for the relapsing patient admitted under Section 2 when psychotic symptoms are not present. It would appear that the less ill the patient the less right the family would have regarding admission to hospital.

4.19   The Commission accepts that it is appropriate, in the circumstances described above, for the patient to be admitted under Section 3. Indeed, one of the pointers listed in the Code of Practice (chapter 5) for the use of Section 3 is that the patient is already known to the clinical team and has been assessed in the recent past by that team. The Commission occasionally finds the need to reinforce this advice where it finds that Section 2 has been used inappropriately, such as in an attempt to avoid the objection of a Nearest Relative. If the objection is felt to be unreasonable, an application should be made to the County Court under Section 29(3)(c) to displace the Nearest Relative. It was held in the case of *R v Central London County Court and another ex parte London [1999]* that an interim order can be made, where necessary, to displace a Nearest Relative, allowing for the expedition of admission under Section 3 where the Nearest Relative was objecting (see 2.50).

4.20   The Code of Practice (5.3b) also advises that if an extended period of treatment is needed, an application for detention under Section 3 should be made at the earliest opportunity and should not be delayed until the end of Section 2 detention. Such action will prevent complications occurring such as illustrated in the following example.

> **Visit to Bay Community NHS Trust; 16 July 98.**
>
> One patient was detained under Section 2 on 2 June 98. In spite of a multi-disciplinary meeting agreeing that the patient was to be further detained under Section 3 when the liability to be detained ceased, nothing was done before the Section expired. On 1 July 98 it became necessary to successively invoke

> the holding powers contained in Section 5(4) and 5(2). On 3 July 98, the patient was detained under Section 3 of the Act. Nursing notes recorded staff concerns that the Section 2 was about to expire with no action regarding the Section 3 recommendation.

4.21   Mental Health Act practitioners do appear to be adhering to the advice in Chapter 5 of the Code of Practice. An increasing proportion of Part II admissions are under Section 3 (see table 4) indicating that more patients are already known to the clinical team, which could be a sign that teams are improving in their ability to keep track of patients and are operating the Care Programme Approach more effectively.

## Section 4 – Admission in cases of Emergency

4.22   This Section provides for temporary admission for up to 72 hours on a single medical recommendation and must only be used in a genuine emergency when there is not enough time to obtain a second medical recommendation. Section 4 is sparingly used and accounts for only 7% of formal admissions to hospital from the community. However, the Department of Health statistics do show a small increase in its use over the past two or three years. One reason for any increase is likely to be difficulties in gaining access to a Section 12 Doctor or a GP (see 4.31 et seq). ASWs report occasions when the patient has become more disturbed while efforts are being made to secure the attendance of a second doctor and an emergency admission becomes necessary. The Commission has noted a particularly high use of this Section in a few units. Some inner city areas may have added difficulties because of the higher numbers of homeless or transient people not registered with a GP.

> **Visit to City & Hackney Community Services NHS Trust (Homerton Hospital); 28, 29 May & 5th June 1998**
>
> The Trust acknowledged that short-term Sections were being used at a high rate of 106 uses of Section 4 and 171 of Section 5(2) in one year and that only about half were converted into longer term detention under the Act. Commissioners were concerned that the majority of Section 5(2)s and a high proportion of Section 4s run for the maximum 72 hours allowed under the Act. An audit of Section 4 from January to March 1998 showed that the majority of the Sections occurred out of hours with about half of these at weekends. The Trust undertook to audit the use of short-term Sections to give a full picture of what happens both "pre" and "post" Section and reminded staff about the appropriate use of short-term Sections with a recommendation that they should be used actively and not allowed to lapse by default.

4.23   A Section 4 admission deprives the patient of the safeguard of being assessed by two doctors rather than one. Many of these admissions occur out of hours when access to alternative methods of dealing with the crisis will be more limited. The ASW and doctor who may not know the patient or, in the case of the doctor, not be approved under Section 12 as having special experience in the diagnosis and treatment of mental disorder, may be more inclined to take the safer option and resort to compulsion. One third (580) of Section 4 admissions are not converted to a longer-term Section (Dept. of Health, 1998b). In order to avoid unnecessary detention in hospital being prolonged, it is particularly important to follow the guidance of the Code of Practice (6.7) that an appropriate second doctor should examine the patient as soon as possible after admission, to decide whether the patient should be detained under Section 2.

## Section 5(2) and 5(4) - Holding Powers

4.24  Section 5 (2) authorises the detention of an informal patient for up to 72 hours where the doctor in charge concludes that compulsory admission is appropriate and the patient might leave the hospital before there is time to give consideration to an application under Section 2 or 3. Section 5(4) empowers nurses of the prescribed class[1] to authorise the detention for up to 6 hours of a patient who is receiving hospital treatment for mental disorder on an informal basis. It is intended for use in an emergency when a doctor is not immediately available and the nurse considers that there might be serious consequences if the patient were to leave the hospital. Most detentions under Section 5(4) are converted to Section 5(2) and a few to Section 2 or 3.

4.25  The 1999 edition of the Code of Practice (8.2, 8.4) has clarified the definition of an informal patient as being a patient receiving in-patient care, including treatment for physical disorders, and who has willingly (or not unwillingly) entered and stayed in hospital. The holding powers cannot be used for out-patients, and admission procedures should not be implemented with the sole purpose of then using Section 5(2).

> **Visit to Lewisham & Guys Mental Health NHS Trust and Lewisham Social Services Department; 12, 17 & 18 November 1997**
>
> A patient who was admitted from Accident and Emergency on 20 September 1997 was detained under Section 5(2) very shortly after arriving on Lister Ward. There was no indication in the notes that the patient agreed to in-patient admission and Commissioners questioned whether this was a genuine informal admission. Similarly, another patient was admitted from Suite Six (out-patients). The plan which was written at out-patients was as follows:- "admit to Lister. Put on Section 5(2)". The plan was that following the Section 5(2) he would be detained under Section 3. The patient arrived on the ward at 7.00 pm, a Section 3 recommendation already having been signed by the doctor who saw him at out-patients, and a Section 5(2) was completed at 7.20 pm which stated: "he needs constant monitoring and restraint ... he is utterly unsafe and unable to assent to, or co-operate consistently with, his management plan." Commissioners doubted whether this patient was a genuine informal admission and they were concerned that Section 5(2) was wrongly used in this case as a short-term admission Section.

---

[1] The Mental Health (Nurses) Order 1998 came into force on 17th November 1998 and extended the categories of nurse who are prescribed for the purposes of Section 5(4). These categories are set out in full in the Code of Practice (footnote to 9.1)

> The Trust indicated that it would continue to monitor the use of Section 5(2) and would draw up a policy. However, Commissioners raised this issue as a matter of concern at their next visit in December 1998.

4.26 The Commission commented in the Seventh Biennial Report on the high usage of Section 5(2) and undertook to monitor the use of this Section closely. It can be seen (table 4) that the use of Sections 5(2) and 5(4) has continued to increase, while the use of other sections has declined. About one in every three detentions involves use of these holding powers and in some units the majority of detentions begin with a Section 5(2). High usage does not necessarily imply misuse, but where this does occur, the Commission will recommend that the unit undertakes an audit to establish the reasons and to ensure that good practice is always observed.

> ### Visit to North Herts NHS Trust; 23 April 1998
>
> Commissioners commented, once again, on the high percentage (71%) of those patients detained under the Mental Health Act who had been held initially on a Section 5(2), although the records reviewed showed that the holding power had been used appropriately. Commissioners were given a breakdown of where the use of Section 5(2) occurred. Managers accepted the Commission's suggestion that a more detailed audit of Section 5(2) should be carried out to try to establish why such a high proportion of detained patients were held on this Section.

4.27 Such audits might include investigating how soon after informal admissions Section 5(2) is imposed, the time between imposing the Section 5(2) and informing the ASW that an assessment is required and the time taken to complete the assessment.

4.28 There is a concern that the Act is sometimes only invoked when the patient attempts to leave or resist treatment and that proper assessments may only be undertaken at that point. For example, Commissioners are aware of instances where patients have been warned that they would be detained under Section 5(2) if they tried to leave. Such a threat, or implied threat, of the use of compulsory powers amounts to de facto detention. It also raises serious questions about the distinction between voluntary and compulsory admission and whether the safeguards under the Act are being denied to those patients coerced into informal admission.

4.29 While patients should be treated on an informal basis where at all possible, it is not appropriate to hold the powers given by Section 5(2) in reserve as a means of delaying an assessment until a crisis occurs. The Section may be used where the patient is clearly indicating that he is no longer willing to stay in hospital, but it must not be used to keep the patient in hospital during a transient period of disturbance where there is no intention to consider an application under Sections 2 or 3. The Code of Practice stipulates that Section 5(2) is not an admission Section under the Act and should only be used if it is not possible or safe to use Sections 2, 3 or 4 (8.9). In the following examples, the desire to avoid the use of compulsion may have led to an unjustified delay in implementing Section 5(2) and then in converting it to a formal admission under the Act.

---

### Visit to a Learning Disabilities unit in February 1998

Three sets of notes relating to patients detained over the last 10 months preceding the visit were examined. Issues on the use of Section 5(2) in relation to these patients gave rise to some concern.

In the first case, a patient was admitted "informally" on 23/9/97 because of aggression towards a family member and challenging behaviour. He indicated his unwillingness to stay by sitting on the floor and shouting, "no, no". He was placed on Section 5(2) at 7.30 pm. There was no further reference to the holding power in the notes until 25/9/97 when it was stated "S 5(2) not necessary as he can be persuaded to stay", but also "needed to be given PRN medication because of upset and aggression". The doctor did not complete a recommendation for detention and, contrary to unit policy, neither a second doctor nor an ASW were asked to assess. Following this period this patient's notes referred at various times between October 1997 and January 1998 to the "need to be restrained" and IM and PRN medication being imposed following an assault on staff.

In the second case, a patient who was admitted informally in mid June 1997 was placed on Section 5(2) on 18/7/97 and on Section 3 on 21/7/97. In fact the notes were clear that from 10/7/97 the patient had been indicating very clearly ("I want to go", "I can't stand it here" etc) that he was not consenting to staying in the unit. In addition, during this period he was threatening and aggressive towards staff.

In the third case, a patient again came into hospital informally on 18/3/97 and, from the early days of the admission, there were references to absconding and aggression towards staff. He was then placed on Section 5(2) on 17/4/97 and Section 3 on 18/4/97.

From these three examples it may be inferred that there was a general intention to treat informally wherever possible; an admirable approach so long as the patient's rights can be fully safeguarded. There are some grounds to conclude that this approach led to patients being treated informally and then dealt with under Section 5(2) where they should have been assessed for compulsory admission at a much earlier stage. The managers were asked to look again at the compliance with the unit policy on the use of Section 5(2), which they undertook to do.

---

4.30   The purpose of Section 5(2) is to prevent the patient leaving the ward only until they can be assessed for further detention. The assessment must be completed as soon as possible. The Section should not be allowed simply to lapse after the 72 hour period and the patient should be discharged from detention under the Section as soon as it is decided that formal admission will not be necessary. The Commission has noted a general improvement in the speed of implementing a full assessment, but still comes across instances where the Section has been prolonged for purposes other than that of completing an assessment.

> **Visit to the Foundation NHS Trust and Staffordshire Social Services Department; 7 & 8 August 1997**
>
> On reviewing the statistical information that was supplied by the Trust, Commissioners noted that approximately 25% of Sections 5(2) were being allowed to lapse.
>
> On scrutinising the legal documents Commissioners found, recorded in patients' notes, instructions to nursing staff requesting them to allow the Section 5(2) to lapse.

## GP and Section 12 Doctor Issues

4.31   Section 12(2) of the Act requires that at least one medical recommendation supporting an application for admission under the Act shall be made by a practitioner approved as having special experience in the diagnosis or treatment of mental disorder and, even if that practitioner has previous acquaintance with the patient, the other recommendation shall, if practicable, be given by a doctor who has such previous acquaintance. Compliance with this Section of the Act continues to present difficulties and is the single issue which is raised most consistently on Commission visits. There is a general difficulty in obtaining reliable and speedy attendance of Section 12 doctors and / or doctors with previous acquaintance.

> **Visit to Bedford and Shires Health and Care NHS Trust and the Social and Community Care Department of Bedfordshire County Council; 9 & 10 July 1998**
>
> There appeared to be no local Section 12 rota and the list provided to ASWs apparently included doctors who were not available or who no longer practised. The Commission was told that, in 10 out of 13 recent assessments, it had taken over four hours to obtain the services of a Section 12 doctor, and in one case two ASWs had approached 16 doctors in a 24-hour period. Delays, particularly during the day, had led to admissions late in the evening, causing distress to families whilst the patient was kept at home. The Trust undertook to work with the Health Authority to address this issue.

4.32   This problem can be exacerbated by the reluctance of GPs to attend assessments in respect of their own patients, whether they are in hospital or the community. There are particular difficulties with regard to out-of-hours cover provided by a GP co-operative, where the doctor refuses to be involved in assessment of patients for compulsory admission, because they have had no previous acquaintance with the patient. It is not sufficient for a deputising doctor simply to have access to the patient's records. The Code of Practice (2.29) now recommends that the second medical recommendation should be provided by a doctor who knows the patient personally in his or her professional capacity. However, it is not uncommon for patients to be detained on the recommendations of two doctors, where the second doctor neither knows the patient nor is approved under Section 12.

> ### Visit to Bournewood Community and Mental Health NHS Trust; 9 March 1998
>
> Commissioners found three examples of applications where neither doctor had previous acquaintance with the patient. In these circumstances, the Code of Practice (2.29)[1] advises that both medical recommendations should be from Section 12 doctors. In the first case, the ASW should have indicated what attempts were made to contact a Section 12 doctor. There was no reference to this in the accompanying ASW report. The same situation was noted on a very recent Section 2 application for the second patient, although the ASW assessment report had not yet arrived. In the third case, the ASW did not give any reason, as required on the application form, why it was not possible to get a medical recommendation from a medical practitioner who did know the patient. However, there was an explanation in the accompanying report.

4.33   The safeguard of a second medical recommendation is negated if both doctors do not fulfill their individual professional responsibility as outlined in the Code of Practice (2.22) and do not conduct a proper medical examination as required by the Mental Health Act itself (Section 12(1)). The GP in the following example reduced his important statutory function merely to a rubber stamping exercise.

> ### Visit to Plymouth Community Services NHS Trust; 19 March 1998
>
> An application form for a Section 2 admission completed by the patient's GP gave the reasons for compulsory admission as "patient's refusal". The Trust's senior managers and senior medical staff had attempted to encourage the GP to be more specific with regard to the reasons for admission. In addition, Commissioners were equally concerned to hear that the GP had not interviewed the patient but simply attended the house, looked at the patient and signed the form.. Commissioners urged the Trust to re-examine the case and to seek further clarification with regard to the legality of this patient's detention.

4.34   Another matter of concern is the level of knowledge of mental health law among medical practitioners. A study in the West Midlands found that even among consultants and senior registrars who were using the Act more frequently than GPs, there was a lack of knowledge in basic areas such as definitions and procedures. This was also despite the fact that NHS Executive guidance on how the approval of practitioners under Section 12 should be undertaken was closely adhered to in the West Midlands (Bhatti et al 1998/99).

4.35   Health authorities have responsibility for the appointment of doctors under Section 12, but lists generated by health authorities may be unhelpful as they may simply list all Section 12 approved doctors in the region (often more than a hundred) irrespective of whether they would be willing to attend to assess a patient. It is not practicable for ASWs to phone through a lengthy list of this nature. A national solution is required, which could include

---

[1] References in all the examples to the Code of Practice have been updated to correspond with the paragraph numbers of the revised edition of the Code.

making Section 12 duties more financially rewarding and which could build in other incentives around education and training of GPs to become approved. It could be made a requirement of any new legislation that all consultant psychiatrists should be approved under Section 12 or equivalent provision. Meanwhile, the Commission welcomes initiatives being taken by a few authorities to remedy the problem. The Commission learned, for example that *Sunderland Health Authority* is considering the possibility of salaried general medical practitioners acting as Section 12 doctors under the Mental Health Act as part of their contractual duties.

### Visit to West London Healthcare NHS Trust and Ealing Social Services Department; 7, 13 & 14 November 1997

Commissioners were informed by ASWs that they experienced considerable difficulties in obtaining the services of Section 12 doctors when asked to carry out an assessment for detention under the Act. They said that there was no rota for obtaining even the first Section 12 doctor and that they regularly had to telephone four doctors and not infrequently up to twelve doctors before they were able to start an assessment. They observed that the psychiatrists on duty at the Resource Centres might not be Section 12 approved and that it was rare for the consultant psychiatrist to come out. Furthermore, their experience was that the integration of the Crisis Intervention Service into the Community Teams had reduced the availability of the Section 12 doctors. As a result of the lack of a workable rota, ASWs often relied on one or two doctors, one of whom appears not to be Section 12 approved.

It is unacceptable that one of the basic requirements of the Act continues to be so poorly provided for in this catchment area. The failure to institute a workable rota of Section 12 doctors was raised as a matter of some concern by the Commission in 1995. Commissioners had understood that funding had been provided to ensure its establishment.

The Commission urged that the matter should be addressed by the Health Authority and the Trust and asked to be provided with an action plan for resolving this together with a report in three month's time on the progress made. Commissioners also asked that the Social Services Department keep detailed records of their activities in relation to arranging assessments during the same period.

In a subsequent meeting with Ealing, Hammersmith and Hounslow Health Authority, the Commission welcomed the fact that the Authority had put £35,000 into funding such a rota, which was finally in place from 12 February 1998.

### Visit to Essex and Herts Community Health NHS Trust (Princess Alexandra Hospital); 30 April 1998

Commissioners commended proposals to improve the availability of Section 12 approved doctors. The proposals had arisen from consultations with the local medical committee and local consultants. Commissioners were informed that a Section 12 rota had been implemented among Trust staff within normal hours, involving not only the consultants but also other doctors. There were proposals to pay all

Section 12 approved doctors a retainer and to develop an innovative training programme, which would not require six months of psychiatric training but would include a six month period of mentoring.

## The Role of the Approved Social Worker (ASW) – Section 13

4.36 ASWs play a crucial role in the process of assessment and admission, and the Commission takes a close interest in the exercise of their powers and duties under the Act. The Commission continues to have concerns that the number of ASWs deployed in some Social Services Departments is insufficient. Difficulties in recruiting ASWs are commonly experienced. A 1996 workforce analysis carried out by the Local Government Management Board and the Association of Directors of Social Services revealed that approximately 40% of local authorities did not have sufficient ASWs. It is not yet known what impact local government re-organisation and the creation of smaller unitary authorities is having on the provision of the ASW service. Smaller local authorities may have difficulty in maintaining a sufficient workforce and can experience particular difficulty when staff leave. It is frequently reported by ASWs that the workload of statutory assessments is such that other responsibilities, e.g. aftercare and key worker roles, cannot be carried out effectively. In some areas the number and availability of ASWs on out-of-hours rotas has been reported as inadequate, leading to delays in carrying out assessments. Where there are difficulties, consideration may need to be given by neighbouring authorities for consortia arrangements for the ASW service, although ASWs still must be appointed by each authority.

4.37 The Commission welcomes the arrangements, often seen, for the appointment of ASWs with specialist expertise with particular groups, including people with learning disability and older people. Where this expertise is not available, ASWs have expressed concern about the quality of the assessment and its outcome:

Visit to Richmond, Twickenham and Roehampton Healthcare NHS Trust and Richmond Social Services Department; 8 September 1997.

Commissioners were told there are no ASWs in the teams for older people and that it is rare for a locality care manager to be available to accompany ASWs on an assessment. ASWs felt that they have insufficient expertise and local knowledge of possible alternatives to admission so that older people may occasionally be detained inappropriately.

4.38 The Commission made a submission to the Central Council for Education and Training (CCETSW) consultation exercise in Autumn 1998, for the review of the requirements for ASW training. Requirements and Guidance are currently set out in CCETSW Paper 19.19. The Commission is concerned that training should adequately equip ASWs with knowledge of, and ability to apply, relevant law and guidance, and that it should address risk assessment, risk management and issues of practice within a multidisciplinary setting.

4.39 ASWs should receive regular, well-planned refresher training. In many areas this is being achieved, although elsewhere refresher training is of variable quality and sometimes non-existent. There have been problems in some of the new unitary authorities where, with the break-up of large county-wide training departments, not all of the new separate authorities have yet been able to establish comprehensive training programmes. Similarly, the quality and accessibility of legal advice which should be available to ASWs remains variable.

4.40 The Commission particularly welcomes the evidence of increasing opportunities for multidisciplinary training, and the establishment of local Mental Health Act forums where ASWs can discuss practice issues with colleagues from other disciplines including doctors, nurses, police and ambulance staff.

4.41 The Commission notes the development of closer partnership between Social Services Departments and Trusts, and the strengthening of working relationships between professionals on the ground. Improved relationships and communications are often reported in those areas where ASWs are members of established multi-disciplinary community mental health teams (CMHTs). In some CMHTs, ASWs report difficulties in gaining understanding by other professionals of their primary statutory role and responsibilities in relation to the overall work of the CMHT.

4.42 Good practice also requires that doctors and ASWs have the opportunity to liaise with each other. It is particularly important that, where possible, there are face to face discussions between ASWs and doctors involved in assessments under the Act. Direct communication can help to ensure that there is an effective sharing of information and different perspectives, leading to good quality assessment and decision-making (Code of Practice, 2.3). However, ASWs are often asked to make applications for detention in hospital on the basis of medical recommendations left by doctors with whom they have had no contact and which, for instance, may have been left on the ward.

> **Visit to Cambridge Social Services Department; 25 June 1998**
>
> Despite generally good working relationships with CMHTs, and with hospital based colleagues, ASWs reported continuing difficulties in securing reliable access to doctors providing medical recommendations under Section 2 or 3, in order to clarify the medical grounds for compulsory detention etc. ASWs also said that they still frequently found that medical recommendations were left on a ward in hospital, in many cases before the ASW had ever been contacted.

> **Visit to Mid Anglia Community NHS Trust and Suffolk Social Services; 22 January 1998**
>
> Despite reporting excellent relationships with some doctors on an individual basis, ASWs wished to highlight the continuing difficulties in complying with the Code of Practice when medical staff failed to notify ASWs in good time of an impending assessment for compulsory admission and/or when an ASW

arrived to find that medical recommendations had been left with the expectation that the ASW would simply go ahead and complete the application.

Further discussions between the Trust and the Social Services Department were planned, following the Commission's Visit, to address these issues.

4.43 The Code of Practice (11.13) has included new guidance that the ASW should leave an outline report at the hospital when the patient is admitted, giving reasons for admission and any practical matters about the patient's circumstances which the hospital should know and, where possible, the name and telephone number of a social worker who can give further information. Commissioners' experience is that copies of ASW assessment reports are increasingly, although not invariably, available on patients' hospital records. These reports are of considerable value, particularly where the format is consistent with the information needs of the receiving hospital. They also confirm ASWs' discharge of their duties including identifying, consulting with, and giving information to Nearest Relatives.

Visit to Aylesbury Vale NHS Trust and Buckinghamshire Social Services; 18 September 1998

Commissioners commended the high standard of the ASWs' assessment reports and also the practice of keeping copies of these together for monitoring and reviewing purposes. Commissioners considered that the practice could be further improved by ensuring that ASWs record the reasons for not consulting with the Nearest Relative where this occurs, and also that the giving of information to the Nearest Relative about rights is also routinely recorded.

4.44 In some areas there are acute problems in accessing beds, and this causes particular difficulties for ASWs. Commissioners are sometimes asked by ASWs whether in these circumstances assessments can be deferred.

Visit to Riverside Mental Health Trust and Hammersmith and Fulham Social Services; 23 October 1997

Commissioners were very concerned to hear that ASWs were, on occasions, not carrying out assessments because of the improbability of a bed being available should the individual require admission. They were told that on one occasion medical recommendations had lapsed because a bed could not be found within 14 days, and patients have had to be held overnight in police cells.

4.45 The Commission advises that ASWs have a duty to carry out their functions as prescribed in the Act, and that the responsibility for finding a bed is clearly laid on health care providers whose duty it is to admit the patient. If the patient cannot be admitted for want of a bed, the relevant social services authority, health authority and police authority will be liable if one or more of them fail to perform for the patient those functions which the law requires them to discharge. In practical terms, this means that in an emergency the ASW should complete the application, making it out to a hospital specified by the relevant health authority in the notice required to be given under Section 140 of the Act, and convey the patient to that hospital. The ASW should inform the hospital that he or she will remain with the patient while a bed is organised, but that it is the hospital managers' responsibility to admit the patient; the patient is *per se* not fit to be in the community.

## The Role of the Nearest Relative

4.46   Section 11(3) of the Act requires that the Nearest Relative must be consulted and informed of the power to discharge the patient under Section 23. Relatives who provide a substantial amount of care to people with mental disorder are an important source of information about the needs of the patient and family. Proper consultation must therefore include information about the hospital to which the patient is to be admitted in order that the Nearest Relative can exercise the power of discharge. Occasionally concerns are referred to the Commission about this requirement, particularly as the ASW has no discretion not to consult an unsuitable person, except where consultation is not practicable or would involve unreasonable delay (Section 11(4)). This dilemma is exacerbated in the case of Section 3 where, additionally, the Nearest Relative has the right to prevent the application being made. As a result, in a small minority of cases, an abusing or potentially abusing person can establish or re-establish contact with a patient in the most vulnerable of circumstances. The Nearest Relative will also retain his or her status even if he or she has severed all geographical and emotional links with the patient.

4.47   The patient has no right to prevent the consultation taking place and is not included amongst those who can apply to the County Court for the displacement of the Nearest Relative by another person. The European Court is being asked to adjudicate on this matter in the case of *J.T.v United Kingdom [1997]*, as it could amount to a violation of Article 8 of the European Convention on Human Rights, i.e. the 'right to respect for private and family life' (see 2.56). In any event, the grounds for displacement relate only to the Nearest Relative's ability to exercise key powers, not to the potentially negative consequences of the relative discovering the patient's whereabouts.

4.48   This problem therefore would appear to stem from two sources; firstly, the Nearest Relative's range of rights and powers under the Mental Health Act (second only to those of the RMO and exceeding those of the Approved Social Worker); secondly, the patient's inability to take any action to prevent the Nearest Relative from being consulted even where there would seem to be a compelling reason to do so.

4.49   The Act itself contains examples of a possible way forward for future legislation. The duty of hospital managers to give information to a Nearest Relative about a patient's detention, Tribunal rights and discharge (Sections 132, 133) do not apply if the patient requests otherwise. Similarly, the power of Supervised Discharge (Sections 25A-J), introduced into the Act in 1996, modifies the Nearest Relative's role to that of a consultee whose views must be taken into account, but with no power to prevent or discharge the order. The Nearest Relative under Supervised Discharge also has a right to apply directly to a Tribunal for the patient's discharge from the order. As with Sections 132 and 133 these rights are subject to the patient's permission unless the RMO feels that special circumstances apply (eg. where the patient could be a risk to others or the Nearest Relative will also play a substantial part in the patient's aftercare).

4.50    It may be that, were the legislation to be amended, extension of these provisions to those parts of the Act dealing with the primary detention of patients would provide protection in such circumstances. The Commission would welcome further consideration as to whether the legal right to object to an application for admission for treatment under the Act provides the best safeguards for both patients and Nearest Relatives. Alternative means of redress, such as the right to apply for an external review of detention and to receive such a review within a specified period, and/or the right to apply to discharge the patient (subject to limitation) could take the place of the right of the Nearest Relative to object to an application. A requirement could also be introduced for the ASW to record, with the application, the Nearest Relative's objection and the reasons for overriding it.

4.51    Alternatively, new legislation could provide for patients to be given the opportunity to object to a particular person acting as Nearest Relative or the equivalent. Currently, unless the Nearest Relative is displaced, there is only provision for the County Court to appoint an individual or a Social Services Authority to act as Nearest Relative if the patient does not have one. However, this opportunity is rarely taken, apart from some notable exceptions.

> **Visit to Chichester Priority Care NHS Trust and West Sussex Social Services; 18 May 1998**
>
> Commissioners were pleased to note that there were several cases where active steps were being taken to seek the appointment of Nearest Relatives where there was no apparent relative identified under Section 26.Commissioners were informed that the Social Services Department had acted on advice to seek private individuals to take on this role rather than allocating the function to a member of staff. There were seven cases where applications to the County Court were being dealt with in this way.

## Section 15 - Scrutinising and Rectifying Statutory Forms

4.52    Commissioners and Second Opinion Appointed Doctors frequently find that statutory forms have not been correctly completed. It may appear to some mental health managers and practitioners that the Commission is being overly fastidious when scrutinising the forms. However, the statutory documentation gives NHS Trusts and mental nursing homes the legal authority to detain and, where necessary, for the RMO to compulsorily treat patients. Where the deprivation of liberty is concerned it is crucial to observe legal and procedural formalities to ensure that patients' legal rights are respected and to protect staff from legal liability. The Commission issued the Guidance Note "Scrutinising and Rectifying Statutory

Forms for Admission under the Mental Health Act" in November 1998 to advise those with responsibilities for administering the Act on the statutory requirements for the completion of the forms, the identification of irregularities and the rectification, where permissible, of mistakes[1].

4.53    Where, during a Commission visit to an NHS Trust or to a mental nursing home, it is suspected that one or more of the statutory forms may be invalid, the managers will be asked to:

•    furnish the Commission with a copy of all the statutory documents relating to the current period of detention;

•    urgently review the authority for the patient's detention and whether there are any other statutory or common law grounds for detention; and

•    notify the Commission of their findings and any steps taken as a result.

The patient should also be informed that there is a possibility that he or she may not be lawfully detained and should be assisted, if required, to obtain independent legal advice.

> **Visit to Park Royal Mental Health Centre, North West London Mental Health NHS Trust; 17 April 1998**
>
> Two examples were found where the legal documentation contained errors which might have had the result that the patient was not legally detained. In the first case, a doctor had completed a medical recommendation for Section 3 based on an examination given for the purposes of Section 2, nearly four weeks previously. Clearly the patient had not been examined by two medical practitioners within five days (Mental Health Act, Section 12.1) and this invalidated the detention. In the second case, an ASW application was wrongly dated a month previously: although this is a rectifiable correction, the 14 day period for such corrections had expired. Commissioners advised that urgent consideration should be given to these two cases and asked that the Commission office be informed on the next working day about the action that had been taken.
>
> Examples were also found of corrections to legal documents which had not been initialled by the signatory to the form.
>
> Commissioners were extremely concerned to find such errors within the legal documentation. They suggested that in addition to the steps requested above, urgent consideration be given to the practice of scrutiny of legal documentation, which was clearly not being carried out to the necessary standard.
>
> The Trust informed the Commission offices of the steps taken to rectify the two errors specifically referred to above within two working days and reviewed the practice of scrutinising documents at the Park Royal Centre.

[1] More detailed advice giving pointers of the completion of forms can be found the in Mental Health Act 1983 Statutory Forms Manual [A Guide for Completion and Scrutiny], Institute of Mental Health Act Practitioners and Trecare NHS Trust, 1998.

4.54 There should be a number of checks within the process of admission to ensure that the documentation is correct. Besides doctors and ASWs making sure that the forms they sign comply with the requirements of the Act, ASWs have the additional duty to check the medical recommendation forms as well as their own application form before admission. It is also the duty of the hospital managers "to ensure that the grounds for admitting the patient are valid and that all relevant admission documents are in order" (Code of Practice, 22.7). It is the managers who are ultimately responsible for the legality of detention.

4.55 A common fault with the medical recommendations under Section 3 is that they do not specifically indicate the reasons for the diagnosis of the type of mental disorder or the alternatives to hospital admission that were considered. For example, on one visit the Commission found one medical recommendation which gave "dishevelled, sleeping in car, denies problems, recently assaulted ex-partner" as the reason for arriving at a diagnosis of mental illness.

> ### Visit to Mid-Anglia Community Health NHS Trust; 16 July 1998
>
> Four statutory documents listed below required amendment, if within the time limit, and in respect of the Forms 11 legal advice regarding their validity. The errors contained in all three stress the importance of thorough scrutiny.
>
> One Form 9 (application by Approved Social Worker for admission for treatment) was found to have omitted the name of the hospital, including only the name of the Trust.
>
> One Form 10 (joint medical recommendation for admission for treatment) was found to have the phrase 'Section 12 approved doctor' deleted and the term 'Police Surgeon' inserted.
>
> In stating "Unable to accept that she is ill or distressed. Not in a stable situation at boyfriends", a Form 11 (medical recommendation for admission for treatment) was not felt to have adequately given the reasons why admission under the Act was necessary.
>
> Similarly on another Form 11, the content of both medical recommendations appeared inadequate. Furthermore, one contained an inaccuracy in stating "the MHA will allow any treatment to be used".
>
> Following the Commission Visit, the Trust copied the Commission's comments to all ASWs and consultants for them to note.

4.56 Rigorous scrutiny is also required to alert Responsible Medical Officers to the need to complete the statutory form to renew detention under Section 3 (Form 30) within two months prior to the expiry date. The failure to complete this form on time where continued detention is necessary has serious consequences for the patient. Late applications for renewal are unacceptable and continued detention is unlawful, unless a new application for a fresh Section 3 is made. In that event the patient is deprived of the consent to treatment provisions of Section 58, as they apply to medication for mental disorder, for another three months and also of an automatic referral to a Mental Health Review Tribunal, which is arranged on renewal of Section 3 if there has not already been a Tribunal application.

## Section 17 – Leave of Absence from Hospital

4.57 Section 17 makes provision for patients who are liable to be detained to be granted leave of absence from hospital. A patient may only be out of that hospital lawfully, for whatever purpose and whether escorted or not, if the RMO has granted leave. Some of the key difficulties that the Commission finds NHS Trusts and mental nursing homes have in implementing this provision are described below.

4.58 Leave is needed if the patient goes outside the grounds of the hospital. However, there is sometimes uncertainty about what constitutes the hospital grounds, particularly now that hospitals and Trusts are not necessarily co-terminous. Where there is more than one Trust on a hospital site, Section 17 leave may not be required for the patient to move from one Trust to another but such authority will be required to leave the hospital site. Where a hospital comprises a number of buildings, leave of absence will be required for any period of absence involved in moving between buildings which are not on the same site. Legal advice may be needed to clearly establish the boundaries of the hospital. Attendance at another hospital site will always require Section 17 leave, even if that hospital is part of the same Trust. However, if a patient is being transferred to another hospital managed by the same Trust, they can be moved without any formality under Section 19(3).

4.59 The RMO has final clinical responsibility for the management of the patient and the Act makes no provision for the responsibility for the granting of leave to be delegated or transferred to another doctor, although it is possible, for instance during periods of leave or illness, that another doctor, preferably another Consultant, may be the RMO[1]. The Commission still finds examples of junior doctors, without RMO status, approving leave. The RMO may direct that a patient remains or is in custody while on leave. The custodian (who will usually be a qualified mental nurse) has certain powers not usually available to others – including the power to detain and to convey. This allows a patient the opportunity to have leave, to receive treatment in another hospital or to have compassionate home leave but with added security. Any relative involved in the care of a patient should be notified before the granting of leave, but would not normally be expected to take on the responsibilities of a custodian. Consequently the recording of leave should avoid giving any misleading impression, (for example, by specifying that the patient must be escorted by a relative), that the patient is in the custody of the relative unless that is what is intended.

---

[1] The Memorandum to the Act now states, at paragraph 60, that the doctor who is for the time being in charge of a patient's treatment in the absence of his or her usual RMO ``should normally be another consultant or specialist registrar approved under Section 12(2) of the Act.'' Section 12 approval is not, however, a *legal* requirement for a RMO. Therefore if, in the absence of the patient's RMO, another consultant is not available or able to take responsibility for that patient there should be no reason why either a locum consultant or a registrar should not undertake the duty.

4.60   The Commission encourages hospitals to devise a simple form upon which the details of the leave and any conditions imposed upon it can be recorded. Forms recording such authorised leave should specify the period for which the leave is valid. Phrases such as "as often as appropriate" are too vague. The frequency of leave should be recorded with the maximum latitude that is granted for a defined period, eg. 'once a day for up to 2 hours' or 'from 2-4pm, up to three times per week' etc. along with any conditions attached to such leave. The authorisation should be regularly reviewed where a programme of leave remains in place over lengthy periods.  Copies of the form should be given to the patient, any appropriate relatives and any professionals in the community who need to know.

### Visit to North West Anglia NHS Trust (Peterborough Sites); 23 & 24 July 1998

Commissioners noted with considerable concern that a Senior Registrar in The Gables had authorised Section 17 leave for a patient in the absence of documented authorisation in the records by the Responsible Medical Officer (RMO). In the absence of the normal RMO, who in this case was on leave, it is essential that responsibility is formally handed over temporarily to another doctor who accepts full responsibility for the patient and that this assignment of responsibility is recorded. RMOs are reminded that they have no authority to delegate responsibility under Section 17 of the Act. The same Senior Registrar in the Lucille Van Geest Centre had authorised Section 17 leave for another patient, again without recorded authorisation by the RMO.

None of the Section 17 leave forms in the Lucille Van Geest Centre conformed with good practice. For example:

- forms contained statements such as "as discussed with the RMO" but there was no written record of what was discussed and authorised by the RMO;

- forms specified "accompanied leave" but did not define who patients were to be accompanied by;

- the period for which the authorisation was valid was not defined; and

- on Ward 5, the space on the form for recording conditions attached to leave was blank on all forms examined.

Commissioners understood that copies of the Section 17 leave forms were not given to involved carers (Code of Practice, 20.6).

Commissioners recommended that RMOs should be reminded of their responsibilities under the Act and that other medical staff should be reminded of the limits to their authority. Following the Commission visit, the Trust organised training for staff on Section 17 and managers reminded staff of the need for a copy of the Section 17 leave form to be given to carers.

4.61   Some hospitals have developed exemplary documentation for recording leave.

> ### Visit to Worthing Priority Care NHS Trust and West Sussex SSD; 19 May 1998
>
> Documentation of Section 17 leave was generally excellent. At Shepherd House and Crescent House, for example, conditions of leave were clearly stated, there was a date for review and the form was sometimes signed by the patient. A circulation list was also included on the form, but representatives from some commissioning bodies told Commissioners that they were not always informed when leave was given to a patient with whom they were involved.

> ### Visit to Horizon NHS Trust; 27 January 1999
>
> Commissioners found good recording and monitoring of leave under Section 17 following the inquiry report in July 1997 into the absconsion of a patient while on escorted leave. Procedures for recording the granting of leave together with regular risk assessments were very good. A new improved leave form was in the process of being introduced at the time of the visit.

4.62 Another area of uncertainty has re-surfaced following the Barker case (see 2.46) concerning whether detention can be renewed under Section 20 if the patient's care alternates between periods as an in-patient and periods on Section 17 leave. The judgment in the Barker case provided a wider definition of what constitutes in-patient treatment.

4.63 The Commission has re-issued its Guidance Note on 'Issues Surrounding Section 17, 18 and 19 of the Mental Health Act 1983', which clarifies the statutory requirements and provides pointers for good practice about arrangements for and recording of leave of absence. It also includes a sample form, which units can adapt to suit their own local circumstances. However, the complexity of applying the leave provisions of the Act within the current configuration of service provision, particularly with the geographical dispersal of units within the same Trust, and treatment approaches that cut across community and hospital ward, is a matter which needs to be considered as part of the review of the Act.

## Part III Issues

4.64 Part III of the Act is concerned with patients involved in criminal proceedings and covers circumstances in which patients may be admitted to, and detained in, hospital on the order of a court, or transferred to hospital from prison on the direction of the Home Secretary.

### Anomalies

4.65 One of the anomalies within the current Act is that Section 35 (remand to hospital for report on accused person's mental condition) is excluded from the Consent to Treatment provisions (Part IV of the Act) and has led to the practice of 'dual detentions' whereby patients are sometimes formally detained under Section 3 to allow treatment. The arguments for and against the legality of this practice are summarised in Jones (5th edition para. 1-324) and need not be repeated here, although the Commission (and the Code of Practice, 17.3) has maintained that it is legal, if not ideal. It is difficult to see the need for the restriction on treatment in the case of any similar power of detention within new legislation.

4.66 Another anomaly which applies to Section 36 (remand of accused person to hospital for treatment) and Section 38 (interim hospital order), as well as Section 35, is that there are no provisions for granting leave under Section 17. This has caused difficulties where patients have required medical attention at another hospital or escorted leave on compassionate grounds. If leave of absence is necessary, the hospital managers need to seek approval from the Court. The Commission is aware of cases where the Court has declined to give consideration to requests for leave on account of the absence of specific authorising provisions in the Act.

## Transfer of Prisoners

4.67 Section 47 enables the Home Office to direct a prisoner serving a sentence to be transferred from prison to hospital. The need for in-patient treatment for a prisoner should be identified and acted upon quickly and the transfer to hospital should take place as soon as possible (Code of Practice, 3.20 and 3.21). However, concerns have been raised with the Commission about considerable delays in effecting the transfer, resulting both from the amount of time it takes for a psychiatric assessment to be completed following a referral from the prison doctor and for a hospital response offering, or declining to offer, a bed. In some cases, there may be a dispute as to the level of security required and a second referral may need to be made to another unit. On occasion, the Home Office may be asked to intervene when there is a disagreement about the level of security required. It is claimed that these transfers are seen as low priority until the release date is approaching because of the low risk to public safety while the patient remains in prison. For example, the Commission has received a copy of correspondence between HM Prison Service and a High Security Hospital about one patient, who was recommended for a transfer in September 1996, but had still not been offered a bed nearly two years later. As he was awaiting a bed, he had failed to progress through the prison system and remained located in the segregation unit because of his threatening behaviour to health care staff when non-compliant with medication. Prisoners transferred close to their release date may feel aggrieved and view their transfer to hospital as a further 'punishment without end'

4.68 During such a period of waiting, the prison medical service is unable to treat the mental illness without the patient's consent, because the Act cannot be applied in prison health centres. Furthermore, the Commission does not have a remit to meet with these patients, as they are not yet detained under the Act. A concern has also been raised about the remission of patients back to prison (Section 50) before they are ready, possibly to relieve the pressure on beds in the secure psychiatric unit or to place discharge responsibilities onto the prison service in an attempt to avoid the duty to provide Section 117 aftercare. The Commission remains of the view that prisoners who require in-patient psychiatric care should be transferred to psychiatric hospitals for treatment and submits that there should be access to some external body, possibly by an extension of the Commission's remit, to keep under review the implementation of transfers between prison and hospital.

4.69 The Commission has discussed the issue of prisoners being transferred close to their earliest date of release at its annual meeting with the Mental Health Unit of the Home Office. The Unit's data showed that in 1997/8 out of 260 transfers to medium secure units, 76 were within 3 months of the expected date of release. Some apparently late transfers may be explained by patients having been sentenced for short periods of time. At the time of the meeting in May 1998, there were 16 prisoners awaiting beds at High Security Hospitals for varying periods up to 19 months.

4.70 Research investigating transfers under Section 48 (which applies to unsentenced prisoners), based upon a sample of prisoners remanded in 1992, concluded that most transfer requests were completed speedily once they had been received by the Home Office. However, a minority of transfer requests were not made until a considerable time after the remand in custody and there was evidence that requests were sometimes not made until a bed was available (Mackay and Machin, 1998). The Commission recommends that further research could usefully investigate the extent of, and reasons for, late transfers for sentenced prisoners.

## Restricted Patients (Sections 41 and 49)

4.71 Under Section 37 of the Act, a court can order a mentally disordered offender to be detained in a psychiatric hospital for treatment. If the offender is also considered to pose a risk of serious harm to the public, a judge can impose a restriction order under Section 41. This places constraints upon the offender's transfer, leave of absence and discharge from hospital. Restriction directions (Section 49) can be imposed on mentally disordered offenders transferred from prison to hospital. Home Office research, which examined the progress of a sample of conditionally discharged restricted patients, found that, on the whole, the orders were effective. The great majority of those discharged were not convicted of further offences that caused or threatened harm to others (Street, 1998).

4.72 In relation to all restricted patients, the consent of the Home Secretary is required for the authorisation of leave into the community and transfer between hospitals. On a number of occasions, the Commission has been informed of delays in obtaining the Home Office consent, which have impeded the patient's rehabilitation. The Commission raised this problem in its annual meeting with the Mental Health Unit of the Home Office and was told that the Unit has performance indicators for leave requests of i) carrying out initial examination and requesting any additional information within 5 working days and ii) completing the paperwork within 2 weeks of receiving all information. The standard is to achieve this target in 70% of cases; it is reached in 74% of cases for escorted leave and 78% for unescorted leave.

4.73    The Home Office will only consent to a restricted patient being granted a period of trial leave under Section 17 to another hospital if the Responsible Medical Officer (RMO) imposes certain conditions; i.e. that the patient submits to such treatment and medication as the doctor in the receiving hospital considers necessary, as directed or agreed by the RMO, and that in the event of the patient's failure to comply the leave shall be revoked and the patient returned to the referring hospital. However Section 17 does not permit a transfer of the authority of the RMO, so that the consultant at the referring hospital remains responsible for any changes in treatment not covered by a Form 38 or 39. Another difficulty is that further leave (i.e. leave from leave) can only be granted by the RMO. At the request of the Commission, the Home Office Mental Health Unit has amended the wording in its letter consenting to trial leave in order to clarify the point that the referring doctor remains the RMO and cannot transfer any part of his or her authority.

## Rights of Detained patients – Section 132

4.74    Generally, the recording of the giving and understanding of rights information is improving. This includes not only giving written information, but also giving explanations and ensuring that the patients understand their legal position.

> Visit To Surrey Heartlands Trust; 23 March 1998
>
> Considerable efforts had been made to ensure that patients understood their rights and this was well documented in the patients' records. A particularly good example was a patient who suffered from short term memory loss and had been provided with a printed card which she was able to carry around with her to remind her of her rights.

4.75    It is important that the giving of information is recorded fully (Code of Practice 14.4d) and it is recommended that a specific form is used for the purpose. Provision should also be made to record when the patient did not understand and when repeated attempts were made.

> Visit to Hellesdon Hospital and Wensum Meadows, Norfolk Mental Healthcare NHS Trust; 7 May 1998.
>
> In some cases patients' notes did not contain evidence in the form of standard documentation that staff had discussed rights issues with detained patients. On the other hand, Commissioners also found that staff were actively engaged in assessing the capacity of patients to understand their rights, particularly on Ward 4, where there was very clear evidence of repeated attempts by staff to give information to an elderly woman detained under Section 3.

4.76    The Commission has decided to monitor the giving of statutory information more closely by selecting it as one of the "Matters Requiring Particular Attention" for 1999/2000 (see 3.36 et seq). The expected standards are that each ward should have the relevant Mental Health

Act leaflets either published by the Department of Health or by the Trust/mental nursing home, that these should be available when required in different languages and in braille and that deaf patients should have access to signers. There should be a standard form to record the name of the person giving the information, the date the information was given, whether the patient understood, whether there are subsequent attempts to give the information and the planned date for the next attempt.

## Police Power to Remove to a Place of Safety – Section 136

4.77    Across the country people detained by police under Section 136 continue to be routinely taken to police cells, pending statutory assessment, despite concerns about the suitability of that environment.

> ### Visit to Bedford and Shires Health and Care NHS Trust and the Social and Community Care Department of Bedfordshire County Council; 9 & 10 July 1998
>
> The Commissioners were disappointed to find that the designated Place of Safety continues to be Bedford Police Station. In 1995 the Commission was sent a copy of the Section 136 Joint Agency Policy for Bedfordshire in which it is stated:
>
> "We are planning to continue to use local Police Stations as the primary Place of Safety until such time as the new designated Place of Safety suites can be built into the revised psychiatric units in the North and South of the County (maximum 2-3 years but probably less than this)"
>
> In February 1997, following a patient focused visit to the Trust, the Commission was informed that the Trust was actively progressing the provision of a Place of Safety on Weller Wing.
>
> During a Visit on 10 July 1998 a Commissioner visited Bedford Police Station, met with the Custody Sergeant and visited cells where patients are taken for assessment under the Act. The physical environment in the Police Station is not suitable for the care of someone considered mentally vulnerable or in crisis. The Custody Sergeant told the Commissioner of a number of incidents involving self-harming behaviour whilst people were held on Section 136 in the cells. He considered that his officers were not trained to deal with this client group.

4.78    The Code of Practice now reflects earlier Commission advice (Seventh Biennial Report, p49 –50) that the preferred Place of Safety should be in a hospital rather than a police station (Code of Practice, 10.5). The Royal College of Psychiatrists' working group on Standards of Places of Safety recommend that, where possible, the Place of Safety should be a specialised assessment unit closely linked to, or at least readily accessible to, a psychiatric facility. However, flexibility is still needed. An alternative Place of Safety should be identified for those whose behaviour makes them unsuitable for the preferred facility (Royal College of Psychiatrists, 1997).

> **Visit to Milton Keynes Community NHS Trust and Milton Keynes Social Services Department; 12 June 1998**
>
> Commissioners were told that there are three places of safety, with an agreed protocol between the police, social services and the Trust as to how they should be used.
>
> The preferred Place of Safety is the Campbell Centre, where there is an appropriately designated room for the assessment of persons held under Section 136 off the unit. The police station is used where there are concerns about violence and the Accident and Emergency Department if the person is physically unwell. The annual statistics on the use of Section 136 provided a breakdown of the places of safety used. 44% of people were taken to the Campbell Centre during the year ending March 1998 and 35% to the police station.

4.79   It may not always be practicable to set aside a single designated facility as a Place of Safety. But there may be problems if acute admission wards are used for this purpose, not only because of possible disruption to other patients, but also because it may lead to an assumption that the patient is about to be formally admitted.

> **Visit to the Hillingdon Hospital NHS Trust; 4 September 1997**
>
> Commissioners were told that an acute admission ward continued to be used as the Place of Safety for the purposes of Section 136. It was considered that the use of such a ward places pressures on staff and other patients during what is often a difficult assessment process. Commissioners prefer the Place of Safety to be a designated room or suite.

4.80   There are continuing concerns about the length of time the patient is held before the statutory assessment is completed. The Commission has submitted to the Mental Health Legislation Review Team that the maximum period of detention in a Place of Safety of 72 hours for the purpose of assessment is too long. It is considerably longer than the 24 hour period during which a criminal suspect may initially be held without charge.

> **Visit to Redbridge Healthcare NHS Trust (Goodmayes Hospital) and Redbridge Social Services; 26 & 27 February 1998**
>
> Commissioners were concerned to see that a high number of Section 136s had run for two or more nights before the patient was assessed. They were told that a detailed audit would be conducted, jointly with Social Services, to establish the reasons for these delays.

4.81   The person must be assessed by both a doctor and an ASW, even if the doctor has seen the patient first and has concluded that admission under the Act is unnecessary. The exception to this, according to new advice in the Code of Practice (10.8), is if the doctor concludes that the person is not mentally disordered within the meaning of the Act[1], in which case, in compliance with Article 5 of the European Convention on Human Rights (the right to liberty and security of the person), he or she can no longer be detained. Otherwise, the patient should not be discharged before the ASW has had the opportunity to assess what alternative arrangements might need to be made for the patient's treatment and care.

4.82    Although it is recommended that records are kept of the use of Section 136, there is still no standard format for such records. Consequently, the extent of use of the power and standards of practice, including the time taken to complete an assessment and dispose of the Section, can only be monitored where local agencies have decided to keep detailed records. There is no reliable information about the use of Section 136, which, in some inner city areas, is known to be high. In London, for example, over the last two years it is estimated that there have been 2000 uses of the Section, approximately three every day (communication at meeting with Metropolitan Police).

> **Visit to Worcester Community Healthcare NHS Trust and Hereford and Worcester Social Services Department; 25 & 26 September 1997**
>
> Commissioners noted that very detailed recording of the use of Section 136 takes place in the Worcester area and asked that this be extended to other areas.

> **Visit to Forest Healthcare NHS Trust and Waltham Forest Social Services; 20 March 1998**
>
> The Commission noted examples of patients subject to Section 136 having waited for up to 72 hours for a full mental health assessment. It was not possible to ascertain how soon after the Section 136 was instituted an Approved Social Worker was asked to assess a patient. It was also reported that a patient spent several days in custody at a local police station on Section 136 awaiting transfer. The Code of Practice is clear on the use of this Section (Chapter 10) and the Trust was advised to formulate an effective policy for the use of Section 136 in conjunction with Social Services and the local Police.

4.83    The Home Office has been considering issuing guidance to police forces to achieve greater standardisation of documentation used in Section 136 cases. This guidance would indicate core information that should be included in the documentation. The Commission would like to see the introduction of a statutory form to record the exercise of the police power to remove to a Place of Safety and the circumstances leading to such use, which as a clinically significant record, would be required to be placed in the patient's notes.

---

[1] In the opinion of the Commission, mental disorder, here, would appear to mean mental disorder within the meaning of Section 1 of the Act rather than the narrower definition of mental disorder of a nature or degree which would justify admission under the Act.

## Mental Health Review Tribunals and Managers' Reviews

4.84   Part V of the Act deals with the function of the Mental Health Review Tribunal (MHRT) to review the justification for a patient's continued detention at the time of the hearing. The administration of MHRTs is not within the remit of the Commission, but the Commission does take an interest in issues raised by detained patients concerning access to the Tribunal. Such matters are raised in 14% of Commission meetings with patients (see table 2, p. 59). Section 23 of the Act provides for an alternative route for a patient to obtain a review of detention by means of a managers' review. Chapter 23 of the Code of Practice substantially revises and expands on the previous guidance on the exercise of the hospital managers' powers of discharge with new sections on the composition of review panels, criteria for review and the conduct of reviews, whether contested or not.

4.85   Table 5 shows the data collected by the Commission, via the Hospital Profile Sheet (see 3.39) on the number of cases heard, and discharges made, by Mental Health Review Tribunals for the three year period between 1995 and 1998. There may be an under-estimation of the number of carers, as the information was obtained from the hospital and not directly from the MHRT Secretariat.

**Table 5. MHRT Tribunals***

|  | Applications | Cases Heard | | | Discharges | | |
|---|---|---|---|---|---|---|---|
|  | 1997/8 (only) | 95/96 | 96/97 | 97/8 | 95/96 | 96/97 | 97/98 |
| Section 2 | 3,243 | 2,480 | 1,934 | 2,096 | 450 | 343 | 348 |
| Section 3 | 6,899 | 3,456 | 3,244 | 3,236 | 410 | 358 | 460 |
| Part III | 1,142 | 784 | 731 | 827 | 147 | 147 | 154 |
| Total | 11,197 | 6,720 | 5,909 | 6,159 | 1007 | 848 | 962 |

* Not including figures from the three High Security Hospitals

4.86   The higher number of Tribunal hearings in 1995/6 may, in part, reflect the increase in the number of detentions for that year (see table 4). The proportion of referrals resulting in discharge remains consistent at between 14.4% and 15.6%.

4.87   The above table does not include Tribunal details held for patients in the three High Secure Hospitals. A recently published study found that out of 661 hearings in 1992, 43 (7%) resulted in a form of discharge of the detention order (Taylor et al, 1999). The authors recommended that consideration should be given in the review of the legislation to an extension of MHRT powers to order transfers between levels of security.

4.88   In 1997/8 there were 3,598 managers' reviews, where detention was contested, resulting in 268 (7.4%) discharges. In 1995/6 and 96/7, there were, respectively, 324 and 232 patients discharged following a managers' review; (the total number of contested reviews is not known for these years).

4.89    A significant number of applications to a Tribunal do not reach a hearing, usually because patients are discharged while the application is being processed. During 1997/8, the Commission collected statistics on the number of applications made to Tribunals and found that 65% of Section 2, 47% of Section 3 and 72% of Part III applications were actually heard. A higher proportion (77%) of the applications for a manager' review were considered by the managers.

4.90    There is a statutory seven day time limit for applications of patients on Section 2 to be heard, but the fact that so many patients on Section 3 do not have their cases heard by a Tribunal is a denial of justice. The Commission commented in some detail in the Seventh Biennial Report about the delays in the system (para. 3.1.4). There is evidence of this problem continuing during the current reporting period.

> **Visit to Coventry Healthcare; 18 July 97**
>
> Commissioners were informed that patients detained under Section 3 of the Act who appealed to the Mental Health Tribunal against detention, were on average having to wait three months for a hearing.

4.91    The MHRT Secretariat is addressing the concerns about the length of time that patients in some areas have to wait to have their application heard. One of the biggest challenges faced is the upsurge in applications during the past decade without a corresponding increase in staffing to process them. A senior manager was appointed in April 1997 to be in overall charge of operational issues in England and a new computerised system has been introduced to streamline the administration and enable the staff to process cases more quickly. In April 1999, the NHS Executive announced  a proposal to tackle the backlog of cases by holding more Tribunal hearings. Mental health service managers were urged to ensure that clinical and professional staff respond by producing Tribunal reports within the statutory period of 3 weeks from the date when the hospital is told of the patient's application.

4.92    For patients subject to restrictions who have been recalled under Section 75(1) of the Act, following discharge from hospital, the Mental Health Tribunal Rules have been amended to introduce a fixed time limit for Tribunal hearings (Mental Health Review Tribunal (Amendment) Rules 1998 (S.I.1189)). This change was prompted by an application to the European Commission on Human Rights alleging a breach of Article 5(4) of the Convention, which gives detained persons a right to a speedy review by a court (*Roux v United Kingdom [1996]*). Tribunal applications must now be heard within eight weeks from the date on which the reference by the Home Office (which must be within a month of the patient's return) is received at the Tribunal Regional Office. Tribunal reports must be submitted to the Tribunal Secretariat within a three-week deadline from the receipt of the notice of the Tribunal application. The number of these cases is relatively small. The Commission would welcome the introduction of time limits for all MHRT hearings. The recognition of the central provisions of the European Convention on Human Rights in domestic law, via the Human Rights Act 1998, (and which underpin the Code of Practice (1.1)) will make it imperative that all cases are heard within the time limits which have been agreed with the Council on Tribunals, i.e. within 8 weeks for unrestricted patients and 20 weeks for restricted patients.

4.93   Doubts have been raised about whether there should be two separate systems for patients to obtain a review of their detention, and the Secretary of State for Health in the last administration announced his intention to abolish the power of managers to discharge detained patients as soon as a legislative opportunity arose. However, managers' hearings do provide an additional and usually speedier safeguard, but this must be seen as being supplementary to a Tribunal hearing and as not undermining the patient's rights to apply to a Tribunal. *Tower Hamlets Healthcare NHS Trust*, in an effort to streamline the process further, has piloted a pre-review system. When a patient requests a review, two managers interview the patient and are in contact with a third manager by telephone. If they are satisfied that a prima facie case exists for discharge from detention, a hearing will be arranged. If not, they will advise the patient that it would be better to wait for a time before requesting a full hearing. Patients are also informed that if they still want a formal review, one will be arranged. There are some concerns that the negative advice of the hospital managers will also discourage the patient from applying for a Tribunal hearing. On a visit to Tower Hamlets, the Commission recommended that a leaflet is prepared for patients with information about the pre-review system and that patients are given adequate warning of the pre-review.

4.94   Hospitals do not have to wait to be asked to review a patient's detention. In the case of Tribunal delays, hospital managers could institute their own review and, if appropriate, discharge the Section.

> **Visit to Heathlands Mental Health Services NHS Trust on 16 March 1998**
>
> Commissioners who visited Arreton Lodge were concerned that three of the four detained patients on that unit had not applied to the Mental Health Review Tribunal (MHRT) within the first 6 months of their Sections and were currently awaiting automatic referral hearings. These hearings were apparently long overdue and Commissioners were unable to discover the reasons for this. They noted, however, that no medical or social work reports to the Tribunal were on the patients' files. They were very concerned that hearings were awaiting the provision of those reports and asked for hospital managers' comments on, and urgent attention to, this matter.
>
> In view of the delays, Commissioners suggested that the hospital managers should review urgently the detentions in each case, irrespective of any applications to them by the patients.
>
> An automatic referral letter had, in fact, been sent to the MHRT the previous December, but there was a difficulty in scheduling the cases. Hearings were held for all three patients within two months of the Commission's visit. The Trust undertook to make sure such delays would not happen again.

4.95 Any body which formally detains a patient should have some role in considering the appropriateness of that detention and must retain the power to end it. However, in its submission to the Mental Health Legislation Review Team, the Commission proposed that, provided an external review of detention is properly available to patients both upon admission and periodically thereafter, the current provision that managers must exercise their right to review detention, whenever, within reason, they are asked to do so by a patient could be reconsidered. A procedure could be established by legislation that required managers to be guided by a patient's RMO when considering a patient's discharge or continued detention. Managers are not necessarily competent to judge the need for treatment, but in the event of uncertainty or disagreement with the RMO, managers could be required to seek an independent medical opinion. Indeed new guidance has been inserted in the Code of Practice (23.17) which recommends that a managers' review panel should consider an adjournment to seek further medical or professional advice, if there is a divergence of views about whether the patient meets the clinical grounds for continued detention.

## Use of the Act in General Hospitals without a Psychiatric Unit

4.96 Patients are occasionally detained under the Act in general hospitals that do not have a psychiatric unit. The Commission has a statutory responsibility to visit all units which may admit patients under the Act. The Commission wrote to all chief executives of general hospitals in 1995 requesting that it be notified and supplied with copies of statutory documentation when a patient is detained under the Act at their hospitals. However, recognising that it is not informed of all such detentions, the Commission decided to gain a more accurate picture of the use of the Act in non-psychiatric hospitals by conducting a survey in one regional area. This was done in collaboration with the West Midlands region of the NHS Executive.

4.97 A short form, to identify the number of times Sections 5(2), 2 and 3 of the Act were used in 1996/7, was sent to 23 Trusts and 21 responses were received, although one hospital was unable to supply any information. Seventeen Trusts reported uses of the Act, of which 15 were able to provide statistics broken down by Section, as follows:

**Table 6. Uses of the Act in General Hospitals in the West Midlands**

| Section | No. |
| --- | --- |
| Section 5(2) | 32 |
| Section 2 | 24 |
| Section 3 | 10 |
| Total | 66 |

nb. The two hospitals without central records had between them detained an estimated 7 or 8 patients.

4.98 The 66 total uses of the Act in the above table may not represent 66 individual patients, as the outcome of each application of the Act is not known: some uses of Section 5(2), for example, may have resulted in further detention under Section 2 or 3.  The following figure shows the range of frequency of use of the Act in the hospitals surveyed.

**Figure 4: Range of Use of the Act in General Hospitals**

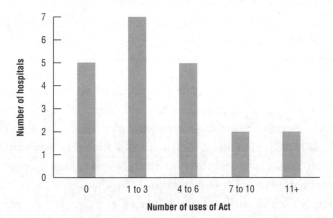

4.99   There was considerable variation in the number of times the Act was used in those hospitals which had detained patients in the period studied. One Trust used Section 5(2) on 12 occasions; three times more frequently than the next highest user of that Section.

4.100  It is evident that general hospitals are making use of the Act for a relatively small but not insignificant number of patients. Where admissions under the Act are infrequent, Trusts may have difficulties in ensuring that the obligations, entitlements and safeguards set out in the Act are observed. However, it is crucial that the necessary arrangements are in place. Following the survey, those hospitals which reported usage of the Act were incorporated into the Commission's visiting programme, each receiving a short visit from a member of the Commission's team, when neighbouring mental health Trusts were visited. The following matters were raised on those visits:

- *Record of admission under the Act*. Many Trusts do not centrally record the use of the Act in a computerised format and therefore there is an under-recording in the annual returns to the Department of Health Statistical Branch. Hospitals visited agreed to keep a central copy of legal papers and a central register.

- *Patient Rights*. Hospitals agreed to maintain Mental Health Act leaflets and to record that an explanation was given to patients about their legal position and rights under the Act.

- *Links to Psychiatric Services*. All hospitals agreed, if they had not already done so, to maintain close links to their neighbouring Mental Health Trust to assist them on an advisory basis on matters relating to the use and implementation of the Act.

- *Role of Managers*. Some Trust Boards were not fully aware of their responsibilities as Mental Health Act managers. None of the Trusts visited had a planned system in place for hearing managers' reviews. Trusts agreed to ensure that managers are aware that they have statutory powers, responsibilities and duties concerning detained patients and to consider using the neighbouring Mental Health Trust managers as associate managers to hear reviews.

- *Staff training in the Mental Health Act.* Hospitals agreed to make training available for key staff, usually to be provided by the local Mental Health Trust.

- *Reference Books / Guidance Notes.* Hospitals agreed to make sure that they had sufficient copies of the Code of Practice, the Mental Health Act Manual (Jones, 1996) and Commission Guidance Notes.

4.101 The need for a compulsory admission to a general hospital can occur where a patient has been assessed as requiring admission to hospital under the Act but, at the same time needs treatment for physical health needs unconnected to the mental disorder, that cannot be met within mental health services. It is legally possible to deal with this situation by formally admitting the patient to the mental health unit and then for the RMO to grant Section 17 leave to a general hospital, where the patient can receive treatment for the physical disorder. However, the preferred approach is for the patient to be admitted directly to the general hospital under the Act and for their assessment and treatment for mental disorder to be started there. It would be helpful if general hospitals had a service level agreement or protocol in place which allowed the care and treatment for the mental disorder to be given under the direction of a consultant psychiatrist from a mental illness unit. There is no reason why the consultant psychiatrist could not carry out the responsibilities of the Responsible Medical Officer, even though not employed by the general hospital.

4.102 The Commission intends to issue a Guidance Note on the use of the Act in general hospitals, which will complement Practice Note 5 'Guidance on Issues Relating to the Administration of the Mental Health Act in Mental Nursing Homes Registered to Receive Detained Patients' (currently under review).

## Use of the Act in Registered Mental Nursing Homes

### Introduction

4.103 In the Seventh Biennial Report the Commission recommended that "the regulations of the Registered Homes Act 1984 be amended so that registering authorities can withhold or withdraw registrations from Mental Nursing Homes to admit detained patients on the grounds of lack of compliance with Mental Health Act procedures". Currently, under Section 23(3)(c) of the Registered Homes Act 1984, an application for registration must, in the case of a mental nursing home, specify whether or not it proposes to receive patients who are liable to be detained under the provisions of the Mental Health Act 1983. The registering authority (the local health authority) can and should refuse registration, when it is first applied for, if the applicant cannot show that he or she, or senior staff proposed to be employed, will be capable of operating in compliance with the Mental Health Act. If this requirement was not satisfied the question of fitness would arise under Section 25 of the Registered Homes Act.

4.104 The Commission is encouraged to see that many registering authorities now issue, in addition to the Mental Health Act Commission's Practice Note 5 on the Mental Health Act in Mental Nursing Homes, their own guidance and standards for receiving and caring for detained patients.

4.105 The House of Commons Health Committee is examining the regulation of the independent health care system and one of the matters of particular concern is mental health. At the request of the Committee, the Commission submitted a memorandum and gave oral evidence setting out concerns and recommending that compliance with the provisions of the Mental Health Act receive greater prominence in the registration requirements. Stronger safeguards are also promised in the White Paper *Improving Protection*, which aims to develop national benchmark standards for residential and nursing homes.

4.106 In the Seventh Biennial Report the Commission declared an intention to draw shortcomings regarding compliance with Mental Health Act procedures to the attention of any relevant NHS commissioning bodies so that standards could be developed and monitored systematically. Reports are now sent directly to the registering health authorities and respective NHS Regional Offices. The Independent Health Association (IHA) has raised concerns about uncorrected reports being sent to purchasing and registering authorities. In response, the Commission agreed to highlight to the recipients that reports are dispatched without hospital or nursing home managers having seen them first.

4.107 The process for addressing issues raised in Commission reports remains variable. Some health authorities formally present the findings at Board meetings and, dependent on whether a contract exists with a specified mental nursing home, the issues are either addressed via contract monitoring meetings or via the registration and inspection (R&I) unit, or both. Other authorities only pass the reports on mental nursing homes to the R&I Unit for their sole attention. The former provides a two-pronged approach which could be seen to exert additional influence on homes to comply with the Mental Health Act. In the interim, and more especially in view of the current emphasis on more 24 hour nursed mental health care which in some areas will be achieved via alliances between the statutory and non-statutory services, the current legislation remains inadequate.

## The Position of the Responsible Medical Officer (RMO) in Mental Nursing Homes

4.108 The *Mental Health Services of Salford NHS Trust* raised a query with the Commission about how the role of the RMO should be fulfilled when they were establishing, in collaboration with a voluntary sector organisation, a 24 hour nursed care facility for patients who were liable to be detained. They questioned whether responsibility for the patients' care could be split between the consultant psychiatrist, filling an RMO role, and a General Practitioner

(GP) fulfilling a primary care role. An RMO has to be identified, because they are granted specific legal powers for detained patients. There is nothing in law which prevents the GP from being the RMO provided that they are the doctor in charge of treatment. However, as a matter of good practice, it would seem difficult to justify detaining patients under the Act and then not having a specialist consultant in charge of their treatment. There should be no reason why a consultant could not undertake RMO responsibilities with the GP taking responsibility for primary care.

4.109 There are other points of confusion in existing guidance. The Mental Health Act Memorandum, 1998 states "all hospital patients should be under the care of a consultant who is in charge in the sense that he is not answerable for the patient's treatment to any other doctor" (para. 60). The definition of 'hospital' in Part II of the Act includes mental nursing homes registered to take detained patients. Where such homes are small with 20 beds or fewer, it is unlikely that they will employ their own medical staff. Issues such as what happens in an emergency situation, as it is only the doctor-in-charge or his or her nominated deputy "on the staff of that hospital" who can apply a Section 5(2), are uncertain. There is also an anomaly that doctors who are on the staff of a mental nursing home cannot provide medical recommendations for admission under the Act, although they can renew the detention under Section 20.

4.110 Another difference between the NHS and the independent sector is that there is a requirement that NHS consultants should be on the General Medical Council's specialist register. The same standard does not apply to the independent sector. However, in 1997, an IHA survey of the qualifications of consultants in the independent sector found that all doctors fulfilled this requirement. But the response rate was only 56% and concerns must therefore remain about the non-responders (communication in Independent (IHA) / Commission meeting). The Royal College of Psychiatrists and the IHA have issued guidelines for all future Consultant appointments, which should be the same as for the NHS and include participation of an assessor from the Royal College. One registering authority (North Yorkshire Health Authority) scrutinises medical appointments (under regulation 12(1)(a) of SI 1984 no. 1578) to test the provision of "adequate professional and technical staff". Such practice is, however, rare.

## Section 17 leave

4.111 There are differing views on whether mental nursing homes not registered to receive detained patients are able to accept patients subject to Section 17 leave. The Commission's Practice Note 5 on the Administration of the Act in Mental Nursing Homes (subject to review) states that "as patients can be sent on Section 17 leave to their own home or a hostel ... in the absence of guidance from the courts, they may be sent on Section 17 leave to a nursing home which is not registered to take detained patients". Section 17 leave does not authorise a transfer of authority and therefore the patient remains liable to be detained by the hospital managers who received the original application for his or her detention. The

Mental Health Act Manual (Jones, 1996; p. 84), advises on this same issue that "as patients on leave under this Section are liable to be detained" the home should be separately registered under Section 23 of the Registered Homes Act 1984. As a consequence of the conflicting advice, practice varies amongst health authorities. For example, the Commission has found that Newcastle Health Authority requires homes to be registered to take patients under Section 17 leave, whilst North Yorkshire Health Authority does not.

## Section 37/41

4.112 The conditional discharge of patients under Sections 37 and 41 is another area of controversy and a similar debate as that surrounding Section 17 leave applies. Contrary to the Mental Health Act Manual (Jones, 1996; p. 191) the Commission takes the view that it is possible for such patients to be conditionally discharged to a nursing home which is not registered to receive detained patients. However, these patients cannot be conditionally discharged to an NHS hospital or to a mental nursing home that is registered to receive detained patients. Discharge means release from hospital and not that the patient should remain in the same or another hospital.

## Implementation of the Act in Smaller Homes

4.113 Commissioners remain concerned about the ability of small homes to fulfil the legal requirements of the Mental Health Act. Registered Person(s) have the same responsibilities as hospital managers, but their experience of the Act may be infrequent and as a result their administration of the statutory procedures may be less than proficient. Certain duties can be delegated and indeed many registering authorities recommend that duties are delegated to the local Trust. However, the advice to homes remains inconsistent, which increases the risk of the possibility of unlawful detention. The Code of Practice now recommends that "Mental nursing home managers, and Trusts and Health Authorities should, where possible, co-operate over exercising their respective functions in relation to the discharge of patients detained in mental nursing homes" (23.5).

4.114 A similar concern relates to the nursing staff in small homes, who can become de-skilled in applying the Act when formal detentions are infrequent. Commissioners have reported situations in which the requirements of Section 132 (patients rights) and Section 58 (treatment requiring consent) were insufficiently understood by the nursing staff and that their access to training in relation to the Code of Practice was either very poor or non-existent. A 'helpline' might prove of benefit to enable staff to access advice and training about the Mental Health Act from the local Trust.

> Visit to Connolly House, Astra Care; 28 August 97
>
> The Commission was pleased to hear that training in the Mental Health Act and Code of Practice had been provided in co-operation with a nurse tutor from Anglia Polytechnic. Provision of rights information to relevant patients was well recorded.

4.115 There has been a rapid growth of providers of health care in the independent sector. There are just over 2,000 mental nursing homes but there are no reliable figures about how many of them are specifically registered to receive detained patients (Munshi, 1999). The Commission currently visits 135 mental nursing homes, which can accept detained patients, but the number continues to increase with the emergence of more smaller 24 hour staffed care facilities. It is vital that the Commission receives notification from registering authorities when such homes are registered. This will enable the Commission to fulfil its statutory obligations, monitor compliance with the Mental Health Act and report its findings to the respective agencies.

## Community Duties and Powers

4.116 The Commission's remit is limited to patients detained or liable to be detained (i.e. those on Section 17 leave) under the Act and does not extend to keeping under review the exercise of powers over patients in the community. However, the Commission is most concerned that there is good continuity of care and one purpose of meeting with Social Services Departments, alongside providers of hospital services, is to monitor the extent to which hospital and community services are able to integrate all aspects of a patient's detention from the initial assessment to the termination of after-care.

### Charging for Section 117 aftercare

4.117 The Commission's observations about how the procedures for the Care Programme Approach, including Section 117, are carried out are discussed in Chapter 5 (see 5.48 et seq.). The particular question, whether patients can be charged for services for after-care provided under Section 117 of the Act, is considered here. The Commission's opinion, discussed in the last Biennial Report (pp. 141), that charges cannot be levied has been confirmed in an answer to a parliamentary question raised on 20 July 1998. Mr Boateng, then Minister of State for Health, also stated in his reply that if a person believes that charges have been levied under these circumstances, they should raise the matter with the appropriate social services authority.

4.118 The duty to provide after-care services continues until both local and health authorities are satisfied that the person concerned is no longer in need of such services, at which point entitlement to free services would cease. However, there is a lack of guidance which would help authorities to decide when a patient should be discharged from Section 117 aftercare. The issue has been considered by the Local Government Ombudsman in one complaint made by the daughter of a patient who had been detained under Section 3 and then discharged to a nursing home. The patient had subsequently also been discharged from Section 117 but the Ombudsman decided that the local authority had failed to address the crucial question of whether she needed and whether she continued to need after-care services. Furthermore, the authority had failed to take account of the daughter's views before ceasing to provide Section 117 after-care (Clements, 1999).

4.119 There are also disputes between health and local authorities about responsibility for funding. When leave is authorised to a residential or nursing home under Section 17, social services departments argue that the person remains liable to be detained and is therefore the responsibility of the Trust. Conversely, health authorities argue that in such circumstances the leave is invariably part of a discharge plan; the person will most likely be receiving social care and should therefore be funded by the social services department. In respect of payments for aftercare under Section 117, problems have arisen where a mental nursing home provides both an acute service and a continuing or nursing home care. Both are part of the one home or hospital and where a patient is discharged from Section 3 and moved into the continuing care service, funding has then been sought from the social services. Under such circumstances, social services departments have argued that the person remains the responsibility of the NHS and they are therefore not liable for funding. It is anticipated that the Department of Health's proposals for improving the scope for pooling health and social care budgets and for commissioning services jointly should reduce such inter-agency disputes.

### After-Care Under Supervision (Supervised Discharge)

4.120 The purpose of supervised discharge is to help ensure that patients who have been detained for treatment receive after-care services provided under Section 117. The patient must present a substantial risk of serious harm to his or her health or safety or the safety of other persons or of being seriously exploited. The Commission's remit only extends as far as the process of making the application while the patient is still detained. There are few applications made; 318 in England in 19987/8 and 11 in Wales. Although this is 50% more than the previous year, it still falls far short of the 3000 patients estimated by the Department of Health (Dept. of Health, 1993) as likely to be suitable for the new power.

4.121 One obstacle is the cumbersome and bureaucratic application procedures. The power is also perceived as ineffective in that treatment cannot be enforced and there are practical difficulties in exercising the powers which do exist. According to one survey, the power to convey the patient was only known to have been used in 10% of cases (Pinfold et al, 1999). However, Supervised Discharge is perceived to have a beneficial effect in improving compliance for those patients who recognise the framework of the law.

### Guardianship

4.122 Against expectation following the advent of Supervised Discharge, the use of Guardianship is increasing. It is thought that the availability of Supervised Discharge has prompted renewed consideration of Guardianship, which may be preferred in relevant cases because it is viewed as a slightly less restrictive alternative. The fact that the application for Guardianship is made by the ASW as opposed to the RMO for Supervised Discharge is another incentive for the latter to encourage the use of Guardianship, thereby relieving him or her of that burden.  There were 434 new Guardianship cases in England during the year ending 31 March 1998, representing a 6% increase on 1997 and almost double the figure of 1992. The number of cases in force at the end of the year was 804 compared to 335 in 1992 (Dept. of Health: Personal Social Services Statistics, 1998). In the case of Supervised Discharge, there is wide variation in use, depending on local policy and practice. There were 8.7 Guardianships per 100,000 population at 31 March 1998 in Southampton whereas it is not used at all in other authorities.

4.123 There are some subtle changes in the wording of the guidance in the revised Code of Practice, which have implications for the use of Guardianship. For example, while a key element of the care plan remains that there should be recognition by the patient of the "authority" of and willingness to work with, the Guardian, there is now a rider which recognises that this depends on the patient's level of capacity (Code of Practice, 13.6a), reinforcing the relevance of Guardianship as a statutory framework for making decisions about the care in the community of the incapacitated patient. The guidance that Guardianship should never be used solely for the purpose of transferring any unwilling person into residential care has now been deleted from the third edition of the Code, thus removing a source of confusion which was putting mental health professionals off its use.

## A New Legislative Framework for Compulsory Powers in the Community

4.124 The position of the Government is that the current legislation does not provide effective safeguards to deal with unacceptable risk to personal or public safety presented by people with a mental disorder when they fail to comply with treatment. Consequently, the Mental Health Legislation Review Team are required to advise on the legislative changes needed to support compulsory compliance with the treatment programme, where deemed necessary for those patients not formally detained. The Commission has taken the opportunity of reiterating in its submission to the Review Team its view that it is vital that the remit of any monitoring organisation such as the Commission should be extended to those patients subject to any new powers of compulsion in the community.

# Chapter 5

# Hospital and Continuing Care

## Summary

*The pressures on in-patient beds highlighted in previous Biennial Reports has continued over the current reporting period. This situation causes serious problems for both patients and staff and can result in delays for urgent admissions, patients frequently moving within and between hospitals, leave beds being used for admissions as a matter of routine, staff spending a disproportionate amount of time finding alternative placements and patients being discharged early. The lack of suitable after-care accommodation often further adds to these pressures. The Commission remains particularly concerned about the placement of patients out of district and the disruption that this can cause in their treatment and after-care.*

*The threshold for admission to hospital has continued to rise and staff are caring for high proportions of detained patients and coping with high levels of disturbance. Pressures such as these can have a deleterious effect on the therapeutic environment of wards.*

*The physical environment in many hospitals has improved but*

Commission Members continue to report sub-standard units that are poorly furnished and decorated and are lacking in privacy. The security of patients' belongings and the safety of the patients themselves is a cause for concern in some units and the Commission continues to recommend that patients are provided, at the very least, with lockable units for their possessions, but preferably with their own bedrooms that can be locked from the inside and accessed by staff with a master key.

Nurse staffing levels on many wards are often highly dependent on the use of agency and bank staff. Where this is the case, and where there is an impoverishment of the ward skill mix, therapeutic regimes are likely to suffer.

Patients often complain of inactivity and boredom. It is essential that some form of organised activity is available for patients in order to support therapeutic engagement and motivation to get better.

Most areas continue to make gradual progress in implementing the Care Programme Approach (CPA), although there remain some variations in policy and practice, sometimes within the same Trust. The Commission continues to find evidence of CPA/Section 117 meetings being held very late, or patients discharged without a meeting being held. The paperwork for CPA may very often be incomplete and the content of care plans can be unclear.

Information technology has a vital role to play in reducing much of the administrative burden. The CPA must integrate as far as possible with social services' care management systems in order to reduce both administrative duplication and confusion over professional responsibilities.

Families and carers very often provide a high level support to patients with severe and enduring mental health problems and their involvement in after-care planning must not be overlooked. Their needs must also be addressed and the Government's *initiatives in the national strategy 'Caring about Carers' are particularly welcomed.*

*There a been a gradual 'silting up' of medium secure units as they find themselves increasingly accommodating patients requiring long-term medium secure care, or conditions of lower security. Women patients, who are in a minority in secure environments, are particularly vulnerable. Staffing shortages can have serious effects upon the quality of patient care and reduce the opportunities for effective therapeutic programmes.*

*The High Security Hospitals are also experiencing significant staffing shortages, with adverse consequences for patients' quality of life and access to rehabilitation and leisure activities. The national shortage of medium and long-term secure places continues to result in inordinate delays in transferring patients out of the high secure environments. The High Security Hospitals have many improvements to make in complying with the requirements of CPA/Section 117, Consent to Treatment and the Code of Practice. The physical environment of some wards is still a cause for considerable concern.*

# 5 Hospital and Continuing Care

## Acute In-Patient Care

### Introduction

5.1 Over the last decade the nature of psychiatric in-patient care has undergone significant change. The closure of the long-stay hospitals and the development of community-based services has resulted in fewer beds and a higher turnover of patients who stay in hospital for shorter periods. As noted in Chapter 4 of this Report, the number of formal admissions has also increased dramatically over this period. Observers have identified high bed occupancy rates and unprecedented levels of disturbance, violence and sexual harassment on acute admission wards, particularly in inner London (e.g. MILMIS Project Group, 1995). Recent large-scale studies have highlighted grave concerns about these pressures and the detrimental effects on the quality of in-patient care, and have concluded that the attention of policy makers and managers must now focus upon the development and improvement of these services as a matter of urgency (Gourney et al., 1998; Ford et al., 1998; Sainsbury Centre for Mental Health, 1998; Higgins et al., 1998).

5.2 In-patient facilities play a vital role in the delivery of modern and comprehensive mental health care and in successive Biennial Reports the Commission has voiced its concerns about the continued and growing pressure on these essential services. The Commission therefore welcomes the Government's determination to address this problem as part of its policy initiative to modernise mental health services (Dept of Health, 1998c), in particular its intention to ensure that there are 'enough beds of the right kind in the right places' and that 'the safety, dignity and privacy of inpatients are protected'. This will include a review across the whole range of accommodation – including 24 hour staffed beds, acute beds and secure beds – in order to provide guidance to help local services assess their needs and to identify and remove blockages in the system. The Government's commitment to provide extra secure places, and to eliminate mixed sex accommodation in 95% of health authorities by the year 2002, is particularly welcomed.

5.3 The Government has pledged an additional £700 million over the next three years to invest in better treatment and care of mental illness, some of which will be available to improve inpatient services. Hospital managers and senior clinicians have a responsibility to ensure that any additional funding is well spent and that inpatient care is provided in an environment that is therapeutic, safe and comfortable. Additional funding available through the Mental Health Grant (formally the Mental Illness Specific Grant) will enable local authorities to develop further the range of residential and respite services required to provide suitable alternatives to hospital admission and support the continuation of patients' care in the community. This will require carefully coordinated planning and close working relationships between Trusts and local authorities.

## Bed Occupancy

5.4    The Commission frequently hears on many of its visits that the heavy pressure on beds described in the last three Biennial reports continues. This situation causes serious problems for both patients and staff and can result in delays for urgent admissions whilst beds are sought elsewhere. Patients are being discharged early or held in settings inappropriate to their care. Leave beds are used for admissions as a matter of routine and are therefore frequently occupied, and in some instances patients returning from leave have been denied re-admission. This situation remains acute particularly, but not exclusively, in urban and inner city areas. Recently published findings from the Commission's National Visit in 1996 estimate a national average bed occupancy rate of 99%. Average bed occupancy rates were found to be significantly higher in Inner and Outer London authorities (107% and 111% respectively) if patients on overnight leave are included, but if these patients are excluded the rates in London may be no higher than elsewhere (Ford et al., 1998).

5.5    The following example from a Commission visit is illustrative of the impact that these pressures can have upon patient care. This includes patients frequently moving within, and between, hospitals; the use of seclusion to contain difficult behaviours that might otherwise respond to conventional nursing; staff having to spend a disproportionate amount time finding placements elsewhere; and difficulties in formulating discharge plans for patients who are being discharged early.

> ### Visit to Richmond, Twickenham and Roehampton Healthcare NHS Trust and Richmond Social Services; 8 September 1997
>
> In their recent reports Commissioners had drawn attention to the serious pressures on the Trust's services and the lack of available intensive care services. It seemed that, despite some measures to alleviate these pressures, they continued.
>
> On the day of the Commissioners' visit, there were 42 patients on the Pagoda 'books', 16 of whom were detained. Three detained patients were on leave. Commissioners were told that only the beds of patients on extended leave were used. One Pagoda patient was on Vine Ward. ASWs reported that patients taken to Pagoda had sometimes had to wait a considerable time before being admitted because the staff were under pressure, and that this created an unwelcoming atmosphere.

An additional five patients were receiving intensive care elsewhere and only one of these five was on the Shamrock Unit (an intensive care unit with which the Trust has a number of contracted beds). Staff confirmed that access to Shamrock beds is extremely difficult and patients are generally sent elsewhere as 'out of area treatments'[1] (OATs) until a Shamrock bed becomes available. The consequences for patient care are serious. For example, one patient had been sent from Pagoda Ward to West Park Hospital where he remained until a bed became available on Shamrock. He was then transferred to Shamrock before returning to Pagoda.

On the day of the visit there were an additional eight Richmond patients on 'out of area treatments' at other hospitals because of a shortage of acute admission beds on Pagoda. The ward was locked and Commissioners were told that this was due to staff shortages on the day, and 4 patients who required level one observation.

The pressures on Vine ward were less but remained high. On the day of the visit there were 39 patients "on the books", 20 of whom were detained. Nine detained patients were on leave. The two available beds at John Meyer provided little help since this was a short term intensive care unit only and did not provide for longer stays. On the day of the visit there were no Richmond, Twickenham and Roehampton Healthcare NHS Trust patients on John Meyer. Three patients were receiving intensive care under OAT arrangements and one patient requiring acute admission was placed in the private sector. Again, patients needing intensive care were frequently transferred from hospital to hospital.

Commissioners were shown details of the times taken to arrange out of area treatments. Between 25th August 1997 and 9th September 1997, 30 OATs were sought and required an average of almost one hour of staff telephone time each.

Commissioners acknowledged that many acute admissions services are under pressure. However, in their experience of similar units, the pressures on this service were extreme and this had serious consequences for patient care. The use of seclusion was declining but it continued to be necessary in order to contain difficult behaviours.

Commissioners were also concerned about the continuity of care of patients who were discharged from the private sector or sent on leave back to their homes and then discharged by the community mental health team. ASWs acknowledged the difficulties in formulating discharge plans for these patients and also the isolation of patients cared for away from their home area and the difficulties for relatives visiting.

Commissioners heard of other factors impacting on bed pressures including a shortage of 24 hour staffed accommodation for short and long stays and a lack of crisis beds as an alternative to admission.

5.6    The lack of suitable after-care accommodation further adds to the pressures on in-patient beds, which in the following example had reached crisis proportions.

---

[1] Previously referred to as Extra-Contractual Referrals (ECRs)

Visit to Porstmouth Healthcare NHS Trust, 25 & 26 February 1998

The lack of suitable facilities for moving patients on was causing a crisis in the Trust. The adult acute mental health wards were seriously overcrowded, with some patients sleeping on the elderly or long-term wards. A patient on the Solent Unit had been allocated four different beds in one day and as a result had lost a number of her possessions.

A patient on Rivendale Ward on a Section 37/41, who was given a deferred conditional discharge by the Mental Health Review Tribunal in the summer of 1996, was still at Rivendele on the day of the visit because it had not been possible to find him alternative accommodation conforming with the condition stipulated by the Tribunal that "he should live in a suitably staffed hostel". The staff in this unit were of the opinion that at least half of the patients were ready to move on but were unable to because suitable accommodation was unavailable.

Of the 12 residents at the Old Vicarage, at least nine needed other supported accommodation but as this was unavailable the waiting list for the unit continued to grow.

Similar problems existed in the learning disability service. There were three clients at Thomas Parr House needing placements elsewhere but there appeared to be no NHS beds in the Portsmouth area for people with a dual diagnosis.

5.7    The threshold of admission in many acute units continues to rise, with staff caring for high proportions of detained patients and very often coping with very high levels of disturbance. This situation continues to present a serious problem for hospitals in urban areas, particularly those in London authorities (Johnson et al., 1997; Gourney et al., 1998) where the proportion of patients detained under the Act is higher than elsewhere in England and Wales (Ford et al., 1998).

Visit to Lambeth Healthcare NHS Trust; 20 October 1997

Commissioners noted the considerably increased pressures on beds on the acute admissions wards at South Western Hospital and on Lloyd Still Ward and the very high numbers of patients in acute phases of their illnesses. This was reflected in the high proportion of detained patients on these wards. On Nelson Ward 19 of 22 patients were detained, and on Luther King Ward 20 of the 22 were detained.

On the day of the visit there were five incidents on Nelson Ward in which patients had to be restrained or other emergency intervention was needed. At Lloyd Still, four patients needing admission could not be placed and alternative beds were being sought. Patients from Lloyd Still were regularly 'slept over' at South Western Hospital which was very disruptive to their care. Nursing staff reported that a considerable amount of their time was taken up with bed searching. It was clear to Commissioners that this was a potentially dangerous situation and that there was little scope for dealing with emergency admissions and re-admissions without displacing very ill patients or using OATs or private beds.

These pressures had knock-on effects on other wards. There were patients on Eden Intensive Care Ward who were ready but unable to move back to open wards because no bed was available. However, five of the patients detained on the day of the visit were patients with long-term challenging behaviours or behaviours requiring medium secure care who were not benefiting from the type of care offered on this ward. These patients were also blocking those beds for patients from the acute admission wards who might have benefited from the higher levels of care offered on Eden. The 'silting-up' of this facility was greatly regretted. Commissioners were told that the Cane Hill Unit rarely had beds available and as consequence the Trust did not have ready access to beds for patients requiring medium secure care. It was unfortunate that those patients must be accommodated in private secure accommodation or in other units far from where the patients families lived. It was the Commissioners' view that urgent attention should be given to problems of bed pressures in the Trust generally and its access to medium secure provision.

5.8    The Commission continues to remain very concerned about the placement of patients out of district. As was highlighted in the Seventh Biennial Report (pp. 67 and 83), this can cause considerable problems for patients in maintaining contact with their relatives, carers and their home area, and also makes difficult any continuity of their treatment and aftercare.

5.9    When a bed cannot be found in an NHS acute ward for a detained patient or other urgent admission, a patient may be sent to a unit in the private sector until an NHS vacancy arises. As a consequence, patients are sometimes resident in private sector units for only very short periods before returning to the NHS, and this can be extremely unsettling for the patient. Alternatively, patients admitted for longer periods and who are beginning to settle into the private ward, may be transferred back suddenly, with the result that their treatment is disrupted. The Commission has heard from NHS consultants about instances where private units have refused to co-operate with the return of a patient in order that a therapeutic programme can be completed. Health authorities, on the other hand, may be reluctant to fund an extended stay in the private sector when an NHS bed is available. The Commissions' view is that the decision to transfer back to the NHS should be based upon the needs and wishes of the patient, and during discussions with the NHS Executive the Commission has recommended the development of protocols to assist in determining clearly the circumstances under which patients should be returned to NHS wards.

5.10   The Commission has found that in some Trusts the appointment of bed managers to oversee and monitor the allocation of beds and to identify existing, or potential, blockages in the system has helped to reduce pressures on beds. Some Trusts have also implemented measures to try to avoid inappropriate admissions. During a visit to *Frenchay Healthcare Trust* in October 1997, the hospital managers informed Commissioners that an interim audit had shown that the Trust's out-of-hours crisis service, established four months earlier, had helped to avoid 27 possible admissions. A study of acute psychiatric provision in Nottingham (Beck et al., 1997) demonstrated that alternatives to acute care could be identified for up to a third of admissions. This would require adequate community facilities and highly co-ordinated care planning to be in place. Alternative models of community-based treatment must also, of necessity, be very selective, as some patients are simply too disturbed or vulnerable for hospital admission to be avoided. Nevertheless, although patients with acute psychotic symptoms may require in-patient care at some stage, models of care based, for example, on intensive home-based treatment or assertive case-management, can also significantly reduce the amount of time that they spend being treated as in-patients (Kluiter, 1997).

5.11 The role of Accident and Emergency (A&E) departments as an important point of access to acute in-patient care should not be overlooked. A six-month study of nine acute psychiatric wards and 215 in-patients undertaken by the Sainsbury Centre for Mental Health (Acute In-patient Care Study [ACIS], 1998), found that A&E departments were the immediate routes to the acute wards for 28% of patients. This figure varied markedly on a regional basis, with nearly half of all admissions in London and the South East using the A&E route, compared to only 5% in the Midlands and the North of England. Improved liaison with A&E departments could, therefore, reduce bed pressures slightly. The use of mental health triage nurses, or nurses specialising in dealing with patients who have deliberately self-harmed, can be used to avoid unnecessary admissions to the acute wards.

> ### Visit to Thameside Community Healthcare NHS Trust; 1 May 1998
>
> The development of the A&E liaison service had had a significant impact on bed occupancy. This was down from 120% to 95%. The liaison nurse guaranteed to see patients in A&E within twenty minutes of their arrival. A recent audit in A&E had shown that the liaison nurses had met the two hour throughput target. Patients were moved from A&E to the ward by their assessing nurse to ensure a smooth hand-over and administration. If the patient was referred to community services, the liaison nurse directed this. Patients were seen in the community within a maximum of two weeks. This eased pressure on general practitioners. It was reported that it had only cost an extra £10,000 to provide the new service, and Commissioners congratulated Trust staff on this economic and effective service innovation.

## Therapeutic Environment

5.12 Commission visits to hospitals and mental nursing homes continue to pay particularly close attention to the quality of the overall therapeutic environment. This includes the levels of nursing staff and the availability and accessibility of psychiatrists, psychologists and occupational therapists, the physical environment of the wards and the quality of care. These issues are, of course, extremely important for all patients, but the Commission considers them particularly so for involuntary patients who, by virtue of their detention, are unable to exercise any choice with regard to the conditions of their stay in hospital.

### Physical Environment

5.13 Admission to an acute psychiatric ward, especially against one's will, can be a distressing and frightening experience. Patients are likely to be very disturbed and vulnerable and in need of a secure, calm and comfortable environment. A recent Council Report by the Royal College of Psychiatrists, 'Not Just Bricks and Mortar' (Royal College of Psychiatrists, 1998), recommends that newly built acute in-patient units should provide standards of accommodation that "act as a statement of investment in quality of care" and "bear comparison with a comfortable modern hotel". Units should be domestic in size and structure, rather than institutional, and include single bedrooms with en-suite facilities for all patients, quiet rooms offering a degree of privacy or somewhere to take visitors, communal sitting rooms and activities areas and a separate smoking room. Anything less than this, the report suggests, is "likely soon to be obsolete".

5.14   While the general improvement in ward environments throughout England and Wales noted in previous Commission reports has continued, there is evidence of some sites continuing to provide extremely poor environmental conditions. There can also be very marked variations in standards within the same Trust. Commission visit reports all too often describe sub-standard units that are poorly decorated and furnished, bathing and toileting facilities that are unhygienic and lacking in privacy, and poor facilities for patients to meet with their visitors or simply find some peace and quiet.

> **Visit to Barnet Healthcare NHS Trust and Barnet Social Services Department; 8 & 9 May 1997**
>
> Commissioners recorded in the strongest terms their dismay at the continuing poor conditions on Hawthorne Ward at Napsbury Hospital. The ward remained much as it was in July 1995 when Commissioners expressed their concerns about the environment for patients on the ward, many of whom were there for several months and were unable to leave the ward without escorts. The Trust were reminded of comments made in reports following visits in July 1995, and February, May and November 1996 when the unacceptable standards and low priority placed on maintaining the environment were noted.
>
> The condition of the ward had a significant detrimental effect on the patients. One mentioned going absent without leave to a previous hospital; another reported feeling positive about treatment until arrival on Hawthorne Ward; and another claimed that the 'progression' from a Regional Secure Unit to Hawthorne Ward appeared to be more of a regression given the facilities, the condition of the ward and the ward ethos.
>
> There had been minor environmental improvements, such as the replacement of broken lavatory seats and mouldy shower curtains, following Commission intervention. However, the decoration and condition of the furniture on the ward was unacceptable and not conducive to good patient care.
>
> Following the visit the managers established a group to examine the therapeutic environment and the activities on the ward.

5.15   The Sainsbury Centre's study of acute in-patient care (ACIS) conducted detailed interviews with 112 patients about their care and the ward environment. The main findings included:

- 55% of patients had no separate bedroom;

- 71% did not have a secure locker for their belongings;

- 47% did not have access to a quiet area where they could take visitors;

- 22 % were unhappy with the cleanliness of the ward;

- 28% did not like the food; and

- 37% did not judge mealtimes pleasant or enjoyable.

One of the most worrying findings was that 32% of the patients did not feel safe on the wards. Similar results were reported in a recent study of patients' satisfaction with in-patient psychiatric services in an inner city mental hospital and a small, purpose-built, suburban district general hospital (Greenwood et al., 1999). In this six month study, 433 patients were interviewed and, of these, 283 (66%) reported at least one adverse experience during their stay in hospital. For these patients, adverse experiences included: feeling unsafe (men, 18%; women, 26%); feeling afraid (men, 30%; women; 44%); being threatened (men, 17%; women 19%); experiencing aggressive behaviour (men, 20%; women, 26%); and experiencing sexual harassment (men, 3%; women 14%).

### Visit to Bradford Community Health NHS Trust: 9 December 1998

Commissioners received an exceptional number of serious complaints from patients during the course of the visit. Commissioners received allegations of physical and sexual assaults on patients, and were told repeatedly that patients felt insecure, vulnerable and afraid. Many patients had no idea how to protect themselves from assault, or their property from damage or theft, and did not feel that the staff were able to offer them protection. Commissioners were not satisfied that many of the complaints being made to staff were taken seriously or that the NHS Complaints Procedure was being complied with.

A carer expressed his concern about the atmosphere on one ward which he felt was explosive. He feared at times for the safety of his daughter and felt that staff did not defuse the situation.

Commissioners were particularly concerned about the safety of patients on the Kestrel Unit, and advised that if this could not be guaranteed then serious consideration would have to be given as to whether or not the unit should remain open.

The Trust responded extremely promptly to this visit report and delivered a detailed action plan to address these and other issues.

5.16 Any psychiatric unit must ensure the provision of a secure environment to protect patients from self-harm, intimidation and assault by other patients and outsiders, and theft and destruction of personal property. With regard to the latter, Commissioners find that whilst it is common practice for ward staff to take patients' money or valuables into safe keeping, patients are very often not provided with lockable drawers or wardrobes in which to secure their personal belongings. Staff may report that lockable furniture space for belongings was originally provided, but the practice was discontinued because patients kept losing the keys or not returning them upon discharge from the ward. However, such problems are not insurmountable and hospital managers have a responsibility to ensure that patients are confident that their personal property is safe and easily accessible by them during their stay in hospital.

> **Visits to Charing Cross Hospital, Riverside Mental Health NHS Trust; 23 May 1997 & 23 October 1997**
>
> Commissioners observed a number of patients on one ward carrying around their possessions, some in overcoats, for fear that they would be stolen. Several patients complained that their belongings had gone missing and they had nowhere to keep them safe, even when they were in their 'bed space' area and asleep at night, as they had no means of securing them. They appeared unaware of how to take up this issue and whether any compensation was available. One relative commented that her son slept in his day clothes for fear of them being stolen.
>
> Only four lockable lockers were available for 24 patients on one ward. The Commission requested that the Trust provide all patients with lockable units, preferably within the patients' personal 'bed space' environment, so that they could have access to them whenever they wanted.

5.17   Where patients sleep in shared dormitories, their bed space should be separated from that of other patients by means of partitioning to provide greater privacy. However, the Commission recommends the provision of single rooms for patients wherever possible. The doors should be lockable from the inside, with an override facility enabling staff to open them with a master key. This level of security and privacy is particularly important for women patients if they cannot be provided with care on either women-only wards, or women-only areas on wards. Sleeping areas for women should be clearly separated from those for men and they should have access to their own amenities for toileting and bathing. These should not have to be reached by passing through mixed areas. As was noted the previous Biennial Report, the Commission's National Visit in 1996 found that whilst only a very small number of women had to share sleeping areas with men (3%), a third of all women patients were provided with toileting and bathing areas that were for mixed use (p. 175). Only 36% of women had the use of self-contained facilities without male patients having any access (Ford et al., 1998) (see 10.57 for further discussion of issues concerning women patients).

5.18   Where in-patient service contraction and relocation is planned, funding for structural improvements to sites destined for eventual closure is likely to be given a relatively low priority. Nevertheless, this must be balanced against the rights and the needs of patients to be cared for in a comfortable and secure environment, especially if the timetable for planned relocation is uncertain or is some time away.

> **Visit to North Birmingham Mental Health NHS Trust; 22 & 23 May 1997**
>
> The run down of in-patient facilities to focus on community resources was seen to be unbalanced, leading to unacceptably low standards of in-patient care. It was stated that in units such as Newbridge House, there was concern that vulnerable women who would expect 'safe' care were seeking to leave hospital because of the difficult environment.
>
> Across a number of sites the level of patient privacy was considered to be less than adequate. The Commission appreciated a reluctance to invest in structural changes whilst a move to new sites was pending. However, with the move then being anticipated as two years away the Commission recommended that a review of the provision of patient privacy was undertaken.

5.19   In this and previous Biennial Reports the Commission has highlighted the increasing incidence of the use of temporary holding powers under Sections 5(2) and 5(4) of the Mental Health Act, and has recommended that where there is a high frequency of use units may wish to undertake audits to explore the reasons for this (see 4.24 et seq.). As the above example demonstrates, managers and clinicians must also be mindful of the fact that the often frightening and distressing experience of admission to a psychiatric hospital is very likely to be exacerbated where the immediate impression, for a vulnerable patient, is of reception into a poor quality environment appearing to offer little in the way of asylum, dignity or security. Under circumstances such as these, it is unsurprising that patients would wish leave the hospital as soon as possible.

5.20   Patients' relatives have also expressed concerns about the environmental conditions in some hospitals. During a visit to High Royds Hospital, *Leeds Community and Mental Health Services Trust* on 26 January 1999, ASWs reported to Commissioners that conditions on the wards of both High Royds Hospital and the Roundhay Wing at St. James' Hospital were so bad that patients' nearest relatives were being displaced under Section 29 of the Act because they were not prepared to allow their relatives to be admitted. Consultant psychiatrists also described the difficulties in persuading patients to enter hospital because of the unsatisfactory conditions. The Commission has, for some time, been concerned about the environmental conditions in these hospitals, and the deleterious effects upon patient care and staff morale. The Trust have acknowledged that there are deficiencies in the service and, following an earlier Commission visit in July 1998, announced plans for capital investment to redesign and redecorate wards in the Roundhay Wing due to commence in March 1999. The Health Authority are providing additional funding for investment in mental health services and members of the national External Reference Group are also being asked to review the mental health services of Leeds.

## Staffing Issues and Patient Activity

5.21   Information collected during the Commission's National Visit in 1996 suggested that, on average, current staffing levels in acute admission and intensive care wards were adequate, with an acceptable mix of qualified and unqualified nursing staff. Subsequent analysis of the data from the 263 wards identified as 'acute admission' units found that 69.5% of the wards had a complement at least 1.16 staff for each patient on the ward (Ford, personal communication). This ratio of staff per patient was adapted from the work of Hurst (1993; 1995) and was used as a benchmark. While this analysis continues to support the original findings of the National Visit, it does mean that the number of staff on duty on nearly one-third of the wards visited was below this level. It should be noted, however, that both of these results do need to be treated with some caution, as staffing levels would need to be varied according to the needs of the patients on the ward.

5.22    Further analysis of the same data also demonstrated that acute admission wards are heavily reliant on agency staff and on staff working overtime on bank systems. It was estimated that 31% of posts - or 4,524 whole time equivalent posts - across England and Wales are being filled by staff not working on a permanent contract with their Trust (Ford et al., 1998). Although the key findings of the National Visit reported that only 5% of staff were unfamiliar with the ward that they were working on, it is unlikely that casual staffing arrangements on this scale would help to secure an appropriate foundation on which to provide high standards of nursing care.

5.23    A nine month study by Gourney et al. (1998), funded by the Institute of Psychiatry and the Royal College of Nursing Institute, collected information about acute and intensive care services from 30 wards across 11 Inner London mental health trusts. The study found high levels of bed occupancy and most wards heavily reliant upon staff who were not members of the ward team. During night shifts one ward in three was staffed solely by bank and agency staff. The study also examined levels of violence and untoward incidents and found that on the average ward there was one assault every three days, and approximately one other untoward incident. This included two threats with weapons, and sexual harassment and physical violence against staff and visitors. During one week, patients had to be placed in seclusion following seven violent incidents. The authors concluded that the high levels of seclusion and physical violence on these wards were undoubtedly compounded by the severe shortages of nursing staff.

5.24    The Department of Health has recognised the acute shortage of nurses in the NHS and has started to address this problem by mounting a large-scale recruitment campaign and increasing the number of places for student nurses (Dept. of Health, January 1999).

5.25    The shift in the provision of mental health care from the hospital to the community has resulted in hospital admission wards providing care for patients who have more acute symptoms but who, on average, spend much less time as in-patients. It can be difficult for staff to provide individualised and intensive therapeutic programmes of care for patients who do not stay on the ward for very long. This problem is exacerbated where patients are cared for on wards with high occupancy levels and high numbers of detained patients who may be difficult to manage. Under such circumstances there is a need for highly skilled and well motivated nursing staff. Where the reliance upon bank and agency staff is high or there has been an impoverishment of the ward skill mix, therapeutic regimes are likely to suffer significantly. For example, agency nursing staff have reported to Commissioners that under such circumstances they are only able to provide custodial care.

### Visit to Bolton Hospitals NHS Trust; 22 August 1997

Commissioners found staff committed to nursing patients therapeutically but who were concerned that they were not meeting patient needs. Although the client population had evidently changed with higher levels of disturbance, the skill mix was increasingly impoverished. The numbers of bank and agency staff was at times very high. At the time of the visit five of the nine staff on one ward were from the bank, three were qualified (two F and one E grade) and six were unqualified. Six of the nine were engaged in special observations.

Commissioners were informed of the need to special/restrain/sedate patients who could be nursed therapeutically. Staff were obliged to concentrate on containment and the control of disturbances. They frequently had to call for police assistance to deal with disturbed behaviour.

Patients in private meetings with Commissioners also commented on the increasing medication levels and the constantly changing staff group. They also expressed their appreciation of individual staff and the care they provided.

Senior nursing officers of the Trust and Health Authority had completed a review of staffing and skill mix and the Trust undertook to ensure that immediate alleviative action, based on the findings of the review, was taken.

### Visit to Broadoak Unit and Windsor House, North Mersey Community NHS Trust; 22 May 1997

Commissioners were informed that staffing levels were improved with the use of overtime and a regular bank of agency staff. However, managers acknowledged continuing difficulties in recruiting qualified staff and were examining the recruitment process.

Patients on both Calder and Greenbank wards drew Commissioners' attention to the effect on patients when staff were not always present. They reported feeling unsafe or neglected when staff remained in the ward office or their attention was diverted to more demanding patients. One patient reported being assaulted by another patient. Management responsibility must extend to ensuring that staffing levels are sufficient and consistent in order to provide a safe and therapeutic environment for patients. The Commission recommended that the managers might wish to consider a review of staffing establishments, particularly in view of the acknowledged pressure on beds. Shortly after this visit the Trust placed an advertisement in the nursing press, with the aim of appointing a number of staff nurses to the acute wards.

5.26    Where the numbers and skill mix of ward staff are inadequately maintained, this can lead to low staff morale, fewer training opportunities and reduced job satisfaction, ultimately discouraging healthcare workers from staying in, or joining, the workforce. Similarly, where services are being reorganised or reprovided, uncertainty about the future can affect staff morale and make recruitment more difficult.

---

Visit to Frenchay NHS Trust; 6 April 1998

It was reported by nursing staff in Oakwood House that there were still severe staffing shortages, that continuity of care for patients was frequently disrupted by the use of bank staff, and that senior staff spent unnecessary time on inducting staff who were only passing through. Commissioners advised that improved physical conditions and safety and more opportunities for training and development activities might assist in recruitment and retention.

---

Visit to Community Health Care, North Durham NHS Trust; 6 January 1998

Throughout the Trust it was apparent that there were difficulties in attracting and retaining qualified nurses. A recent internal inquiry had recommended cessation of the use of agency nurses but they were still being employed. The problem applied to Registered Mental Nurses (RMNs) as well as RNMHs. Some staff told Commissioners of their perception of a poor career structure and more attractive conditions of service at other neighbouring Trusts.

On Helmsford Ward there were vacancies for three qualified nurses, a situation aggravated by maternity leave. This was being covered by overtime and the use of bank and part-time nurses, detrimentally affecting the continuity of patient care. Opportunities for post-basic training were reported to be good but often staff could not attend due to the staffing situation.

---

5.27   An important indicator of the quality of patient care is the level of interaction between nurses and their patients. The most effective care is likely to occur where there is a high level of staff and patient interaction. However, as has been highlighted in previous Commission reports, patients continue to express concerns to Commissioners about nursing staff being so busy that they have little time to talk to them. The ACIS study found that patients identified the lack of availability of nurses as one of the factors that they would most like to change on the wards. During the National Visit, Commissioners found that there was no nurse interacting with patients on a quarter of the wards visited (Ford et al., 1998) and where there was interaction on other wards, staff were mainly engaged in one-to-one observations. The amount of time that nurses can devote to direct contact with most patients will be influenced by the presence of others who are displaying challenging and disruptive behaviour, the numbers of which can sometimes be very high. Nurses may also be spending an increasing amount of their time involved in non-direct patient care and administrative duties.

5.28   A study by Higgins et al. (1998) examined in-patient psychiatric nursing activity in 11 sites across the former NHS Regions of Yorkshire and Northern and Inner London and found that in those sites with difficult patient populations (increased severity of patients' illness and more compulsorily detained patients) and high bed occupancy, nurses reported a shift from a therapeutic to a custodial model of care. In these sites, the nurses' work increasingly involved stabilising patients prior to discharge, rather than participating in the complete care process, with the volume of administrative duties and paperwork cutting down their contact time with patients. Across all of the areas, between 1985 and 1996, the time spent in direct patient care by G and F grade nurses decreased by over 20 per cent, while their 'associated work' (meetings with medical staff, office duties, teaching junior staff etc.) increased by 39 per cent and 15 per cent respectively. During the same period, E and D grade nurses reported spending 13 and 17 per cent less time respectively involved in direct patient care and an increase in associated duties (mainly office work) of 17 per cent and 26 per cent respectively. Senior nurses (G and F grades) claimed that up to 60 per cent of their paperwork was not directly relevant to patient care and was completed as a matter of routine for the benefit of finance and personnel departments, for example. The introduction of the Care Programme Approach had also introduced a large volume of extra paperwork.

5.29   The study also conducted interviews with a small number of patients and found that across all of the sites they had little contact with ward staff. They frequently mentioned the 'boredom' of hospital life and spent much of their time on their own 'doing nothing', watching television or talking to other patients. Patients reported spending only four per cent of their time with ward staff and identified the lack of sufficient 'quality time' with nurses as a specific problem.

5.30   The nursing profession has recognised the current pressures and difficulties experienced by its membership, in particular high levels of stress, low morale, staff shortages and increasing exposure to violence and aggression. In March 1999, the Royal College of Nursing published a Mental Health Nursing Strategy which argued that some of the Government's policy objectives in *Modernising Mental Health Services* may be difficult to achieve unless the core problems facing the nursing profession are tackled effectively. The strategy outlines seven areas of service development regarded as critical in realising positive change. These are:

- a greater emphasis on the therapeutic possibilities offered by in-patient nursing care and better access to training in skills-based treatment strategies for in-patient nurses;

- a recognition of the high levels of risk of violence faced by mental health nurses and the need to develop and promote national guidance on violence in health care settings;

- the development of national protocols to enable in-patient nurses to adequately assess and manage risk;

- the provision of nursed beds in the community, for patients in the post-acute phase of their illness, in order to ease demand on acute admission wards;

- the need to ensure that nurses and patients from ethnic groups receive equitable support and opportunities within the mental health services;

- fostering further recruitment and retention initiatives specific to mental health nursing; and

- ensuring that mental health nursing receives recognition and support for its research and practice development needs.

5.31 If effective therapeutic in-patient care is to be provided, hospital managers must review the availability of their staff and ensure that high priority is given to engaging with patients. This will include ensuring that staff have access to support and training opportunities adequate to the task. The Commission has found that the current emphasis in the NHS on 'evidence-based' practice appears to be in little evidence on psychiatric wards. The ACIS study found a marked absence of such practice, with only 5% of patients receiving specific psychological therapies. The most common interventions were creative therapies (46%), social activities (33%), ward groups (23%) and relaxation (21%). Medication regimes may also fail to conform with 'evidence-based' standards. In an earlier study, Geddes et al. (1996) found that fewer than two-thirds of patients admitted to one ward over a one month period received medication regimes that could be said to conform with evidence-based criteria.

5.32 The Commission recognises that the time and ability to deliver evidence-based therapeutic care will, undoubtedly, be influenced by the pressures on in-patient services described above. For this reason it is all the more important that there are strong links between ward-based staff and other professional groups, such as psychologists, occupational therapists and community-based staff, in order to make comprehensive assessments of the patients' needs, deliver effective therapeutic care and to plan effective strategies for community management before discharge.

5.33 The ACIS study also highlighted the need for improved communication between the professions and a clearer understanding of each other's contribution and role; particularly between nurses and occupational therapists (OTs). The study found that nurses very often felt that OTs would not accept some of the most disturbed patients and did not attend the ward often enough. On the other hand OTs felt that they did not receive referrals soon enough, or that the referrals were inappropriate, and that when they had started a programme of care patients might be discharged without their being informed.

5.34 Patients very often complain to Commissioners of inactivity and boredom. Some form of organised activity is essential, particularly on acute wards, in order to support therapeutic engagement and maintain the patients' interest in their care. It can also serve to reduce tensions on the ward that can arise from boredom and may therefore reduce the likelihood of aggressive and violent behaviour. This is particularly important for patients who are detained and confined to the ward. However, Commissioners regularly hear of shortages of occupational therapists. This is mainly due to difficulties in recruitment, although shortages in local funding can also be a significant factor. Occupational therapists are able to offer diversional therapies that are not only aimed at re-skilling individuals and improving their self-esteem, but also assist in reducing feelings of frustration and containment when patients are confined to a single ward. However, as reported in the Seventh Biennial Report, nurses and nursing assistants continue to be called upon to fulfil these duties but often lack the necessary skills.

> ### Visit to Barnet Healthcare NHS Trust and Barnet Social Services Department; 8 & 9 May 1997
>
> There was inadequate occupational therapy provision on Hawthorne Ward (where an occupational therapist attended once a week) and at Barnet Psychiatric Unit. This had been raised by Commissioners on previous visits, particularly in relation to Hawthorne Ward.
>
> The reading material available to patients at Barnet consisted of four copies of the Watchtower, Women's magazines, which were over one year old and a few Mills and Boon novels. There were no daily newspapers and on Ken Porter Ward a number of patients were observed unoccupied, looking bored or asleep.
>
> Following the Commission's visit, the Trust established a group of senior nurses and occupational therapists to facilitate and develop activities for patients on the unit.

5.35   The Commission is particularly concerned that patients should also have sufficient access to fresh air. This is especially important for those on crowded wards in order to relieve feelings of oppressive confinement. However, Commissioners very often hear reports from patients that such access is denied them, either because staff are unavailable for escort duties or the design and siting of the ward does not permit it.

> ### Visit to The Ladywell Mental Health Unit, Lewisham Hospital; 12 May 1998
>
> The weather on the day of the Commissioners' visit to the Unit was hot and sunny. Many patients complained to Commissioners of the heat and the body smells on the wards and expressed the need for adequate air conditioning. The Commissioners confirmed that all the wards were unpleasantly hot and stuffy and the absence of any outside area to which the patients could have access to obtain fresh air exacerbated the problem. The Commissioners were told of plans to provide air conditioning in the dining rooms with fans in other parts of the upstairs wards and air conditioning throughout the Johnson Unit.

> ### Visit to Riverside Mental Health Trust, Hammersmith & Fulham Mental Health Service; Visit 24 April 98
>
> Although it had been accepted for some time that there were serious problems with the environment, on some wards Commissioners had never seen patients more distressed by their living conditions. There were major problems with access to fresh air and facilities for exercise, particularly for patients on high level observation. During the previous week the temperature reached 100°F on Ward 3 West, and Commissioners were told of other wards being too hot for comfort at times.

## Physical Examinations

5.36   Patients suffering from psychiatric illnesses are particularly vulnerable to problems with their physical health (e.g. Meltzer et al, 1997) - especially those with long-term mental illness

(Brugha et al, 1989) - and there is an increased risk of premature death from natural causes for all mental disorders (Harris & Barraclough, 1998). It is, therefore, extremely important that adequate attention is given to patients' physical well-being, as well as their mental health, during their stay in hospital. During the current reporting period the Commission included the routine provision of physical examinations for detained patients among the 'matters requiring particular attention'.

5.37   Commission members gathered information on the arrangements for physical examinations during visits to over 1,200 wards, and found that in only a quarter of these were staff able to produce evidence of a discrete policy requirement for a physical examination to take place within a given period following admission, or for regular examinations for long-term in-patients. However, some units may have included such a requirement within their general admission policy. The Commission also recognises that clinicians consider physical examinations a routine component of care and are, therefore, likely to regard this as obviating the need for a specific policy statement. Where a policy was in place, Commissioners found that in the majority of cases (90%) the requirement was for a physical examination to take place within seven days of admission and, in the case of patients resident for long periods, just under half (44%) clearly specified that physical examinations should take place at least annually.

5.38   The majority of wards (80%) had at least one detained patient who had been resident for longer than a month, and on each of these wards the Commissioners examined the medical notes of the patient who had most recently been admitted and who fell into this category. In just under a quarter (23%) of these cases, they were unable to find any recorded evidence of a physical examination having taken place following admission. Nearly half (48%) of these wards also had at least one detained patient who had been resident for over one year. In examining the records of the patient who had been resident for the longest period, Commissioners found that in 47% of these cases there was no record of the patient having received a routine physical examination during the preceding 12 months.

5.39   These findings are based on a relatively small sample of detained patients' records and it is very important to recognise that they are not suggestive of the fact that that physical examinations had not taken place, only that they had not been clearly recorded in the patients' medical notes. Nevertheless, adequate recording of events such as assessments and medical examinations are fundamental to the delivery of care and findings such as these are a matter for concern. As a result, the Commission would recommend that Trusts ensure that clear guidelines for the physical examination of patients, and the recording of these events, are in place. Adherence to these guidelines must be monitored and Trusts might wish to consider including them among their standards for Clinical Governance.

# Ensuring Quality of Care

## Legislating for Quality

5.40   One of the questions posed by the Mental Health Legislation Review Team was whether legislation should be used to ensure the provision of high quality care – improving buildings, staffing and skill levels, environmental conditions on the ward and facilities in the community. The House of Commons debated a Private Member's Bill[1], that sought to legislate for standards by imposing a duty on Health Authorities to provide single sex wards, including the fixture of appropriate security devices to doors and to prepare a strategy for the provision of in-patient care for people going through acute episodes of mental illness. While this always had a very limited chance of reaching the statute books, it demonstrated the concerns of the legislature for enhancing standards in in-patient care.

5.41   There are extreme difficulties in legislating for quality. One possible model for such legislation, however, is the Children Act 1989, which does set out some broad principles of care in Part I and some requirements for local authorities' provision of service in Part III[1]. The fact that the Children Act itself does not set out specific remedies relating to each of these principles has, in the understanding of the Commission, not detracted from the value of having such principles stated in legislation. The Commission believes that the principles reinforce professionals' awareness of their duties to provide the most appropriate care in their practical implementation of the law. The Commission would suggest, therefore, that new mental health legislation could incorporate principles based upon the *Guiding Principles* listed in Chapter 1 of the Code of Practice. In addition to such a clear statement of principle that, for example, supports the provision of services that are non-discriminatory with regard to ethnicity and gender, specific provision could be made within the legislation requiring professionals to record and demonstrate that account has been taken of such issues.

5.42   In terms of ensuring quality of care on a more sophisticated level than the 'blunt instrument' of legislation, different levels of quality standards could provide the most comprehensive and practical model for quality assurance. Firstly, a *legislative* standard, setting minimum legal standards; secondly, some form of *registration* or *accreditation* of service providers, providing more exacting and, possibly, locally agreed standards; and finally, the *Code of Practice*.

## Setting Standards into New Legislation

5.43   The 1983 Act does impose a number of duties upon mental health professionals that protect the patients' rights (such as, for example, the statutory procedures for admission under the Act, consent to treatment provisions etc.) and, to a considerably lesser extent, sets standards for their care in hospital and continuing care following discharge. It seems logical that any

---

[1] Mental Health (Amentment) No. 2 Bill, 12 December 1997.

legislation that primarily deals with the imposition of compulsory powers should have, at its core, a set of powers and duties that enable such imposition to be achieved with the minimum inconsistency and with full regard to the rights of individuals to not be subject to compulsion without pressing need. The Commission has suggested to the Mental Health Legislation Review Team that if new legislation were kept within such parameters, more prescriptive regulation of services could be set by authorities empowered to do so by statute.

## Registration/Accreditation for the Regulation of Mental Health Services

5.44    One suggested model for setting service standards into new legislation is that all mental health services providing a service to people subject to compulsory care and treatment for mental disorder should be required to be registered by a registration and inspection authority and approved to provide services. Such registration would require the satisfaction of basic standards such as, for example, the keeping of records in relation to leave, seclusion and physical examinations, and the provision of information to patients and relatives. Providers could be required to publish records relating to the incidence of seclusion, suicides, patients who have been absent without leave etc., and could be required to show the existence of procedures for the regular review of care. Periodic inspections by a regulatory body would police the system and the results of such inspections could be made public. Failure to adhere to standards could result in warnings, with the ultimate sanction of outside managers being brought in to oversee the failing mental health provider.

5.45    A similar model for setting standards into new legislation is an accreditation system as established in Canada, Australia, Holland and the USA. Accreditation differs from registration in that, as opposed to a set of minimum standards that would be uniform to all providers, it requires a judgment about whether a set of agreed quality standards has been met by providers. Under such systems a set of agreed standards (categorised according to the size and nature of the service offered) would have to be met by mental health services to receive accreditation, which would be provided by a monitoring body. Failure to meet the set standards after an opportunity for improvement had been provided could result in the same sanctions as suggested above.

## The Code of Practice

5.46    The Commission believes that the Mental Health Act Code of Practice is an essential tool in ensuring quality of care for patients subject to the Act. The Code does enshrine good practice and provides guidance to responsible authorities on how to proceed when undertaking duties under the Act, particularly concerning compulsory powers.

5.47    The Code of Practice does not impose legal duties on providers. The guidance that it does give is perhaps best served by its current status and would be unlikely to be enhanced if its provisions were given statutory force. The effect of giving statutory weight to the provisions of the Code in new legislation might have the effect of watering down those provisions until they became a set of minimum standards; whereas such minimum standards could themselves be enshrined in legislation, or enforced through statutory requirements upon providers to be registered or accredited, as a more effective way of imposing statutory duties upon providers.

## Continuity of Care

### Section 117 and the Care Programme Approach

5.48    The Care Programme Approach (CPA) was introduced in 1991 to provide a framework for the care of seriously mentally ill people in the community in order to 'minimise the possibility of their losing contact with services and [to maximise] the effect of any therapeutic intervention' (Circular HC(90)23). All detained patients should benefit from the CPA. Providers' statutory obligations to provide aftercare under Section 117 must be integrated with the provisions of the CPA, but patients entitled to Section 117 aftercare must be clearly identifiable within the CPA recording system (Code of Practice, 27.3). Continuity of patient care between in-patient and community-based services is fundamental to the delivery of high quality mental health services. If treatment in hospital is to be successful it must be complemented by the availability of well co-ordinated care at the point of discharge, followed up by regular review in the community. A failure to implement the CPA risks the breakdown of care and further compulsory admission.

5.49    The principal requirements of the CPA are clear and well established, but they are worth reiterating. All patients must:

*    receive a thorough and systematic assessment of their health and social care needs;

*    have in place an individualised care plan addressing those needs;

*    have a keyworker who will maintain contact with them and who will monitor the implementation of the care plan; and

*    have their care regularly reviewed, and modified or changed where necessary.

Care planning should seek to ensure the active involvement of patients, carers and, where necessary, other appropriate agencies, and all decisions and activities relating to the CPA must be adequately recorded. The Code of Practice (1.2) now includes extensive reference to the CPA; and health authorities, Trusts and social service departments are responsible for ensuring that the Act is always applied in that context.

5.50    The Commission has found that most providers continue to make gradual progress towards the implementation of the CPA. However, the process is still far from complete and there remain some variations in policy and practice, sometimes within the same Trust. Most providers have adhered to the 3-tiered approach to the CPA, where the CPA procedures are adjusted according to the complexity of the case.

---

[1] Children Act 1989, Chapter 41.

5.51   For the CPA to form the cornerstone of good practice in the delivery of co-ordinated and individualised psychiatric care, mental health professionals should work closely as part of multidisciplinary teams. The links between community-based workers and their hospital-based colleagues must be effective to avoid inadequately planned discharges and the likelihood of later inappropriate admissions.

> ### Visit to Hounslow & Spelthorne Community & Mental Health NHS Trust; 21 & 22 May 1998
>
> Practice in this area was some of the best that Commissioners had come across and professionals in all areas of the services were clearly committed to the CPA process. Examples of high quality assessments were found and Commissioners commended the practice of inviting patients to identify their own needs. The integration of community and hospital services had apparently contributed to the high standard of practice and Commissioners were told of easy and frequent contact between hospital and community based staff.

5.52   Where community staff are not in regular contact with the ward, there is a danger that they may only get involved in planning for the patient's discharge at the last minute, if at all. Although detailed CPA planning for discharge might not be realistically undertaken until late in the patient's hospital stay, outline planning involving all interested parties should nevertheless begin soon after admission (Code of Practice, 27.1). However, as reported in the previous two Biennial Reports, Commissioners continue to find evidence of CPA/Section 117 meetings being held very late, or of detained patients being discharged without a multidisciplinary Section 117 meeting being held. Problems can also include discharge planning taking place during routine ward rounds without appropriate discussion with community staff, or CPA meetings called simply to ratify previous plans which had not been made in a full multidisciplinary team meeting. ASWs have sometimes complained to Commissioners of being given only a few days notice of CPA meetings, and of the meeting minutes not being circulated until several weeks, and in some cases months, after the patient's review.

> ### Visit to Cambridge Social Services Department; 25 June 1998
>
> Commissioners heard concerns expressed by service users, ASWs and staff from statutory and voluntary groups about the adequacy of discharge arrangements. All four of the service users seen during the visit, two of whom received services from Peterborough units and the other two from the Fermoy Unit, said that they had not been told of arrangements for further support after their discharge from detention. Commissioners requested that they should be followed up after the visit to assess the need for services. Staff of residential and day care facilities also reported that some patients were discharged from hospital without prior warning to the community services, with no review systems in place, and with very scanty follow-up available. ASWs also pointed out that CPA implementation was still incomplete, with major concerns over North West Anglian Healthcare Trust. Senior managers

> acknowledged these concerns, but indicated that a new CPA policy had been implemented in that area on 1st June 1998, backed up by joint training

5.53   Social services managers must also ensure that social workers are allocated cases in a timely manner in order that full assessments of patients' social care needs can be made. Where this does not happen patients' discharges are likely to be delayed. This is particularly important where patients must be provided with suitable accommodation before they can be discharged.

5.54   Commissioners usually find that the paperwork for the CPA is in place in patients' records but that it is very often incomplete, containing only basic demographic information and no records of CPA meetings or care plans. The Commission's observations are also supported by independent research. The Sainsbury Centre for Mental Health ACIS study examined the case notes of 215 patients soon after discharge, and found that for 102 (48%) of the patients the notes did not contain any care plans, or that the notes could not be found. Only 34 (16%) of the 215 patents had a CPA meeting arranged before discharge. In another recent national study, the Social Services Inspectorate interviewed 528 mental health service users and found that only 282 (53%) had a care plan, with just over half of these actually having a copy of their care plan (Social Services Inspectorate, 1999).

5.55   During private meetings with Commissioners some patients have indicated concerns that they did not fully understand the CPA process or that they were uncertain about the plans for their future care.

> **Visit to Tameside & Glossop Community and Priority Services NHS Trust; 11 December 1997**
>
> A number of patients who met with Commissioners indicated that they had little understanding of what their care plans involved and how the plans related to their weekly programmes or long term goals. The majority of patients interviewed wished to have more information about their care plans. The Trust was asked to consider providing patients with their own copies of the care plans that are in place

5.56   Commissioners have also found that the content of care plans may be unclear or badly written and can very often lapse into jargon. A small scale study by McDermott (1998) examined the self-reported views and experiences of 43 patients who were identified as having complex mental health and social care needs and who were in receipt of 'full multidisciplinary' CPA. Whilst in this study 95% of the patients reported having copies of their care plan, only 26% claimed to have a full understanding of its contents.

5.57   Some patients and their carers have also reported to Commissioners that they find the formality of large multidisciplinary CPA review meetings very intimidating, and as a result feel unable to participate effectively in the planning process. These kinds of experiences are likely to exacerbate the psychological distress that patients may already be feeling and which may be preventing them from active involvement in their care. It is imperative that mental healthcare professionals find ways to demonstrate to patients that their needs and concerns are well understood and have been taken into account in planning their care. Comprehensive and comprehensible care plans are fundamental for communicating information to all parties, including the users and their carers.

5.58    Where CPA forms are not well designed, or the CPA is not well integrated with nursing and medical records in order to avoid duplication, staff can find the process of recording and care planning a burdensome and time-consuming administrative procedure, which in turn can result in further delays in service delivery and patients' needs remaining unmet. Where the process is viewed as simply one more piece of paperwork to be completed, the Commission has found that this leads to an erosion of staff commitment to the principles of the CPA.

5.59    Comprehensive training in the local policies and procedures for CPA is essential for all clinical staff groups and must be constantly monitored and reviewed in order to ensure that staff are kept abreast of developments in policy and practice. CPA training should integrate with training in health and social care needs assessment and recording, and in particular with risk assessment protocols. Most importantly, members of multidisciplinary teams should train together "to ensure that potential key workers from different professional backgrounds develop a shared approach to the key worker role" (Building Bridges, Dept. of Health, 1995, p. 86/87).

5.60    The Commission recognises that information technology has a vital role to play in reducing much of the duplication in CPA recording, and can provide staff with immediate access to the information that they need in order ensure continuity of patient care. The Government has recently published 'Information for Health: An Information Strategy for the Modern NHS' (Dept. of Health 1998d), which outlines a plan for substantial investment in information technology throughout the NHS in order to support service delivery and to eliminate much of the frustration engendered by inaccessible records, repeated form-filling and poorly co-ordinated services. The Commission hopes that mental health services and service users will benefit significantly from this investment.

> **Visit to North Birmingham Mental Health NHS Trust and Birmingham Social Services Department; 22 & 23 May 1997**
>
> Commissioners were able to spend time with the Care Programme Approach manager to discuss progress in the implementation of the CPA. It was clear that this implementation reflected many of the challenges present in North Birmingham, e.g. the size of the population, large numbers of teams and multi-agency working. There were currently over 12,000 patients registered on the CPA, of whom 5,000 were identified as having complex needs. The manager received up to 300 forms each day. There was only limited information technology available to handle this mass of information. The Commissioners felt that it was difficult to see how the aims and objectives of CPA could be met without it.

## Care Management

5.61 Social services departments have a responsibility to undertake assessments of individuals' social care needs and to design and implement care plans in accordance with Care Management procedures. The guidance set out by the Department of Health in *Building Bridges* (1995) advises that "although Social Services Departments have responsibility for Care Management, and Health Authorities for CPA, the principles underlying the two processes are the same. It is therefore essential that health and social services departments co-ordinate the implementation of the two processes to avoid duplication and the waste of precious resources. If properly implemented, multi-disciplinary assessment will ensure that the duty to make a community care assessment is fully discharged as part of the CPA, and there should be no need for separate assessments" (p. 15).

5.62 The CPA and Care Management systems must, therefore, be integrated as far as possible. The requirement for integration has also been reinforced in the Code of Practice (1.2), and should have the effect of ensuring that patients benefit from continuity of care between hospital and the community through fully co-ordinated multi-disciplinary and multi-agency care planning. However, evidence from Commission visits to many social services departments suggests that the successful integration of the CPA (including Section 117) with Care Management is still to be realised. In discussions with Approved Social Workers (ASWs), Commissioners frequently hear that the administrative duplication that is involved in working within two separate systems is not only an additional burden for them, but can also delay the delivery of care. The lack of clarity and integration of CPA and Care Management systems is also reported as a problem by hospital-based staff, and can result in confusion over responsibilities and subsequent delays in care planning.

5.63 A national inspection by the Social Services Inspectorate (SSI) of the integration of the CPA and Care Management, found that few Social Services Departments had achieved the level of integration described in 'Building Bridges': hence the title of the final report, 'Still Building Bridges' (Social Services Inspectorate, 1999). The SSI found, among other things, that where multidisciplinary community mental health teams had been established with clear terms of reference and an understanding by all staff of the 'mental health worker' role, care planning and care management had integrated well. This is also the experience of the Commission. A few Trusts and Social Services Departments appear have made significant progress in integrating the CPA and Care Management service delivery systems.

> Visit to Northumberland Social Services Department; 29 January 1998
>
> The 'Northumberland Mental Health Strategy', published in June 1997, proved extremely helpful in updating the visiting Commissioners in developments in the county. Particularly pleasing was the development of the tiered approach (incorporating four levels of need) providing a common framework within which health and social care agencies carried out their responsibilities.

It appeared that all agencies involved in mental health services in Northumberland were committed to the objective of an effective partnership as the only means of developing a high quality comprehensive service. During the course of this visit it became apparent that this objective had been achieved.

CPA and care management were reported to be working well through integrated care management teams. ASWs reflected good morale and were complimentary of joint working with health colleagues. Peer group support and multidisciplinary relationships were reported to be good, and mention was made of effective user representation.

Commissioners gained the impression of some excellent multi-disciplinary team work, with mutual respect and confidence in an area of difficult geography and the potential for isolation. Team members appeared to have overcome these difficulties and were achieving their objectives. Without doubt this was due to some sound leadership and good motivation.

5.64    As the above example demonstrates, successful integration is largely dependent upon co-operation, joint planning and a shared commitment to the delivery of high quality services by health authorities, Trusts and social services departments. However, this can often be difficult to achieve where service boundaries or service providers change and established patterns of service delivery are interrupted. Where such changes do occur, Trusts and social service departments must be especially vigilant and ensure early consultation with all agencies.

**Visit to North Tyneside Council Care in the Community Function; 2 February 1998**

In 1995 the NHS provider of psychiatric care for adults under 65 years of age became the Newcastle City NHS Trust. The NHS provider for those over 65 years remained the North Tyneside Health Care NHS Trust. In the North West of the Council's geographical area, the NHS service for the over 65s was still provided by the Newcastle City NHS Trust.

The change of provider for people under 65 years with mental health problems had brought about changes which were discussed with the Commissioners. Communication with Newcastle City NHS Trust personnel, particularly consultant psychiatrists, was said to be poor. Examples included:

- ASWs not being informed of CPA/Section 117 after-care meetings;

- the use of Consultant Psychiatrists' secretaries to arrange CPA meetings without any consultation with the North Tyneside Council;

- the decision of the City NHS Trust to re-organise consultant work in North Tyneside, so that some consultants saw only in-patients while others did only community work, was taken, Commissioners were told, without any consultation with the North Tyneside Council; and

- the initiative to establish a multi-agency Code of Practice Group, which the Commissioners supported when they visited in 1994, had made no progress, and the change in provider seemed to be a factor in this (the first meeting of the Code of Practice Group took place later in April 1998).

5.65   In *'Modernising Mental Health Services: Safe, Sound and Supportive'*, the Government has identified the failure to integrate the CPA and Care Management systems as a major obstacle to effective aftercare (para. 3.13), and has announced its intention to review and harmonise these procedures (paras 4.46 to 4.48). At the time of writing, a recent NHS Executive consultation paper has outlined the Department of Health's view that care must be delivered as part of a single system combining mental health and social care, in which service users would expect one assessment process, one principal or primary contact person, one care plan and one review process (Dept. of Health, 1999c) The features of a truly integrated system of CPA and Care Management would include:

- a single operational policy;

- joint training for health and social care staff;

- one lead officer for care co-ordination across health and social care;

- a single complaints procedure;

- a shared information system across health and social care;

- agreed risk assessment and risk management processes; and

- an agreed protocol for the allocation of resources.

## The Needs of Carers

5.66   Families and carers very often provide a high level of support to service users with severe and enduring mental health problems, and their involvement in after-care planning is a vital aspect of the CPA and Care Management. Carers must always be involved in meaningful discussions about the plans for the patient's care upon discharge. In *Building Bridges*, the Department of Health further advised that carers' own needs for support should also be assessed. In the previous Biennial Report the Commission expressed the hope that the Carers (Recognition and Services) Act 1995 would "encourage a more systematic approach to carers' ability to provide care and their need for support" (p.140). Although the Commission has previously noted some gradual improvements in this regard, recent reports by the Social Services Inspectorate have revealed little evidence of the routine use of carers' assessments or that carers have fully understood their statutory rights (Social Services Inspectorate, 1999). Carers themselves were also found to be very critical that social services departments and other agencies did not take their views and needs into account (Social Services Inspectorate, 1998).

5.67   The Commission therefore welcomes the Government's initiative in recognising the vital role played by informal carers and the recently published National Strategy - *'Caring about Carers'*. This strategy records the Government's intention to provide carers with better information (e.g. the NHS Direct helpline for carer information and Government information on the Internet), improvements in the consistency of charging for services and a new charter on what support carers can expect from long-term care services. The strategy also recognises the importance of carers' involvement in planning and providing services, and the need for service providers to consult local caring organisations. Carers' own health needs will also be addressed through the introduction of new powers for local authorities to provide services for carers, particularly through special grants to help them to take a break. This will be funded by an additional £140 million, to be used in a targeted way over the next three years.

5.68    The Commission hopes that these initiatives will place carers high on the agenda of the statutory services, who must recognise that they can no longer focus on the client, patient or user and must see the person requiring support within the whole environment of family, friends and the local community.

## Medium Secure Care

### Service Pressures

5.69    Over recent years there has been an increasing demand for places offering medium and low secure psychiatric care. Factors that are generally recognised as contributing to this increased demand include the closure of the long-stay psychiatric hospitals, the size and siting of which usually allowed staff to cope with quite high degrees of challenging behaviour, and a general increase in the levels of violence in society which is reflected in the psychiatric population. A growing awareness of the incidence of psychiatric problems among prison populations has also increased the pressures upon secure units.

> **Visits to the Caswell Clinic, Bridgend and District NHS Trust; 17 October 1997 & 25 March 1998**
>
> Parc Prison, within a few miles of the Caswell Clinic, opened in November 1997 and was designed to hold, by March 1998, approximately 800 male prisoners. This included 500 adults (remand and detained), 200 young offenders (aged 18-21) and 100 juveniles (aged 15-17). The new prison doubled the prison population of Wales and was expected to make considerable demands on the forensic services at the Caswell Clinic. Bridgend and District Trust had been given the contract to plan and provide psychiatric medical and nursing services in an 18-bedded Medical Centre in the prison. However, the Medical Centre would not be regarded as a hospital unit but as providing primary care. Patients requiring hospital treatment would have to be transferred to a suitable hospital unit.
>
> Following the opening of the prison, a large number of prisoners with substance misuse problems, self-harm tendencies and suicide risk were identified, and the Trust experienced difficulties in meeting the growing demand for services. Conflicts also arose between the custody and care regimes. The Trust recognised the need for improved protocols and procedures, and for team building between security staff and health professionals.

5.70    In February 1996, the NHS Executive published a review of the existing and planned provision of mental health services in England (Dept. of Health, 1996). In terms of the provision of medium secure places, the review noted that, by March 1997:

- there would be 1,200 beds available in purpose built units for patients requiring medium secure care;

- 450 places of medium secure standard would be available in interim secure units;

- 300 additional places were included in Trusts' development plans; and

- 400 secure places would be purchased from independent sector providers.

In 1998, approximately 55% of all low and medium secure places were provided within the independent sector, in both the profit making and not-for-profit sectors. This substantial growth in independent sector provision is a result of previous Governments' commitment to the expansion of independent sector health and social care, and a marked reduction in the availability of NHS capital for building new facilities, although the latter is now recovering. During the current reporting period, the Commission has visited 72 medium secure units throughout England and Wales, 38% of which were in the independent sector. The majority of these independent sector places are purchased by the NHS. A small number of these are purchased on a contract basis, but most are provided on the basis of individual case purchasing (Out of Area Treatments).

5.71 One of the greatest areas of concern for the managers and staff of the medium secure facilities is that the demand for beds is exacerbated by a gradual 'silting-up' of the units as they increasingly find themselves accommodating patients requiring long-term medium secure care, or conditions of lower security.

> Visit to the Butler Clinic, Exeter and District Community Health Service NHS Trust; 8 January 1998
>
> Ward staff confirmed that as many as nine patients on the two wards could be ready for discharge if appropriate placement was available locally. Delays of this nature caused frustration for patients and staff alike, and seemed to reflect a lack of low-security or intensive care facilities for longer-term patients elsewhere in this part of the Region. The Clinic is seen as virtually the only unit in the south of the Region with the capacity to cope with patients who present significant management problems, whether or not there is a forensic element. Commissioners were advised that interim arrangements were planned for a unit for patients with longer-term needs on the Langdon Hospital site to become available later in 1998, which it was hoped would relieve some of the pressure on the Butler Clinic, as well as allowing for the return of a number of 'out of area treatment' patients.
>
> However, other factors, notably the need to retain 'leave' beds for discharged patients who are subject to Home Office restriction for up to 6 months, added to the pressures. Purchasers carry financial responsibility in the latter case to pay for the retained bed as well as for the new placement. Pressures of this nature are not unique to the South West, but Commissioners meet regularly with Officers of the Regional NHS Executive, and agreed to raise the item for discussion at the next meeting.

5.72 There are service developments being planned in different parts of the country to relieve the pressure on the medium secure services. The *Reaside Clinic* in Birmingham has undertaken a survey of the needs of patients in the High Security Hospitals and has submitted proposals to health authorities and social services departments in the West Midlands for the development of further medium secure provision, including long-stay accommodation on-site and smaller low-secure hostels in the community. During a visit to *Eastbourne and County NHS Trust* in May 1998, Commissioners were advised that the Health Authority had commissioned a four-place rehabilitation hostel for the forensic service near the entrance to the grounds of Hellingly Hospital, which was due to open in the near future. It was anticipated that this would assist with the rehabilitation of patients in Southview and Ashen Hill who no longer needed a secure environment but were not yet ready for, or were unable to access, suitable community accommodation and support. At this time there continued to be almost 100% occupancy within Ashen Hill Medium Secure Unit, with East Sussex making use of up to 16 beds at a time against a contracted level of 13 beds. It is hoped that the hostel development will ease this situation. The *Mental Health Services of Salford NHS Trust* has submitted a Business Case to the NHS Executive (North-West) and the High Security Services Commissioning Board to improve provision in the North West Region for patients needing long-term medium secure care. The Trust has also developed plans, in partnership with the independent sector, to provide a number of smaller units offering high supervision, but lower levels of security.

## Quality Standards

5.73 In the Seventh Biennial Report, the Commission emphasised the importance of the monitoring of independent sector provision from the perspective of a lead purchaser for each of these services. Over the current reporting period the Commission has observed that this arrangement is increasingly becoming the norm. NHS purchasers are inspecting these facilities and building quality standards into their contracts, as they do with NHS providers. Independent sector units, as statutorily registered mental nursing homes, are inspected by the local health authority's nursing homes inspectorate, and all members of the Independent Healthcare Association have given a commitment to accreditation by an appropriate external accreditation body.

5.74 The Commission's Special Interest Group on Medium Secure Care has conducted a review of the Commission's Visiting Policy in relation to patients in all medium secure facilities, with a view to strengthening the policy and ensuring the standardisation of visiting procedures. The Commission will conduct Full Visits to units every two years and endeavor to see all patients and examine their case records at least annually. Out-of-hours and unannounced visits will continue. Commissioners will pay particular attention to the following general issues.

5.75 Good quality psychiatric and general medical treatment should include out-of-hours and weekend cover for emergencies. Care should be provided by a multi-disciplinary team offering assessment, counselling and psychotherapy, and treatment regimes for specific problems such as eating disorders and self-harm. The unit should also provide access to well women's clinics, although these might not necessarily be on site, as well as advice on general health and sexual and relationship matters. Commissioners will pay particular attention to medication regimes and the use of 'as required' (PRN) medication, and will seek to ensure that the principles and requirements of patients' consent to treatment are being scrupulously observed. Care and treatment plans relating to the CPA/Section 117 after-care and Section 17 leave should be easily accessible by staff and patients. Any performance and outcome measures adopted by the unit should be understood by staff and be of value to them.

5.76 As patients are likely to be in hospital for long periods it is important to ensure the availability of a healthy diet that ensures that ethnic and special needs are satisfied. Equally important is access to occupational, work and educational facilities, together with physical exercise, leisure and fresh air. Hygiene and clothing issues will need consideration, as will benefit payments and rewards and sanctions.

5.77 Particular account should be taken of the needs of women patients and vulnerable patients. The design of the building should allow for effective observation and supervision in all patient areas, and locked areas must be easily accessible in an emergency. The location and design of bedrooms is particularly important for those units accommodating sex offenders or potentially assaultive patients. Commissioners will pay particular attention to the provision of call alarms for patients and staff, and to whether patients have the facility to lock their bedroom doors and the circumstances under which this may be permitted.

5.78 Units should have policies in place relating to visiting arrangements, including visits by children (Code of Practice, 26.3), searching patients, and the safe storage of, and access to, personal property, including the confiscation of patients belongings. Management strategies should be in place for dealing with individual and group disturbances, particularly if there are no seclusion facilities. Where there are seclusion facilities they should conform to the standards set in the Code of Practice (19.16 to 19.23). Where 'time out' or therapeutic isolation is used as an alternative to seclusion, this should be correctly recorded and reviewed by senior managers and care teams. Commissioners will also pay attention to the standards, training and monitoring in place for the use of control and restraint techniques.

5.79 A major incident plan should be in place to deal with emergencies that are likely to involve external agencies such as the police and the fire department. Such incidents will include fire, severe violence beyond the control of staff and absconding. Staff training programmes should be in place.

5.80 Independent advocacy services should be available to all patients in secure facilities in order to negotiate as much personal choice as is clinically acceptable and safe within the setting. Interpretation services should be available, as should access to legal representation, including facilities for private interviews when necessary.

## Staffing Issues and Patient Activity

5.81   As reported in the previous section, staffing shortages can have serious effects upon the quality of patient care and will significantly reduce the opportunities for therapeutic programmes and patients' leisure activities. This is of particular importance in secure units, given the fact that patients may be resident in these units for long periods and living under very constraining regimes of care. In such circumstances, the delivery of individualised treatment relevant to the patients' needs, in an environment offering an appropriate degree of stimulation, may be difficult to achieve.

> ### Visit to the Eric Shepherd Unit, Horizon NHS Unit; 12 September 1997
>
> Commissioners were concerned about the number of nursing and medical vacancies in the unit. This was having an effect on patient care and the range of activities and therapies available to patients. Commissioners appreciated that the Trust had made arrangements to cover the vacant posts but hoped that the Trust would be able to recruit to its establishment as a matter of urgency. They were particularly concerned about the long hours some nursing staff worked and that patient activity was being restricted due to non-availability of nurses for escort duties. Commissioners were told that on occasion hospital appointments had been cancelled due to the lack of available escorts.
>
> This situation was worsened by some restrictions of the environment. Patients complained to Commissioners that they were bored and that there was nothing to do at weekends. A number of patients were particularly concerned that they were no longer able to play football in the courtyard. The suggestion that they play behind House 4 was not considered by Commissioners to be a suitable alternative, as the area was not developed to accommodate this and a number of patients were not able to join in as they did not have the appropriate leave entitlement. This was a young, physically active group of patients and Commissioners urged managers as a matter of priority to address the problem of where all the patients may play football and other ball games.

> ### Visit to Redford Lodge, Edmonton, North London; 11 July 1997
>
> A specific issue regarding staffing levels was raised on Vincent Ward. There was a problem with staff vacancies, which Commissioners were told would be resolved in the near future, but the ward was presently reliant on bank staff. Of perhaps more concern was the effect of the general staffing levels on both staff and patients. Given the high level of need of patients on the ward, and the large number needing special observation at any one time, the staff were reported to be under extreme pressure, and patients were sometimes not being granted escorted leave because there was not sufficient staff to carry out escort duties. However, the ward management were commended for organising a weekly support session for staff, but it was considered more appropriate to review staffing levels on the ward, in order to reduce stress and to ensure that patients were not confined to the ward more than was necessary.

5.82    The provision of further education can be an important feature in the programme of activities offered in secure units. Many mentally disordered offenders have limited educational achievements, resulting in poor job opportunities and low self-esteem. Educational courses, such as those that improve literacy and numeracy skills, or new areas such as computing, can be a route to reversing these disadvantages and offering hope for the future. These courses can also provide an opportunity for the patient to be engaged in an activity that they have chosen for themselves, and to be in contact with a tutor with whom they are not in a custodial or therapeutic relationship.

5.83    However, Section 60 of the Further and Higher Education Act 1992 specifically prevents the Further Education Funding Council (FEFC) from funding further education provision for "people otherwise than at school, in pursuance of an order made by a court or an order of recall made by the Secretary of State". This has been interpreted as applying to patients detained under Part III of the Mental Health Act and creates an anomaly between them and other patients. One unit is attempting to levy additional charges from the Health Authority to pay for further education for these patients. *Northgate and Prudhoe NHS Trust* lost funding for further education for detained patients and from the 1 April 1997 the service was discontinued and two teachers were made redundant.

5.84    A meeting was held in May 1998 between the Department of Health, the Department of Further Education and Employment (DFEE) and the Mental Health Act Commission to discuss this issue, but the DFEE informed the meeting that there was unlikely to be any amendment to the legislation or change of policy in the foreseeable future.

## Services for Women Patients

5.85    The Commission continues to remain very concerned about the welfare of women patients in secure facilities, where they usually represent a minority in a male dominated culture (also see 5.128 et seq. on the High Security Hospitals). A major concern is that many may have been the victims of physical, emotional or sexual abuse and can find themselves sharing a ward with male patients who may have committed physical or sexual offences against women. Standards of care for women can often be inconsistent and insufficiently defined.

> **Visit to Eastbourne and County Healthcare NHS Trust; 10 November 1997**
>
> Commissioners found that there were no locks fitted to the doors of the women's rooms although they understood that the ward manager was endeavouring to correct this. There appeared to be little privacy for the women and Commissioners were told that men wander into their rooms at night apparently unhindered. They were informed that there are not always female staff on duty, particularly at night, and consequently level 4 observations on women patients are sometimes conducted by male staff. Female patients reported that they felt humiliated, embarrassed and degraded by this and on such occasions would not wear night clothes, preferring to remain in day wear.

> **Visit to Arnold Lodge, Leicester; 16 October 1997**
>
> The Commissioners have drawn attention in the past to the problems of women's issues and wish to do so again. The very small number of women patients presents problems to the women themselves and to the staff. An example of this is that the notes of several male patients make reference to serious sexual assaults in the past and the dangers that this may present for female staff. Commissioners were struck by the fact that little or no mention was made of the possible dangers to women patients. The managers acted upon the Commissioners' recommendation that WISH (Women in Special Hospitals ) be contacted to see if the organisation could support the women patients and guide the staff.

5.86   There is a need for a consistent strategic approach to standards for the care of women in secure environments, and the foundations for this approach were proposed by the Special Hospitals Service Authority in 1995 (Kaye, 1998). For example, a preferred arrangement might be for women to be cared for in separate living units. These may be on the same campus as men in order to provide opportunities for shared activities and preparation for rejoining a mixed society. However, the small numbers of women requiring medium secure care might suggest grouping them in one unit within each Region, although this type of solution may run the risk of exacerbating the problem of the patients becoming distanced from their areas of origin.

5.87   The experience of Commission Visiting Teams suggests that most secure units are making concerted efforts to address the problems of providing effective treatment and support for this challenging group of patients.

> **Visit to Cane Hill Forensic Mental Health Unit, Lambeth Healthcare Trust; 3 November 1997**
>
> Commissioners were pleased to note the efforts being made to avoid the isolation of the women patients, which was commented on at the time of the last visit. All three women patients are currently accommodated in Glencairn and have the second floor as an exclusively female area.

> **Visit to Redford Lodge, Edmonton, North London; 11 July 1997**
>
> A women's forum has been established, including a patient representative, which has conducted a survey of women patients about services and the attitudes of staff. The Commissioners commended the managers for this initiative and hoped that it would continue to highlight and prioritise women's needs within the service

> **Visit to the Edenfield Centre, Mental Health Services of Salford NHS Trust; 13 March 1998**
>
> Commissioners were informed that plans were proceeding to provide a self contained five-bedded area for women on Keswick Ward, the present intensive care facility. Two posts, a nurse and a psychologist,

> have designated responsibility for women's issues. Staffing requirements had been finalised and work was proceeding with WISH (Women in Special Hospitals) to develop a service philosophy and research.

5.88 The problem of vulnerability is, however, not just confined to women patients. Over the current reporting period the Commission has also noted increasing references by patients to the problems of bullying in medium secure units. To some degree, given the characteristics and mental health problems of some of the patient population, this may be unsurprising, but it is nevertheless important that managers give consideration to this matter and act appropriately.

> **Visit to Kneesworth House Hospital (Partnerships in Care Ltd.); 14, 15 & 19 August 1997**
>
> On this and previous visits, some patients have told Commissioners that they have been exposed to threats of physical and sexual assault and have been coerced into actions that they would not otherwise have undertaken. This 'bullying' has been in the form of verbal abuse, mild to severe physical assault, goading, name-calling and some incidents involving sexual assault. Most of these incidents are well-documented in patients' notes and the names of individuals are known to staff. In some cases the patients are willing to be, and have been, identified to staff. As is normal in bullying behaviour, both victims and perpetrators of this behaviour seem to be restricted to certain types of individuals. However, the same victims can be subjected to this behaviour by different bullies in different wards. Two patients also complained of bullying by staff, although they were not willing to have their names released.
>
> As this issue had been raised on the previous Commission visit, it was recommended that the hospital should develop its policy on bullying. Such a policy should guide the implementation of effective measures and standards to monitor and counter the problem. Following the visit the managers undertook a review of the Hospital's policy in conjunction with an independent quality consultant.

## Arrangements for After-care

5.89 Medium secure units in the independent sector are heavily reliant upon 'out of area treatments' and patients can be placed in units which are some distance from their area of origin. This problem is not unique to the independent sector, and under such circumstances it can be difficult to maintain satisfactory relationships with the patient's home area. The Commission has, therefore, emphasised the importance of the correct implementation of CPA and Section 117 procedures.

5.90 The view is sometimes expressed that, because most patients are transferred on to other hospitals rather than direct into the community, the Care Programme Approach may not need to be initiated in medium secure units. However, circular HC(90)23 clearly refers to all in-patients considered for discharge, and all new patients accepted, and the circular also makes clear that the requirements even apply to the High Security Hospitals. Care Programme Approach arrangements should be built into the established conferencing procedures, so that all patients are clearly seen to benefit from individual care plans, as set out in the circular.

5.91 The Commission has also drawn attention to the need to hold Section 117 meetings before a Tribunal hearing, in order that suitable after-care arrangements can be implemented in the event of the patient's discharge (Code of Practice, 27.7).

> **Visits to Kneesworth House; 1,2 & 9 May 1997, and 14,15 & 19 August 1997**
>
> The Hospital was commended for its excellent records and evidence of planning meetings held at regular intervals. However, Commissioners noted that implementation of Section 117 appeared to be deferred until the hospital was certain the patient was leaving. Commissioners found that two patients, who had been given a deferred conditional discharge by a Tribunal, were still in hospital several months later because not all of the community support team had been identified. Commissioners suggested that if Section 117 meetings were scheduled in advance of Tribunals, delays of this nature - which meant that a patient had to wait in medium security longer than was considered necessary by the Tribunal - might be avoided. The problem of obtaining attendance of the local authority social worker and relevant clinical team members to contribute to adequate planning was acknowledged.

## High Security Hospitals

### Introduction

5.92 In September 1998 the Parliamentary Under Secretary of State wrote to the Chairman of the High Security Psychiatric Services Commissioning Board (HSPSCB) indicating the direction that the Government proposed to take in delivering and managing high security psychiatric services. The stated intention is that the three high security hospitals, Ashworth, Broadmoor and Rampton, will remain, with the Regional Offices of the NHS Executive taking a role in integrating the hospitals into the wider spectrum of regional mental health services. The hospitals will either become NHS Trusts in their own right, changing from their Special Health Authority status, or merge with an existing Trust providing wider mental health services; probably in an adjacent area. The intention is that the hospitals will no longer be seen to stand in isolation from other mental health services. It is proposed that responsibility for commissioning these services will pass from the HSPSCB to a lead purchaser within the Regional network, with a transitional hand over period for this complex set of services.

5.93 The population of the hospitals is likely to continue to decline slowly as discharges and transfers of patients continue to outnumber admissions. The Report of the Committee of Inquiry into the Personality Disorder Unit at Ashworth Special Hospital might also lead to a reduction in the admission of offenders with a severe personality disorder.

5.94    These changes are likely to bring uncertainty for the patients and the staff of the High Security Hospitals. The Commission will continue to be primarily concerned with the continuing improvement of patients' care and treatment. The new arrangements must result in the right patients being treated in the right setting and must ensure their timely transfer to conditions of lesser security when appropriate. As well as transfer and discharge activity, the Commission will pay particular attention to the admission and assessment processes. The Commission will also continue to look for improvements in services for women, with an emphasis on developments out of the high secure environments.

5.95    In addition to monitoring the implementation of the Act and the Code of Practice, the Commissioners visiting the High Security Hospitals systematically examine issues directly related to the care and quality of life of patients. Quality standards are set by the HSPSCB through their contracts with each hospital and the Commission has maintained a dialogue with the HSPSCB on these matters throughout the current reporting period. Under the proposed future arrangements, the Commission intends that this dialogue will continue with the lead purchasers in each of the Regions in which the hospitals are located.

5.96    The Report of the Committee of Inquiry into the Personality Disorder Unit, Ashworth Special Hospital, Cm. 4149-11 was published on 12 January 1999 and in its covering letter to the Secretary of State for Health recorded that the patient's description of the environment and practices on Lawrence Ward in the Personality Disorder Unit, which led to the Inquiry, was largely accurate. Matters of concern included the misuse of drugs and alcohol, financial irregularities, possible paedophile activity and the availability of pornographic material in the Unit. The child at the centre of the allegations of paedophilia was, in the Committee's view, being groomed for paedophile purposes.

5.97    The Committee had no confidence in the ability of Ashworth Hospital to flourish under any management and recommended that it should close. However, the Secretary of State did not accept this recommendation. The Committee offered a view as to how high security services could develop within regional forensic networks involving both the NHS and the Prison Service and suggested changes to the law to introduce reviewable sentences for severely personality disordered offenders.

5.98    The accountability arrangements between the NHS Executive and the Hospital Authority were found to be unclear and unsatisfactory, and the Committee recommended that they should change. At the time of writing, the results of the joint deliberations between the Department of Health and the Home Office concerning the future management and treatment of severely personality disordered offenders are awaited.

## Staffing

5.99    There are serious difficulties in recruiting and retaining appropriately trained consultant forensic psychiatrists in the high security services. This has been a recurring theme in previous Biennial Reports. However, the Commission is pleased to learn of recent success at

**Rampton** Hospital in its recruitment efforts. For a long time many of the consultant vacancies were covered by long-term locum staff. An audit of the care of 153 patients, undertaken by the Commission found that, on average, patients had more than two changes of RMO during a two year period and one patient had seven changes during the same period. Only 39 patients had the same RMO throughout the two year period. The compilation of accurate reports to the Mental Health Review Tribunal or the Home Office will present difficulties for the RMO, who may have only limited personal knowledge of the patient.

5.100 At Rampton Hospital the nursing staff have been under considerable pressure and there has been heavy reliance on staff overtime and bank staff. Nursing staff have sometimes moved between wards at short notice to cover for absence or sickness and a skill mix review has resulted in an increase in the number of unqualified nursing assistants. The Commission has observed that this has had an adverse effect on patients' treatment and quality of life. Patients have claimed that the reduction in staffing levels has lessened their access to rehabilitation and social activities, and their access to fresh air. Also, the reduced opportunity for patients to benefit from contact with their named nurse, or any qualified nurse, at times of stress is a matter of considerable concern.

5.101 At **Broadmoor,** serious nursing staff shortages of a similar nature, particularly between May and November 1998 (but also continuing into 1999) resulted in cancellations and curtailments of patients access to recreational, social and therapeutic activities. This included very limited access to fresh air and effective withdrawal of direct nursing observation at night on some wards, where 'locking-off' of parts of the wards was carried out late in the evening. Commissioners have expressed serious concerns at the limitations imposed upon patients and the potential risks to safety of 'locking-off' ward areas at night. The Commission has paid additional unannounced visits to the hospital in order to monitor the consequences for patient care, and has formally raised its concerns with the Chief Executive of Broadmoor Hospital Authority, the HSPSCB and the NHS Executive.

5.102 More recently, the hospital has also experienced particular problems because of the need to provide escorts for patients requiring medical attention in acute hospitals. On one occasion three patients required urgent treatment and each had to have four escorts. Although attempts have been made to improve the management of overtime working, sickness levels among nursing staff continue to remain very high, which, in the opinion of managers, may be indicative of the fact that staff are succumbing to the continuous and unremitting pressures upon them.

5.103 During 1998 the Prison Officers Association (POA) repeatedly threatened industrial action because of concerns about the severe shortages of nursing staff and the consequences for the safety of staff. The POA was also concerned about planned changes in shift patterns for nurses and attempts to reduce overtime levels because of the hospital's financial position. However, negotiations between hospital managers and the POA resulted in shift revisions on a number of wards for a pilot period.

5.104 The hospital has made substantial efforts to address the shortage of nurses and recently recruited 27 qualified nursing staff from Australia and New Zealand, although these recruits have yet to feature in ward establishments. There have been some problems with obtaining registration with the UK Central Council for Nursing, and Broadmoor Hospital was seeking to negotiate with local hospitals to arrange for additional practical experience in order to fully meet registration requirements.

5.105 The numbers of medical staff have also improved during 1998 and at the time of writing there are no current vacancies for RMOs. However, the ratio of RMOs to patients continues to compare very poorly with that found in medium secure facilities. Throughout 1998, staff shortages also resulted in problems with patients accessing dental care within the hospital.

5.106 The Commission is concerned to note that five patients committed suicide between October 1998 and January 1999, which raises questions about the adequacy of staffing to assess and manage risk. The Hospital has commissioned an external, independent audit into the incidents.

5.107 At **Ashworth** Hospital, the public inquiry and the introduction of new management arrangements have had a detrimental impact upon staff morale, with the result that experienced nurses and medical staff, including the Medical Director, have left the hospital. At the time of writing, the services for women patients now have only one forensic consultant psychiatrist for an extremely challenging patient group.

5.108 Staffing difficulties at Ashworth Hospital are primarily responsible for the under-utilisation of a project to provide patients in the Personality Disorders Unit (PDU) with the skills to enable them to cope in the community upon discharge (the Wordsworth Project). This facility, recently constructed on the hospital's East site and designed to accommodate sixteen patients in self-contained flats, has been ready for occupation for over a year but has not functioned as intended because of the absence of an RMO to oversee the project. Social therapists, specifically trained and employed for this work, have also left the hospital. The building is currently used for group work which takes place during the mornings only. This arrangement has caused difficulties because patients have to be transported across sites to attend. The Commission is very concerned to witness a much needed facility being underused.

## Transfer delays

5.109 The United Kingdom has been held to be in breach of the European Convention on Human Rights in a case where a patient was held in **Rampton** Hospital for more than three years after being assessed as no longer suffering from a mental disorder, and a Mental Health Review Tribunal decision that he should be discharged on the condition that he live in a supervised hostel. No hostel placement was found and the patient was given an absolute discharge and awarded compensation (*Stanley Johnson v United Kingdom*, 2.57).

5.110 While this case was being heard, in June 1997 an Executive Letter was sent by the Department of Health to the Chief Executives of the Health Authorities and Directors of Social Services requesting their help in ensuring prompt action to implement decisions made by Mental Health Review Tribunals (MHRTs) directing the conditional discharge of detained patients. The delay in securing transfers for patients who no longer require the level of security offered by the High Security Hospitals has long been a major concern and a recent review found a number of cases where the period of deferment of MHRT directions for a patient's conditional discharge had been in excess of twelve months. This situation was deemed to be unacceptable and health authorities and social service departments were required to give priority to ensuring that such decisions are implemented within six months of the MHRT's decision. The landmark case above, and the Executive Letter, should have the effect of expediting some of these transfers.

5.111 These cases involve patients who are subject to special restrictions under the Act where the MHRT has decided that the patient should be discharged from detention subject to specified conditions being met. They require comprehensive aftercare planning. Medical and social supervision is invariably specified, covering, among other things, attendance for medical treatment, compliance with medication, and place of residence. Where problems arise in identifying suitable placements or supervision arrangements, the Department of Health has advised that Social Services Inspectorate or NHS Executive regional mental health leads may be able to provide advice, while any serious difficulties should be brought to the immediate attention of the MHRT office. In the event of responsible authorities finding it impossible to meet the discharge conditions, they are advised to contact the Home Office so that consideration may be given to referring the case back to the MHRT. In the meantime, MHRT offices are compiling a list of cases where discharge has been deferred for more than six months. This list will be circulated to chief executives of health authorities, directors of social services and regional mental health leads in the Social Services Inspectorate and the NHS Executive in order that they can monitor progress in complying with the decisions of the MHRTs.

5.112 Throughout the current reporting period, the Commission has found that delays in the transfer of patients out of the high security hospitals continue to remain a very significant problem, the principal contributory factor being the national shortage of medium and long-term secure places. For example, Edenfield Regional Secure Unit has only a few beds designated for **Ashworth** Hospital and patients have to wait some considerable time for vacancies to arise. In Ashworth there are an estimated 200 patients who do not require high levels of security. However, health authorities appear unwilling to fund expensive placements elsewhere.

5.113 At **Rampton Hospital**, the Commission has highlighted the cases of four patients who were granted conditional discharges by Mental Health Review Tribunals but who continued to be resident in the hospital over six months later. Commissioners have found many instances of patients being obliged to remain at Rampton despite recognition by clinical teams, and the decisions and recommendations of Mental Health Review Tribunals, that they no longer require the level of security provided by that hospital. Despite the efforts of clinical teams there are very considerable problems in arranging suitable transfers to some areas of the country. These problems are also compounded by the frequent changes of RMO for many patients and also by the variable application of the Care Programme Approach.

5.114 At **Broadmoor** Hospital, Commissioners have noted many similar difficulties and the Visiting Panel has identified transfer delays as a core theme activity for continued monitoring. Nevertheless, the hospital staff have made efforts to transfer and discharge patients and, although both long-term and medium secure facilities remain in very short supply, during 1998 sixteen patients were successfully transferred to Thornwood Park and two women patients were transferred to Pastoral Homes. However, both Commissioners and the hospital executive remain very concerned about 'entrapped patients' awaiting discharge or transfer to less secure settings. At the time of writing, there were 112 patients detained in Broadmoor Hospital who had been identified as progressing towards transfer or discharge, and seventeen restricted patients were awaiting the agreement of the Home Office. In respect of the latter, the Commission noted documentation in the patients' medical records indicating a significant problem in terms of communication with the Home Office, and subsequent delays. It is clear that the Home Office has become more exacting in its approach to this issue and there are instances of patients who have been under consideration for up to five years. Funding for placements in medium secure or other settings, both in the NHS and the independent sector, is also causing delays, in some instances of up to two years.

5.115 The phenomenon of the 'aging patient' is also beginning to emerge as a problem, with several elderly patients either unwilling to move from the hospital or for whom suitable placements cannot be found. For example, one elderly man has been resident in the hospital for 53 years and has never been outside in that time, but he no longer requires psychotropic medication and adequately manages his financial and other affairs.

5.116 The Commission remains particularly concerned about patients who are unnecessarily detained in the High Security Hospitals, not only because of the severe and clinically unwarranted curtailment of their liberty, but also because this can restrict immediate access to scarce places for those who require treatment in such a setting, and who may, for example, be obliged to remain in prison despite their deteriorating mental health. The Government has made a commitment to the provision of additional medium secure beds, and the Commission trusts that this action will go some way towards alleviating the current pressures on the high security services.

## The Care Programme Approach and Section 117

5.117 The Commission has found that the Care Programme Approach has been developed and implemented to differing degrees throughout the three hospitals. As noted elsewhere in this Report (see 5.48), an accessible recording system, that does not require information to be duplicated, is fundamental to the successful implementation of the CPA. The system should make explicit the patient's needs, a plan of care and the identity of the keyworker. **Ashworth** Hospital has undertaken an ambitious programme to develop a bespoke computer-based Patient and Clinical Information System to record all aspects of care planning and delivery. Although this has yet to be implemented on all the wards, where the system has been introduced the level of communication between disciplines and departments is reported to have improved markedly and important information about the patients' care and treatment is now readily available to those staff who have access rights to the system.

5.118 The last Biennial Report registered concerns that RMOs at **Broadmoor Hospital** had shown little enthusiasm in applying the hospital's policy for Section 117 and the CPA. The CPA forms in the casenotes were often absent or incomplete, with much activity remaining unrecorded, and there were separate records for some disciplines (p. 86). The hospital managers have attempted to address some of these problems and have developed a new hospital policy and revised documentation. However, this appears to have met with little success and some nursing staff have complained that they do not consider it to be part of their job to complete the paperwork, whilst some medical staff continue to display little commitment to the concept of the CPA. Although the hospital has continued with the implementation of the new procedures, and all staff are aware of the policy and revised documentation, the Commission has found that where this has been accepted it has yet to have a significant impact at ward level and will be looking for clear evidence of progress in the near future.

5.119 Although the Commission recognises that the CPA can be perceived, for a variety of reasons, as an additional administrative burden for nursing and medical staff, it would remind those concerned that the principles of the CPA are an important part of the Government's strategy for the delivery of effective treatment and care for mental illness and must apply to all patients (Dept. of Health, 1990; Dept. of Health, 1998c).

5.120 **Rampton** Hospital has, over the last two years, made a considerable effort to effectively implement the CPA. However, when Commissioners carried out a detailed review of the application of the CPA during May 1998, they found that at ward level, knowledge about policy, and commitment to the appropriate documentation, were extremely variable. The Commission intends to undertake a further review in due course and will hope to see a marked improvement. As has been highlighted above, the ineffective implementation of the CPA has potentially serious consequences for both the review of patients' care and treatment, and for progressing their rehabilitation.

5.121 It has been argued that the provisions of Section 117 do not apply to patients in the High Security Hospitals when preparation is being made to transfer them to medium secure care, rather than discharge from hospital. The CPA and Section 117 overlap in many respects and the principles of both procedures require that matters relating to the eventual discharge are addressed throughout the period of the patient's treatment in hospital. Section 117 planning and consideration of longer term plans for eventual discharge are relevant at the point of transfer from high to medium secure units, as the latter are likely to need some indication, even if only in outline form, about future plans and the patient's likely length of stay in the unit. In addition, Section 117 plans should be in place for each patient in advance of their case being considered by a Mental Health Review Tribunal, in order to cater for the possibility that the patient might be discharged by the Tribunal (Code of Practice, 27.7). In the absence of a discharge plan stating what services would be provided in the community, it will be more difficult for a tribunal to satisfy itself whether the patient can be discharged from hospital and what conditions would be appropriate (see recent case of *MHRT and Others ex parte Hall Times Law Report 20 May 1999*)

## Consent to Treatment

5.122 One of the Commission's primary activities in the High Security Hospitals is to monitor the implementation of the Consent to Treatment safeguards set out in Part IV of the Act. In the last Biennial Report the Commission indicated its concern that all three High Security Hospitals were exhibiting serious shortcomings in the completion by RMOs of Form 38 certifying patients' consent (p. 87). Unfortunately, during the current reporting period the Commission has found that, with some exceptions, this area of practice continues to require attention and improvement.

5.123 At **Broadmoor** Hospital, Commissioners have noted continuing improvement in clinical practice regarding Consent to Treatment matters. This includes good recording in the medical records relating to discussions with patients about consent and Forms 38 being subject to regular review. However, some wards continue to pay insufficient attention to the quality of the completed forms which regularly fail to comply with the guidance in the Code of Practice. The specific concerns of the Commission are that the Forms 38 are not always signed by the current Responsible Medical Officer - a situation which is all the more likely to occur if there are frequent changes of RMO (see 5.99 with reference to Rampton Hospital) – and they are not always subject to annual review. The number of preparations in each British National Formulary category is not always specified and the route of administration is also rarely stated. In relation to Clozapine, Commissioners have continued to recommend that its inclusion or exclusion is specified when prescribing anti-psychotic medication. The Commission has welcomed the decision to arrange a clinical audit of Consent to Treatment forms across the hospital and will continue to include these issues as a matter for particular attention for visiting Commissioners.

5.124 Similarly, at **Ashworth** Hospital the Commission has been very concerned about the inadequate attention given to Forms 38 by a number of RMOs and has pressed for a comprehensive training and monitoring system to be introduced. Of particular concern has been the lack of understanding by nursing staff of the serious consequences of treatment administration without authority. Commission members have often had to remind nurses of their professional responsibility to ensure that all drugs they administer are given legally.

5.125 During 1998, the Commission conducted a detailed review of the operation of Consent to Treatment provisions at Ashworth Hospital. The review found that:

- discussion with the patient regarding consent to treatment was very often undocumented in the clinical record;

- outdated forms were not being cancelled, resulting in occasional confusion as to the correct treatment plan, which was sometimes compounded by more than one medication card being in use;

- many treatment plans were very specific with regard to named drugs and dosage, with the result that relatively minor changes in the treatment plan were resulting in treatment plans becoming outdated, requiring a new one to be issued[1]; and

- there were many examples of unauthorised medication being prescribed and administered.

One of the most worrying observations of the review was that staff appeared to be showing a marked lack of knowledge, and sometimes indifference, to the requirements of Section 58 of the Act. Pharmacy staff also appeared to be taking no steps to address this situation. The review concluded that there were pockets of good practice in the Hospital, and that there was some improvement over the period of the review. However, the understanding of and implementation of Part IV of the Act, by doctors, nurses and pharmacists, was deficient and needed to be addressed urgently.

5.126  Towards the end of 1998, Commissioners visiting **Rampton** Hospital carried out a detailed review of the use of Form 38. They found that in the majority of cases, but regrettably not in all, patients indicated that their RMO had discussed a medication plan with them at or around the date recorded on the form, although a number of patients complained that the possible side-effects had not been explained to them. However, Commissioners also found a poor standard of recording of the interview at which the RMO should have assessed capacity and sought consent. Commissioners trust that the clear guidance set out the Code of Practice (16.13) will be observed in the future. Failure to comply with this guidance will result in the validity of the Forms 38 being left open to question. Like their colleagues at Ashworth Hospital, Commissioners visiting Rampton Hospital have also been very concerned about those instances where the medication recorded on the treatment cards fails to accord with that authorised on the Forms 38 or 39. Commissioners will pay particular attention to this issue during future visits.

## Mental Health Act Training and the Code of Practice

5.127  The Commission has found that, in all of the three High Security Hospitals, staff training in the use of the Mental Health Act 1983 and the Code of Practice is regarded as a relatively low priority. Commissioners have noted when visiting many of the wards that the staff are unable to produce either a copy of the Act or the Code of Practice. This finding is often reported to the hospitals' managers but little progress appears to have been made in rectifying the problem. The publication of the revised Code of Practice will have provided an opportunity for the hospitals to improve their compliance with the principles of the Code.

[1] Paragraph 16.14 of the revised Code of Practice now allows for named drugs to be recorded on Forms 38 and 39, although any changes to the treatment plan, however minor, will still require a new Form to be issued.

The three High Security Hospitals have accepted the Commission's offer to run briefing sessions on the revised Code, specifically geared to the needs of the hospitals.

## The Care and Treatment of Women Patients

5.128 One of the major problems facing women in the High Security Hospitals is that they constitute a minority patient group, representing between only 15% and 20% of the total population. The hospitals continue to operate in a predominantly male culture and as a consequence women's special needs can be overlooked. These will include the availability of therapeutic or other programmes of care for eating disorders, self-harm, and issues concerning self-care and sexuality. The Commission has expressed concern in previous Biennial Reports that, for the majority of women patients, these special needs attract little attention. However, consultant forensic psychiatrists at **Broadmoor** Hospital have informed the Commission that they have conducted an analysis of the needs of women patients and have identified and implemented several initiatives to specifically address them. These include the establishment of a Deliberate Self Harm Group, through which the women's services have been able to stimulate the development of practices and culture to address self-harm, and multi-disciplinary training and education in new treatment modalities such as Dialectical Behaviour Therapy for personality disordered women. The hospital has also identified the general absence of treatment for eating disorders within medium secure services and has developed an expanding training package in this area. Similarly, a working group, based at Broadmoor, has identified specific problems in relation to women's sexuality and self-care that are not being addressed within medium secure services.

5.129 Commissioners have welcomed the continued evidence of high standards of care and treatment for women on several of the wards in this hospital, particularly those providing intensive care facilities. However, on others, Commissioners have repeatedly expressed concerns regarding the suitability of the environment for women because of limited staffing levels and inappropriate patient mix. Under such circumstances the atmosphere can become volatile and challenging and can, as has been the case on one ward, result in high numbers of incidents such as self-harm.

5.130 A significant proportion of women patients in the High Security Hospitals are likely to have been either physically, emotionally or sexually abused by men, and many of the male patients have committed crimes against women. This situation has the potential of making the environment particularly unsafe for women, and exposing them to the risk or fear of abuse. Some activities, whether therapeutic or educational, will place women in close proximity to male patients and if they find this threatening or intimidating they may refuse to attend. For example, the educational facilities at **Rampton** Hospital have, historically, never been particularly well attended by women patients. In all three hospitals recreational and social activities appear to remain geared towards the male population and women patients have complained to Commissioners that the facilities available to them are not as varied as those for male patients. This is particularly important in relation to activities that provide weekly income. Rampton has made particular efforts to integrate women into traditionally male dominated areas and has tried to provide facilities for women-only activities or 'male-free zones', although this initiative has met with only limited success. Where managers and staff wish to implement schemes to broaden the range of social and recreational opportunities available to women, the Commission has observed that it is important to ensure, for example, that there are adequate numbers of female staff on duty and that there are suitable facilities, such as toilets. Failure to attend to such details can result in well-intentioned initiatives not being utilised by the women patients.

5.131  At **Rampton** Hospital a senior manager was appointed specifically to lead the development of women's services, with the result that attempts to improve access to activities for women were fully supported by the hospital management. Similarly, at **Ashworth** Hospital, as a result of a searching review by the hospital and the HSPSCB, a far reaching action plan was developed to improve women's services. This service was experiencing serious problems with poor day care facilities, high levels of staff sickness and the use of bank staff or staff from other wards, and a lack of clinical and team leaders. Unfortunately, the action plan was halted because of a shortage of funds for capital and revenue projects and, at the time of writing, is under review. The Commission is aware of a very variable service for women patients in this hospital, particularly in relation to the management of self-harm, and attention to this issue will remain high on the Commission's agenda for future visits.

5.132 The Commission recognises that a significant proportion of women in the High Security Hospitals do not require conditions of maximum security. However, there are also insufficient numbers of suitable, or women-only, facilities to which they could be transferred. In the Regional Secure Units it is not uncommon for there to be only one or two women patients. As a result, they can remain relatively isolated in a predominantly male culture, with inadequate attention given to their needs, and can experience similar problems to those endured in the high security environments. The Commission trusts that the Government's commitment to the provision of additional medium secure places will take into account the needs of this challenging patient group.

## Withholding of Mail

5.133  The Commission has a statutory duty under Section 121(7) of the Act to review decisions by the managers of the High Security Hospitals to withhold postal packets when requested by the patient or correspondent. During the period covered by this Report, the Commission received twenty-four such requests, compared with nine during the previous reporting period, and six during the period 1993-1995. At the end of the current reporting period, six requests remained to be decided. Of the remainder, twelve decisions were upheld, three were reversed, one upheld in part, one request was withdrawn, and in one case it was found that no item had been withheld. The case that was partially upheld involved consideration of 23 items withheld over a period of 18 months. The Commission reconsidered an earlier adjudication in this case and finally decided that 20 of the items should remain withheld.

5.134 The Commission has received a number of requests to review decisions to withhold patients' mail in the Personality Disorders Unit at **Ashworth** Hospital. The Commission recognises the difficulties in applying Section 134 of Act (correspondence of patients) and has held discussions with senior managers about this issue. The hospital has now developed a policy to provide guidelines for staff when dealing with patients' mail. It is important for managers and clinicians in the high secure services to understand that once an appeal against withholding has been upheld, the piece of mail in question cannot again be withheld from the patient.

## Environment

5.135 At **Broadmoor** Hospital, Commissioners have noted a convivial atmosphere and clean environment on many of the wards visiting during the reporting period. However, some environmental issues have continued to be a source of concern for Commissioners, particularly the poor states of decoration and furnishings in some of the older blocks. These are old institutional type wards providing accommodation for up to 25 patients and the Commission appreciates that if they were removed further pressures would result because of the loss of beds. Nevertheless, the accommodation that they provide is cramped and lacking in privacy. The garden area for one ward, serving the needs of 25 male patients and disparagingly referred to by them as "the cage", is a small area of tarmac surrounded by a high wire fence with, aside from two benches, few facilities. The area affords no privacy and the patients are in full view of all who walk along the busy adjoining footpath.

5.136 Of particular concern to visiting Commissioners and patients at Broadmoor Hospital are the inadequate indoor recreational facilities. There are poor gymnasium facilities, a large, institutional recreation hall, which is also used for patients to receive their visitors, and no swimming pool. Broadmoor is the only High Security Hospital without adequate recreational facilities and patients transferred to Broadmoor from other High Security Hospitals, most Medium Secure Units or from prison, are considerably worse off in this respect.

5.137 At **Rampton** Hospital a substantial programme of refurbishment has been undertaken and the Commission recognises that this has improved the quality of life for some patients. However, the physical state of many wards, particularly those in the older blocks, is still a cause for considerable concern, although many of the concerns relate to poor domestic arrangements and maintenance rather than the physical structure of the buildings. Commissioners have found environmental conditions at **Ashworth** Hospital to be generally very drab on some of the wards on the hospital's North site, and there are reported to have been repeated problems with the heating system and patients' showers. Work on a plan of significant refurbishment, mainly on the North site, commenced late in 1997, including, on one ward, the adaptation of several rooms for the use of disabled patients.

## Access to Fresh Air

5.138  An important feature of the environment for long-term detained patients is that the siting of wards should permit patients' access to a garden or other outside area for fresh air. Patients' access to fresh air has been a long-standing concern for the Commission and has been highlighted in previous Biennial Reports. The Special Health Services Authority (SHSA) established the minimum quality standard of 10 hours access to fresh air per week for each patient during the summer months and four hours per week during the winter. At **Broadmoor** Hospital, meeting these minimum standards has been a major problem during 1998 and an audit undertaken during the latter half of the year revealed that only 40% of the wards were realising these targets. Major contributory factors to this low figure are the shortages of staff to supervise patients and the necessary alterations to garden deck areas on some wards. Accurate recording of patients' access to fresh air is essential if this important element of patient care is to be effective, but the Commission has noted that this is not done consistently across the hospital.

5.139  At **Ashworth** Hospital, Commissioners have found that access to fresh air appears to be adequate, although no detailed records are being kept. Commissioners visiting **Rampton** Hospital have actively sought to ensure that the standards of the former SHSA are offered to patients as a *minimum*, rather than a *standard* requirement. Most wards have been recording when each patient has been offered access to fresh air and when this offer has been accepted. Where standards have not been reached, changes in staffing levels is the most common explanation. As noted in the last Biennial Report, the Commission expects staff in the High Security Hospitals to pursue these standards with vigour and for systematic monitoring to continue (p. 90). It is a matter which the Commission intends to keep under constant review.

## Advocacy

5.140  In the Seventh Biennial Report the Commission emphasised the vital importance of an advocacy service for patients who are subject to severe and prolonged curtailment of liberty (p. 96). At both **Ashworth** and **Rampton** Hospitals, Commissioners have noted that comprehensive services continue to offer support to the regular meetings of the Patients' Councils. At **Broadmoor** Hospital, the Commission has been pressing for the introduction of an advocacy service for at least five years and the Patients' Council has repeatedly expressed concern to visiting Commissioners about the inordinate and unacceptable delay in establishing this important service. However, the Commission has recently learned that additional funding for the Advocacy Service will be forthcoming from the Commissioning Board.

# Chapter 6

# Consent to Treatment

## Summary

There are continuing concerns over the validity of some patients' consent. The need for information provision and the recording of consent discussions is highlighted.

The Commission has arranged 14,800 Second Opinions in this reporting period, an increase of roughly one third from the previous period. Some, but not all of this increase can be attributed to the Bournewood case. Data about Second Opinions completed for patients by Mental Health Act category, gender, age and ethnicity is given.

RMOs are reminded that it is a statutory duty to complete Section 61 reports and of their importance for the effective monitoring of treatments.

Seventeen neurosurgery for mental disorder (NMD) treatments were proposed during this reporting period.

# 6 Consent to Treatment

## Introduction

6.1    Consent to treatment issues continue to play a significant role in the Commission's activities, not only in its statutory role of administering the consent to treatment provisions of Part IV of the Act but also as a major area of focus on its visits to hospitals and in its meetings with detained patients.

## Validating the Authenticity of Consent

6.2    One of the main issues pertaining to consent to treatment that was highlighted in the Commission's Seventh Biennial Report was the authenticity of consent. The Responsible Medical Officer (RMO) should only deem a patient to be consenting to a proposed treatment if he or she has ensured that the patient understands its nature, purpose and likely effects as well as the likely consequences of it not being given, the likelihood of its success and whether there are alternatives to it. "Consent" itself is defined in the Code of Practice (15.13) as "the voluntary and continuing permission" of a patient based on an "adequate knowledge" of the above.

6.3    The Commission would welcome the further development of written information on psychiatric treatments to complement that which should be provided orally by RMOs when they discuss proposed treatments with patients and seek their consent to such proposals. Few Trusts or drug manufacturers have produced patient information leaflets. The revision of the Code of Practice has strengthened the previous recommendation that patients who are treated with ECT should receive a leaflet which helps them understand and remember advice about its nature, purpose and likely effects, so that it is now a requirement of good practice (Code of Practice 16.10). Some units show exemplary practice in respect of giving patients information:

> **Visit to Exeter and District Community Health Service NHS Trust; 4 March 1999**
>
> Commissioners noted good practice where patients are invited to sign a hospital form confirming that they have been given leaflets explaining the action and side effects of their medication.

6.4    Section 58 (3) of the Act requires that for certain treatments (the administration of medicine for mental disorder beyond three months in any continuous period of detention and ECT at any time), the RMO must certify on Form 38 that the patient has the capacity to consent and does so or a Second Opinion Appointed Doctor must authorise the treatment on Form 39. It is often pointed out, as an apparent anomaly in the 1983 Act, that patients do not themselves sign Forms 38 indicating their consent to treatment. It is not uncommon for patients, particularly those who have consented to ECT and must therefore undergo an anaesthetic, to be asked by hospitals also to sign hospital consent forms. Such practice may not in itself be a bad thing, but staff must be clear that it is the Form 38 that gives the legal authority for the treatment of a consenting detained patient and, even if a patient countersigns an authorisation made under Section 58(3)(a), both that patient and staff must clearly understand that consent may be withdrawn at any time. It is important that hospital staff are aware that a patient's consent may fluctuate and that real consent is the continuing permission of a patient rather than a one-off agreement. Nurses responsible for administering medication should be particularly careful to be attentive to the patient's expressed wishes every time they administer treatment authorised under Form 38.

> ### Visit to East Surrey Priority Care NHS Trust; 10 March 1998
>
> Several of the Forms 38 were completed with no limit as to the number of drugs of a particular class e.g. "oral anti-psychotic medication". The Commissioners doubted whether patients do, in practice, give blanket consent to medication without reference to the number of drugs in any one class. Following the visit the managers reminded consultants of the need to specify the maximum number of drugs authorised in any class and arranged for the Pharmacy Department to monitor consent forms.
>
> In addition, Commissioners had noted that one patient had a Form 38 that referred to "depot or oral anti-psychotic medication within BNF dose (BNF 4.2.1)". Apart from the obvious error that depot medication is, of course, BNF 4.2.2, the Commissioners' main concern was that the record of the interview with the RMO, which was in the nursing notes rather than the medical notes, stated that the patient had been "seen by Dr F agreed to take his medication and new Form 38 done". At that time his medication was an oral anti-psychotic and it appeared to the Commissioner from other entries in the notes that the patient was not consenting to a depot when he gave his consent to continue with the medication, despite the fact that he countersigned the Form 38. It seemed, therefore, that the Form 38 was misleading. It was appreciated that the patient had not been given a depot since the form had been completed and had not been written up for it, but nevertheless the Commissioners questioned whether the Form 38 accurately reflected the true consent of the patient. Upon review, a Second Opinion was sought for this patient.
>
> The Commissioners also questioned the practice of obtaining the patient's signature to the consent to treatment form as this only reflects a patient's consent on the day the form is signed. Consent to medication is a continuing state of mind rather than a single event.

6.5    The Commission noted in its last Biennial Report that, where the consent of a patient to a particular treatment plan was certified by an RMO, there was often no record made in that patient's clinical notes of any discussion between that patient and the RMO. The Code of Practice now specifically requires that a record of such discussions should be placed in the patient's medical notes (16.9a, 16.13).

6.6 The recording of consent was monitored systematically during 1998 as one of the items on the Commission's procedure for 'Matters Requiring Particular Attention' (see 3.36 et seq). Of 789 Forms 38 looked at on Commission visits to hospitals in 1998, nearly half (386) showed no corroborative record of a discussion between the patient and the RMO in the seven days before the doctor's signing of the Form.

6.7 Forms 38 should be regularly reviewed by the RMO, who should discuss the treatment with the patient and, if consent is still given, complete a new Form 38. No Form 38 should be regarded as effective for over a year (Code of Practice, 16.35). The Commission found that a small but significant proportion (58; 7%) of Forms 38 had not been signed by the current RMO and 72 (9%) were over a year old.

6.8 The requirement that discussions between patients and RMOs about consent to treatment are recorded could improve practice in meeting the obligation to provide the patient with adequate information about the proposed treatment and to ensure that those who do not consent are given access to a second opinion.

> **Visit to Stockport Healthcare NHS Trust; 14 May 1998**
>
> Generally, Forms 38 and 39 were appropriately completed. However, Commissioners did discover areas of particular concern regarding Forms 38. Firstly, it was difficult to find any record in patient files of the discussion on consent to treatment associated with the completion of Form 38. Further, in the case of one patient, while the Form 38 was satisfactorily completed, the record on the file that had been documented seemed to indicate that the particular patient was objecting to treatment. The Trust re-advised staff on consent procedures following the visit.

6.9 The Commission has noted some good practice in this area.

> **Visit to Norwich Community Health Partnership NHS Trust (Broadlands Clinic and Little Plumstead Hospital); 17 April 1998**
>
> Forms 38 were well completed in accordance with guidance in the Code of Practice, with few exceptions, and records of discussion of consent with the patient were usually documented in the clinical notes. Consent was regularly renegotiated on at least an annual basis.

> **Visit to Whorlton Hall Nursing Home (Barnard Castle) and Hollyhurst Nursing Home (Darlington); 26 February 1998**
>
> The Commissioners located a "model" entry by an RMO in the clinical records of one patient, in which he had set out clearly and legibly an account of his meeting with that patient before the completion of a Form 38. The RMO gave full details of the patient's capacity and consent, and not only signed the entry himself but also had the entry countersigned by two qualified nursing staff who were in attendance at this important doctor/patient consultation. There was no room for doubt that the patient had capacity and had consented to treatment.

6.10    The Commission continues to recommend to RMOs that it is generally advisable to complete Forms 38 authorising medication for mental disorder by reference to BNF categories and dose-ranges. The Commission recognises, however, that there are likely to be circumstances where it is more appropriate to specify named drugs on such Forms, such as when a patient actively consents to a specific preparation but not to any other drug in its generic category, and it advised the Secretary of State that the revision of the Code of Practice should make provision for this. The Code now states that drugs proposed should be certified "by name or, ensuring that the number of drugs authorised in each class is indicated, by the classes described in the British National Formulary" (16.14). The Commission does come across examples where the practice of authorising named drugs rather than categories of drugs leads to their unlawful administration to patients, when Forms that specify named drugs are not rewritten when one drug in a specific BNF category is substituted for another.

> **Visit to Wexham Park Hospital;11 July 1997**
>
> Commissioners were very concerned to note the continuing problems in the implementation of Section 58 of the Act. Although time constraints are now being observed the content of the forms did not comply with Code of Practice guidance on seven of the eight forms operative on the day of the visit. Several patients were receiving medication that was not covered by Form 38 and the problem was apparently exacerbated by the naming of specific preparations and dosages rather than BNF categories.

## The Limitations of Part IV of the Act

6.11    The consent to treatment provisions of the Act apply to detained patients, including those on Section 17 leave, but not those detained under Sections 4, 5(2) or (4), 35,135, 136 and 37(4), and do not apply to patients conditionally discharged under Sections 42(2), 73 and 74. Despite this, Commissioners still encounter occasions of the mistaken use of the consent to treatment provisions to "authorise" treatment for patients detained under these Sections.

Visit to Heathlands Mental Health Services NHS Trust; 16 March 1998

Commissioners noted that one patient had a Form 38 completed even though he was a conditionally discharged patient who had been re-admitted on an informal basis and to whom Section 58 did not apply. His consent should have been recorded in the medical notes.

Another patient had been given Acuphase while detained under Section 136. Presumably this had been given under the common law (Code of Practice, 15.25) although no record of this was available in the notes.

The Trust undertook to take active steps following the visit to ensure that these issues were addressed.

## Treatments Requiring Neither Consent Nor a Second Opinion - Section 63

6.12   Section 63 of the Act provides that the consent of a patient shall not be required for medical treatment for mental disorder that does not fall under Sections 57 or 58 if that treatment is given under the direction of the RMO. In the Seventh Biennial Report the Commission noted its concern that case-law concerning the use of Section 63 to authorise medical interventions not usually regarded as medical treatment for mental disorder had been misleadingly reported in the press. The Commission was concerned that such reporting could lead to incorrect assumptions as to the extent of the legal precedents created by those judgments and therefore to the inappropriate use of this Section. Further guidelines on the general principles which apply in cases involving incapacity where any surgical or invasive procedure might be needed were established by the Court of Appeal in *St George's Healthcare NHS Trust v S (no 2) (Re S) [1998] 3 All ER (see discussion at 2.28 et seq)*. The Department of Health has issued a Health Service Circular (HSC1999/031) that sets out the principles as laid down by the Court, which should be read alongside the Department of Health publication *A Guide to Consent for Examination for Treatment* (originally issued with HC(90)22) and the revised Code of Practice.

6.13   The intention of Section 63 was that it should extend only to "routine" treatment and "general nursing and other general care" (ref: Kenneth Clarke, Minister of Health, Hansard vol 20, No 82, 22 March 1982). There is no requirement for any special procedures to be followed before such treatment is given, although treatments falling under Section 63 are not excluded from the Code of Practice's provision that "the patient's consent should be sought for all proposed treatments" (16.4).  Case-law has widened the scope of Section 63 to include treatment for physical disorders where there is a direct link between the physical disorder and the mental disorder, but the Commission considers that the circumstances where treatment for physical disorders can be imposed under this section will be limited.

6.14 The Commission's Guidance Note '*The Treatment of Anorexia Nervosa under the Mental Health Act 1983*', published in August 1997, offers further clarification on the limitations of Section 63 to authorise treatment for physical conditions, in that medical treatment may only be given if it is sufficiently connected to the treatment for the patient's mental disorder. The courts have ruled that feeding a patient by artificial means to treat the physical complications of anorexia nervosa can reasonably be regarded as medical treatment for mental disorder. However, the Commission advises that such treatment must be carefully and regularly reviewed and discontinued when the patient's compliance can be secured for normal methods of feeding to which compulsion would not apply. The Commission's suggestion, made in its last Biennial Report, that naso-gastric feeding for detained anorectic patients should be included under those treatments falling within Section 58(3) of the Act, thereby ensuring that such feeding is only administered (in the absence of consent) on the authority of a Second Opinion, has been broadly welcomed by most organisations canvassed by the Department of Health in 1998. The Commission's recommendations on this matter were restated in its written submission to the Mental Health Legislation Review Team. The Commission also proposed that Section 63 or its equivalent in new legislation should be carefully reconsidered during the review of mental health legislation.

6.15 In practice, the reports on case law on the scope of Section 63 do seem to have led to a number of queries from RMOs and other hospital staff requesting advice on whether proposed treatments may be considered to fall under this Section. Such treatments have included blood-tests for diabetes, drugs for insomnia and blood transfusions. In the third example, the Commission was approached to give its approval to the transfusion of blood to a self-harming patient if that patient's haemoglobin fell below a safe level. The Commission responded that the legal authority for such treatment could probably be found in the common law. Common law allows that treatment in accord with accepted medical practice and which is in the patient's best interests (meaning that it should save life or prevent a deterioration in the patient's physical or mental condition) may be given without the patient's consent. If there is any doubt as to whether a treatment may be given without the patient's consent, the Commission recommends that practitioners seek legal advice without delay.

6.16 The Commission occasionally is asked for its view on the administration of placebos to patients detained under the Act. The Commission does have serious legal and ethical concerns about the administration of placebos to detained patients. The Commission is anxious that questions of the legal authority for and the ethical problems involved in such use should be considered, not only by consultants who may ultimately be responsible for their administration, but also by other professionals and managers involved.

6.17 The legal authority for the administration of placebos to patients detained under the Mental Health Act is unclear and, unless the matter is tested in the courts, no definitive legal interpretation is likely to be available. It is submitted that, as an inert substance, a placebo does not fall within the definition of "medicine" and, therefore, falls outside the provisions of Section 58. However, given the very broad definition of medical treatment in Section 145, even if a placebo is not "medicine" it may arguably still be regarded as "treatment." As such, the authority to administer placebos could be provided by Section 63, where a treatment may be given without a patient's consent under the authority of the patient's RMO. Whilst this is the interpretation of the law generally favoured in discussions within the Commission, it does not entirely resolve the legal and ethical problems allied to placebo treatment. In particular, it does not absolve an RMO who is considering such treatments from addressing the wider ethical implications. It is, for example, a basic premise of the Mental Health Act that as much information as possible is given to detained patients about the reasons for their being in hospital and for their treatment whilst they are there. The requirement of the Code of Practice that even those treatments whose authority derives from Section 63 should not be given without an attempt to gain the patient's consent is a reflection of this. In most cases it would seem that the use of placebo medication would necessarily involve the deception of a patient. Whether or not such deception may be justified clinically, it may be very difficult to justify with reference to the expectations of the Mental Health Act and Code of Practice.

6.18   Whilst the consultant who is a detained patient's RMO will bear the ultimate responsibility for administering placebo medication, any placebo treatment necessarily will involve a number of other disciplines, such as nurses and pharmacists. Both of these groups, as well as any other medical staff involved, have their own ethical codes of conduct and it does seem likely, for example, that the use of placebo treatments would cause professional difficulties for nursing staff within the UK Central Council for Nursing guidelines. The Commission would strongly recommend that, where placebo medication is considered, its use should have the consensus backing of a multi-disciplinary team. The Commission would further recommend that a formal policy, widely debated amongst and agreed by the professional and managerial structures of Trusts and other service providers, should be a minimum framework within which such procedures may be considered.

6.19   The Commission first raised its concerns about the involvement of detained patients in research in its Sixth Biennial Report (pp. 57) and, in 1997, published a Position Paper on Research and Detained Patients. The Commission's Position Paper has now been reviewed, following correspondence with the Royal College of Psychiatrists and the Maudsley Hospital Research Ethical Committee, and a revised version is to be published in 1999.

6.20   The Commission's concerns over research and detained patients stem partly from the use of placebo medication in such research, but the Commission does recognise that not all therapeutic research involves placebos. A great majority of contemporary drug trials compare a new treatment against an established one, so that no patient involved in the research is actually deprived of treatment through their participation. Nevertheless, the Commission remains of the view that every patient detained under the Act should receive the best and most appropriate treatment available and that this must be the overriding principle upon which any research is considered.

# Emergency Treatment - Section 62

6.21  Treatments normally requiring either a patient's consent or a Second Opinion can be given in an emergency without either safeguard provided that one of the criteria listed in Section 62 of the Act is met. The least stringent criterion allows for treatments to be continued pending the visit of a SOAD if discontinuation of treatment would cause serious suffering to the patient. The initiation of any treatment under Section 62 must meet the criterion of being immediately necessary, either to save the patient's life, or to prevent a serious deterioration of the patient's condition, or to either alleviate serious suffering by the patient or to prevent the patient behaving dangerously. The Code of Practice (16.40) states that the decision to authorise treatment under this Section is the responsibility of the patient's RMO or, in the RMO's absence, the doctor who is for the time being in charge of the patient's treatment. The Code also requires hospital managers to produce a form for recording the use of Section 62, stating details of the treatment, why it was immediately necessary, and for how long such treatment was continued. Managers are also required to monitor the use of Section 62 (Code of Practice 16.41).

> ### Visit to Huntersombe Manor Hospital; 12 February 1998
>
> Commissioners were extremely concerned to note that two patients had been given intra-muscular injections on several occasions without consent or a Second Opinion and commented that the legal basis for so doing was not at all clear. They urged that a clear policy and procedural guidelines be implemented as a matter of urgency and drew attention to the Code of Practice guidance that managers should ensure that a form is devised to be completed by the patient's RMO every time urgent treatment is given under Section 62. Commissioners advised that the form should require details to be given of the treatment, why it was of urgent necessity to give the treatment and the length of time for which the treatment was given. The managers were asked to monitor the use of Section 62 in their hospital.

> ### Visit to Bethlem Royal Hospital; 26 May 1998
>
> Commissioners considered that with the high numbers of detained patients subject to the consent to treatment provisions the implementation was mostly very good and the number of errors seen gratifyingly few. There was clearly a good flagging system in place for reminding RMOs of critical time periods. However, Commissioners found several examples of the use of Section 62 and wondered whether the Trust might wish to monitor the reasons for its use. For example, documentation of the reasons for the use of emergency treatment was not apparent for two patients.

6.22  The Commission has noted records of authorisations being made under Section 62(1) for a course of ECT or multiple administrations of medication. The Commission advises that each application of ECT or administration of medication should be considered as a discrete intervention for the purposes of this Section, so that each administration should be justifiable against its criteria. Commissioners occasionally have cause to question whether treatment given under Section 62(1) was immediately necessary at that time.

> ### Visit to Bay Community NHS Trust; 16 July 1998
>
> Commissioners noted that a Form recording the authorisation of emergency treatment under Section 62 was completed without detailing why the treatment was, in fact, urgent. As the treatment was administered four days after the completion of the form, the urgency of the intervention was questionable.

6.23 The Commission has asked that Trusts include the total number of times that emergency treatment has been administered to detained patients under Section 62 as a part of the information submitted to the Commission on annual Hospital Profile Sheets (see 3.39). This specific information is primarily of use to Commissioners when visiting the Trust concerned. The Commission has noted that the vast majority of units which returned the information (95% in 1996/7, 94% in 1997/8) reported fewer than 10 occasions when emergency treatment was administered under Section 62 over the year.

## The Commission's Administration of Second Opinions

6.24 The Commission has a statutory responsibility for appointing registered medical practitioners to consider authorising non-consenting detained patients' treatment with medication for mental disorder after an initial three months of treatment or with ECT at any time. The Commission appoints registered medical practitioners with suitable experience to its Second Opinion Appointed Doctors (SOAD) panel for renewable periods of up to three years; the Commission then appoints individual members of this panel to undertake specific Second Opinions. Such specific appointments, which the Commission makes on behalf of the Secretary of State, are made according to geographic and other availability on a rotational basis. In 1998, 37 new appointments were made to the SOAD panel, increasing its active membership to 164 doctors (see appendix 3 for full list). Most of the newly appointed doctors completed their induction training soon after appointment and all but 12 of existing SOADs were provided with refresher training, through seminars held in Stockport, Nottingham and London. The Royal College of Psychiatrists accredited the Commission's SOAD training seminars as being suitable for the Continuing Professional Development of Psychiatrists.

6.25 The administration of the service of providing statutory Second Opinions takes up roughly a third of the Commission's budget and considerable secretariat time, but the Commission's administration of Second Opinions, from the receipt of requests from hospitals through to the appointment of a doctor and the monitoring of authorisations and treatment subsequent to such authorisations, ensures that patients who are detained under the Act are assured of the overview of a national, independent organisation when certain forms of compulsory treatment are considered.

## SOAD Activity

6.26 Between March 1997 and March 1999 there were 15,470 requests for a second opinion. At the time of writing, 14,808 (95.7%) of these had been attended by SOADs and the data returns processed. In 333 (2.2%) of these cases, SOADs had attended but the second opinion was not completed. The principal reasons for this included: the RMO changing their mind about continued treatment (35.4%); unavailability of the patient or the consultees (14.7%); and the SOAD being unable to reach agreement with the RMO (14.1%). Five patients were also found to be illegally detained.

6.27 The completed second opinions are shown in table 7, according to the Mental Health Act categories of mental disorder. The majority of these patients (82.5%) were detained under Section 3 of the Act.

**Table 7. Mental Health Act categories for completed second opinions**

| Mental Health Act Category | n | % |
| --- | --- | --- |
| Mental Illness | 12,960 | 89.5 |
| Mental Impairment | 313 | 2.2 |
| Severe Mental Impairment | 233 | 1.6 |
| Psychopathic Disorder | 120 | 0.8 |
| Dual Diagnosis | 751 | 5.2 |
| Not Recorded | 98 | 0.7 |
| Total | 14,475 | 100 |

6.28 The Commission is concerned that a second opinion review of treatment falling within the provisions of Section 58 of the Act should be completed as soon as possible following the request from the RMO. It has set attendance targets of three days following a request concerning ECT, and five days following a request concerning medication alone. During this period, 73.6% of second opinions for ECT were completed within three days and 94.5% were completed within 5 days. Sixty-three per cent of second opinions for treatment involving medication alone were completed within five days and 87.7% were completed within seven days.

6.29 Of the completed second opinions, 661 (4.6%) patients had been given emergency treatment under Section 62 of the Act prior to the second opinion. In these cases, SOADs were able to complete a greater proportion of their assessments within the target times. Where ECT was involved, 78.3% of cases were seen within three days, and where the patient was also under the age of 18, this increased to 84.2%. Sixty-eight per cent of cases involving medication alone were seen in five days or less.

6.30   Slightly over half of the second opinions were required because the patient was judged to be incapable of informed consent and the remainder were refusing treatment. More men than women patients were judged as being incapable of understanding the purpose and likely effects of the treatment (51.1% compared to 48.9%). The women tended to be a much older group with over a third (35.3%) aged 65 or over, compared to 14% of men. A much higher proportion of women were also referred for ECT (see table 8), and the majority (52%) of these were over 65 years of age.

**Table 8. Completed second opinions: Treatment by gender (%)**

| Treatment | Men (n=7,709) | Women (n=6,766) | All (n=14,475) |
|---|---|---|---|
| Medication | 83.8 | 56.3 | 70.9 |
| ECT | 15.4 | 42.7 | 28.2 |
| Medication and ECT | 0.8 | 1.0 | 0.9 |

6.31   A significantly higher proportion of black patients were referred for medication alone (table 9). Similar findings were reported in the Seventh Biennial Report (p. 103). As then, the present findings may be a reflection of the gender balance, as the majority of the black patients were male .

**Table 9. Completed second opinions: Treatment by ethnic group (%)**

| Treatment | White (n=11,173) | Black (n=1,662) | Asian (n=442) | Other (n=318) | Not recorded (n=880) |
|---|---|---|---|---|---|
| Medication | 67.4 | 92.0 | 74.9 | 81.8 | 70.3 |
| ECT | 31.7 | 7.3 | 24.2 | 17.3 | 29.1 |
| Medication and ECT | 0.9 | 0.7 | 0.9 | 0.9 | 0.6 |

**Table 10. Completed second opinions: Ethnic group by gender**

| Ethnic Group | Gender | | | | All | |
| | Men | | Women | | | |
| | n | % | n | % | n | % |
|---|---|---|---|---|---|---|
| White | 5,567 | 72.7 | 5,606 | 82.9 | 11,173 | 77.2 |
| Black Caribbean | 857 | 11.1 | 333 | 4.9 | 1,190 | 8.2 |
| Black African | 266 | 3.5 | 112 | 1.7 | 378 | 2.6 |
| Black Other | 67 | 0.9 | 27 | 0.4 | 94 | 0.6 |
| Indian | 131 | 1.7 | 81 | 1.2 | 212 | 1.5 |
| Pakistani | 103 | 1.3 | 60 | 0.9 | 163 | 1.1 |
| Bangladeshi | 47 | 0.6 | 20 | 0.3 | 67 | 0.5 |
| Chinese | 14 | 0.2 | 19 | 0.3 | 33 | 0.2 |
| Other | 195 | 2.5 | 90 | 1.3 | 285 | 2.0 |
| Not recorded | 462 | 6.0 | 418 | 6.2 | 880 | 6.1 |

6.32    Table 11 shows the age groups of patients and the treatment for which they were referred for a second opinion. Of the 192 patients under the age of 18 years, 16 had a treatment plan that included ECT. Forty-one of these patients were also under the age of 16 years, although the treatment of only one of these involved ECT.

**Table 11. Completed second opinions: Treatment by age group (%)**

| Age group | Treatment | | | All | |
| | Medication | ECT | Medication and ECT | | |
| | (n=10,269) | (n=4,077) | (n=129) | n | % |
|---|---|---|---|---|---|
| Under 18 | 1.7 | 0.3 | 1.6 | 192 | 1.3 |
| 18 - 25 | 13.7 | 5.0 | 4.7 | 1,613 | 11.1 |
| 26 - 40 | 41.5 | 15.6 | 33.3 | 4,936 | 34.1 |
| 41 - 64 | 28.9 | 30.5 | 38.8 | 4,260 | 29.4 |
| 65 and over | 14.2 | 47.8 | 20.7 | 3,535 | 23.9 |
| Total | 100 | 100 | 100 | 14,470 | 100 |

6.33    The treatment plan proposed by the RMO was amended, to some degree, by the SOAD in 12.6% of cases (see table 12). A greater proportion of treatment plans (15.6%) were amended for patients under 18 years of age than for patients in other age groups. Changes to the treatment plan were less likely for those patients over the age of 65, where only 9.2% of treatment plans involved some degree of change.

**Table 12. Completed Second Opinions: Changes to RMO's treatment plan by treatment type (%)**

| Degree of change to RMOs treatment plan | Treatment Type | | | All | |
|---|---|---|---|---|---|
| | Medication | ECT | Medication and ECT | | |
| | (n=10,269) | (n=4,077) | (n=129) | n | % |
| No change | 85.3 | 92.9 | 83.7 | 12,655 | 87.4 |
| Slight change | 12.8 | 6.4 | 9.3 | 1,588 | 11.0 |
| Significant change | 1.9 | 0.7 | 7.0 | 232 | 1.6 |

6.34   In 1166 (8.1%) cases the final treatment plans included a medication dosage above the BNF limits, and 131 cases (0.9%) included ECT exceeding 12 treatments. For the patients aged under 18 years in receipt of medication, 14 (7.9%) were treated with dosages above BNF limits. Of the 16 patients in the same age group receiving ECT, one case involved the administration of ECT in excess of 12 treatments.

6.35   A survey of child and adolescent psychiatrists carried out by the Child and Adolescent Section of the Royal College of Psychiatrists in 1991 showed that there were some 65 cases under the age of 18 years that had been treated with ECT in the previous 10 years (cited in Freeman, 1995). A more recent survey of ECT clinics in Scotland found only six cases of ECT given to those under 18 years in the preceding five years (Robertson & Freeman, 1995). As shown above, the Commission is aware of 16 patients under the age of 18 years who have been given ECT during the current two year reporting period. Taken together, these figures suggest a very low rate of treatment for this age group overall.

6.36   The number of Second Opinions the Commission arranged and monitored between 1997 and 1999 (nearly 15,000) represent an increase of over 25% from the previous biennial reporting period. A major factor in this increase was the sudden rise in the detained patient population as a consequence of the Court of Appeal decision in December 1997 in the *Bournewood* case (see 2.12 et seq). The Commission estimated, based upon data supplied by the Trusts and registered mental nursing homes which it visits, that up to 22,000 patients who were cared for on an informal basis prior to that ruling would need to be formally detained under the Act as a result of it. Before the overturning of the decision by the House of Lords in June 1998, the Commission was aware that a significant number of mentally incapacitated patients who were previously informally residing in hospitals and receiving medication for mental disorder were being detained under the Act, and that this newly detained population would be likely to require Second Opinions for such treatment after the first three months of detention. The number of requests for Second Opinions in June 1998 was, in line with this prediction, 27% higher than that for the same month in 1997. Whilst this source of the increase in requests for Second Opinions is now levelling off, as most

*Bournewood* patients will no longer be detained under the Act, the Commission continues to receive more requests for Second Opinions under Part IV of the Act than ever before.

6.37   The Commission contacted SOADs in anticipation of the increase in Second Opinions due to the Court of Appeal's *Bournewood* ruling and requested that they set aside additional time for SOAD work and/or make themselves available for work at weekends to manage the expected increase. The Commission wishes to record its gratitude to all SOADs for their positive response to this request and for meeting the increased demand for Second Opinions.

## The Monitoring of SOAD Work and Section 61 Reports

6.38   In addition to the Commission's statutory function of appointing SOADs to meet requests for Second Opinions under Part IV of the Act, the Commission also undertakes to monitor SOADs' work. This monitoring has a threefold purpose:

- to ensure that uniformly high standards of documentation and clinical practice are observed by SOADs;

- to oversee the treatment of patients subject to treatment without consent by considering SOAD authorisations and reports alongside reports made to the Commission by RMOs under Section 61 of the Act; and

- to inform the Commission's decision concerning the re-appointment of SOADs

6.39   The Commission requires SOADs to submit a report to it for each patient visited, and all such reports and SOAD authorisations are monitored weekly by clinically experienced members of the Commission's Consent to Treatment Special Interest Group. Monitoring SOAD work ensures that appropriate action is taken when discrepancies in documentation or procedure occur. Such discrepancies are usually of a minor nature and result in a letter being sent to the SOAD concerned pointing out the problem as an aid to practice improvement and, where necessary, requesting that Forms issued are amended. Rarely such discrepancies are serious enough to warrant the Commission initiating a further SOAD visit.

6.40   SOAD reports on their visits also inform the Commission of any problems encountered in accessing relevant records, such as a written treatment plan provided by the RMO, or in contacting relevant professionals to undertake the statutory and other consultations required to complete a Second Opinion. Particular difficulties may be taken up with the hospital managers, with whom responsibility ultimately rests for these procedural arrangements. The Commission was pleased to learn that a study is to be undertaken at the Reaside Clinic, South Birmingham NHS Trust, to audit whether, in the view of the SOADs concerned, the procedural arrangements made by the Clinic are satisfactory and whether any improvements can be made. The audit will be undertaken over six months through the use of a short questionnaire supplied to SOADs during their visits to undertake Second Opinions. The Commission welcomes this unprecedented study, which potentially is a model of a pro-active approach for Trusts to adopt to ensure that the best possible arrangements are made for Second Opinions.

6.41 Informed by its experience of monitoring SOADs' work and in response to changes in the Code of Practice, the Commission has produced a revised Guidance to SOADs, which the Code encourages RMOs to obtain for their own information.

6.42 The Act (Section 61) requires RMOs to submit a report to the Commission at specified times on patients' treatment and condition when such patients' treatment has been authorised on a Form 39 by a SOAD. Such reports should be furnished to the Commission upon the renewal of a patient's detention under the Act or, in the case of restricted patients, six months from the date of the detention order and then whenever the RMO makes a report to the Secretary of State under Section 41(6) or 49(3). The Commission is also empowered to require a report under Section 61 at any time. Commission members check that such reports have been submitted to the Commission for those patients that it encounters on visits and continues to discover occasions where RMOs have not fulfilled their statutory duty in this respect. This not only denies patients their legal right to have their treatment reviewed by an external body but is also, in the experience of the Commission, often indicative of further problems in hospitals' compliance with Part IV of the Act.

---

### Visit to Littlemore Hospital, Oxfordshire Mental Health NHS Trust in June 1998

Commissioners were disappointed with the inconsistent application across the Hospital of the consent to treatment provisions of the Mental Health Act 1983. A number of errors and omissions were again found in the documentation.

One patient's most recent Form 39 appeared to be dated 20 February 1995. The most recent MHAC1 form was dated 1996. The last report to the Home Office on this restricted patient was dated October 1997 and an MHAC1 should have been completed at that time. Commissioners requested that RMOs should be reminded to complete an MHAC1 on each occasion when a section is renewed, or for restricted patients, when a report is submitted to the Home Office

On one ward, Commissioners observed a number of other errors/omissions. One Form 38 related to ECT but failed to specify the maximum number of treatments. There was no evidence of discussions between the RMO and the patient about consent. This was particularly important in one case where a patient had previously been considered incapable of consenting. One Form 38 was dated 2 July 1998 and old forms were not crossed through. Some forms did not specify British National Formulary (BNF) categories or dose limits.

On another ward one Form 38 included medicine that was not for a mental disorder. The number of preparations was not recorded on the consent form. Medication that was not included on the Form 39 certificate of second opinion was being prescribed to one patient. However, Commissioners commented on the excellent records in patients' notes of discussions between RMOs and patients over consent on Ashurst, Phoenix and Wenric II. On both Ashurst and Phoenix Wards, documentation was satisfactory.

The Commission recommended that medical staff should introduce regular peer group audit or, alternatively, a pharmacist to monitor these vital procedures and regulations. Following the Visit, the Trust's Medical Records Officer arranged training on consent issues for medical staff and set up a

---

system with the chief pharmacist whereby the pharmacy would be supplied with copies of current consent to treatment forms to ensure that only authorised medication would be issued.

6.43   The Commission will on occasion initiate further SOAD visits as a result of its monitoring of Section 61 Reports. In some cases this will be because patients' current medication falls outside that authorised on their extant Forms 39, in which case the Commission writes to RMOs informing them of the unlawful treatment. More often, a further SOAD visit is arranged to review an authorisation on the grounds of the length of time that it has been allowed to run. In general, it is the Commission's view that no Form 39 should remain operative without review for more than two years, but in certain circumstances (such as for refusing, rather than incapable patients, patients in the High Security Hospitals or medium secure units, or patients whose medication is above BNF recommended doses) the Commission will usually initiate a further Second Opinion after one year.

## Neurosurgery for Mental Disorder

6.44   Section 57 of the Mental Health Act stipulates that Neurosurgery for Mental Disorder (NMD) may only be undertaken if a registered medical practitioner and two lay persons, who are all appointed by the Commission, have certified that the patient is capable of understanding the nature, purpose and likely effects of the treatment and consents to it, and the registered medical practitioner certifies that the treatment is likely to alleviate or prevent a deterioration in the patient's condition and that it should be given. This Section applies to any proposed treatment with NMD, whether the patient is detained under the Act or not.

6.45   In this reporting period 17 referrals were made to the Commission to consider certifying NMD treatment. This figure is considerably lower than for any previous period.

**Table 13.  Referrals for Neurosurgery**

| Biennial Reporting Period | NMD Referrals |
|---|---|
| 1983-1985 | 57 |
| 1985-1987 | 54 |
| 1987-1989 | No statistics collected |
| 1989-1991 | 52 |
| 1991-1993 | 46 |
| 1993-1995 | 30 |
| 1995-1997 | 30 |
| 1997-1999 | 17 |

6.46 All were certified although one patient withdrew consent before the operation took place. However, 17 operations have taken place in this period, as one operation which was certified in the last reporting period was performed in this period. Fourteen of the total referrals were women and 16 were white and one Pakistani. Of the 17 referrals, one was to consider authorising a repeat operation for a patient treated at the University Hospital of Wales, Cardiff, whose first operation had failed to achieve the desired result either in terms of the relief of symptoms or in producing an adequate lesion. As with the three similar repeat operations in Cardiff in the previous reporting period, this operation was authorised after careful consideration. Also in this period, for only the second time since the introduction of the Act, a detained patient was referred for NMD. That operation was also authorised.

6.47 The youngest patient was 28 years old at the time of referral, the eldest were both 66 years old. The distribution by age and gender of referrals is given below:

**Table 14. Age and Gender of Patients Referred for Neurosurgery**

| Age range | Male | Female |
|---|---|---|
| 21-30 years | 0 | 1 |
| 31-40 years | 1 | 5 |
| 41-50 years | 0 | 4 |
| 51-60 years | 2 | 2 |
| 61-70 years | 0 | 2 |

6.48 One patient was referred from the Republic of Ireland, and the Section 57 Appointees visited that patient at St Brigid's Hospital, County Louth, to undertake the assessment. The operation was authorised.

**Table 15. Operation Details for Neurosurgery**

| Operating Centre | Procedure | Number of operations |
|---|---|---|
| University Hospital of Wales | Bilateral Capsulotomy | 11 |
| Kings College Hospital | Stereotactic Subcaudate Tractotomy | 5 |
| National Hospital for Neurology and Neurosurgery | Stereotactic Subcaudate Tractotomy | 1 |

6.49 The Commission has produced, following discussions with the Neurosurgeon and Psychiatrists at the University Hospital of Wales, a short information leaflet that is given to patients who are offered NMD. Patients are also invited to complete a self-report to the Commission six months following their operations. The Commission has produced a semi-structured form to facilitate the submission of progress reports from practitioners, as required by the Commission under the authority of Section 61 of the Act, six months from the date of any NMD operation. The Commission has previously acknowledged the difficulty in evaluating outcomes of NMD (Seventh Biennial Report p. 112) but it is apparent that insufficient after-care arrangements are partly responsible for this difficulty. Whilst some patients may not wish to participate in after-care arrangements or follow-up assessments, the Commission recommends that patients should be encouraged to do so and that the neurosurgeon who undertook the operation should be routinely involved. Of the 31 such reports received during this period, 19 indicated that patients had benefited from their NMD operations, 8 reported little or no progress and four patients' conditions appeared to have deteriorated.

# Chapter 7

# Complaints of Detained Patients

## Summary

The Commission received approximately 1300 complaints over the two year reporting period. The Commission advises and supports the complainant through the NHS complaints procedures. It now investigates few complaints itself.

A judicial review (in May 1998) clarified and extended the complaints remit of the Commission, so that it is now allowed to investigate complaints from relatives of patients about those aspects of care and treatment, which are of a serious nature. Previously, the Commission only investigated complaints from relatives and people other than the detained patient if they concerned very specifically defined powers and duties in the Act.

Considerable efforts are made in High Security Hospitals to ensure thorough and timely investigations of complaints. There are still some unacceptable delays in concluding investigations and formally responding to patients.

The NHS Complaints handling has markedly improved, but the Commission considers that it or any successor body should retain a role in the investigation of complaints of patients subject to compulsory powers.

# 7 Complaints of Detained Patients

## Introduction

7.1 The Commission's complaints remit is set out in Section 120 of the Mental Health Act 1983 and has two distinct elements. The first enables the Commission to investigate "any complaint made by a person in respect of a matter that occurred while he was detained and which he considers has not been satisfactorily dealt with by the managers of that hospital" (Section 120 (b) (i)). The Commission can investigate any complaint from a detained patient, but only after hospital managers have investigated and have failed to satisfy the complainant. The second enables the Commission to investigate "any other complaint as to the exercise of the powers or the discharge of the duties conferred or imposed by this Act in respect of a person who is or has been so detained" (Section 120 (b) (ii)). This part of the remit allows the Commission to investigate complaints from relatives and third parties. The Commission does not have to refer such complaints to hospital managers as long as they concern "powers and duties" in the Act. This second part of the Commission remit has been the subject of a judicial review in May 1998 (see 2.23 – 2.26). The Commission has discretion not to investigate a complaint or to discontinue investigating, if it considers it appropriate to do so (Section 120 (2) ).

## Complaints From Detained Patients

7.2 The Commission received some 1300 complaints over the two year reporting period from detained patients or their carers by letter or telephone calls. A large number of these complaints were about detention or medication and the Commission offered advice about patients' rights regarding the Mental Health Review Tribunals and entitlement to Second Opinions.

**Figure 5: Complaints by Category 11/3/97 - 10/3/99**

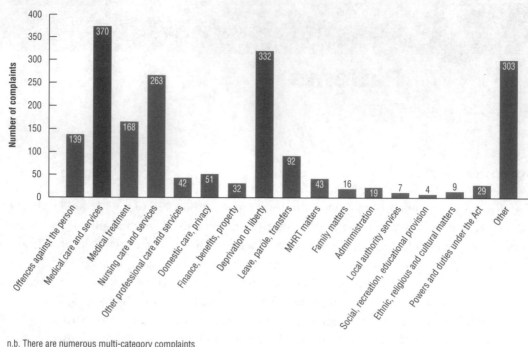

n.b. There are numerous multi-category complaints

7.3   Where patients complain about any aspect of their care and treatment, they are advised about the requirement to refer such complaints to hospital managers, sent a copy of the NHS complaints leaflet and asked whether they wish the Commission to pass on their complaint to the managers of the hospitals concerned. A substantial number of complainants do not give their permission and do not pursue their complaint beyond this stage, some undoubtedly because they are worried that this may have unpleasant repercussions for them. The Commission does what it can to reassure patients, but ultimately has to respect their wishes.

7.4   The Commission asks hospital managers to provide a copy of their response to detained patients' complaints and, when this has been received, the Commission writes to patients, asking them whether they are satisfied and informing them about their right to ask for an Independent Review Panel (IRP). In many cases, Trusts decide, or are advised by the Complaints Convenor, to try again to achieve local resolution before a decision about an IRP is made. The Commission can and does exercise discretion about whether to investigate at this stage, i.e. the end of "local resolution" but in the vast majority of cases will advise the complainant to seek an IRP. If an IRP is refused and the Commission considers that such a refusal may be unreasonable, it will, where appropriate, advise the complainant that the Health Service Commissioner (HSC) has powers to ask Trust Complaints Convenors (whose role is to decide whether an IRP is convened) to reconsider their decision.

7.5   If patients are dissatisfied either with the decision not to grant an IRP, or with the outcome of an IRP, they can again ask the Commission to investigate. The Commission will consider, in the light of all the available information, whether it should undertake an investigation and will inform the complainant of its decision. If the Commission decides not to investigate, it will give its reasons for this to the complainant and will advise about the right to refer the complaint to the HSC. If the Commission decides to investigate, it will identify a Commissioner from its team of Complaints Investigators who will undertake the investigation and produce a report, which will be sent to the complainant and the Trust concerned. Patients are advised of their right to refer their complaints to the HSC if they are not satisfied with the Commission's findings and the HSC will decide whether to investigate.

7.6 Since the introduction of the new NHS Complaints Procedure in April 1996 the Commission's role in relation to complaints from detained patients has changed substantially. In the vast majority of complaints which the Commission deals with, its primary function has become one of advising and supporting detained patients through the complaints process, advising them of their rights and corresponding with Trusts either on their behalf or in relation to perceived shortcomings in the way complaints are being handled. In doing so, the Commission tries to ensure that patients receive an appropriate response to their complaints. If matters of general concern are raised these are followed up by one of the Commission's visiting teams.

7.7 The following are examples of how the Commission has assisted detained patients to pursue a complaint.

### Case 1

A visually impaired patient complained by phone to the Commission about her care and treatment. She provided a cassette recording of her concerns, which the Complaints Unit transcribed and forwarded to the hospital managers for investigation of the complaints made.

In reply to the managers' response, the patient provided a further tape for transcription by the Complaints Unit. Her additional concerns were forwarded to the hospital managers, with a request for a further response, or the convening of an Independent Review Panel (IRP).

A further response was received from the managers in due course, which satisfied the patient's concerns. The Commission finalised the matter by writing to the hospital managers, thanking them for a refreshingly frank and open response, which had acknowledged faults, offered apologies and brought the matter to a satisfactory conclusion.

### Case 2 (June 98)

A relative of a patient who had been detained under Section 3, complained that he had been required to sell the patient's house, to pay for her aftercare under Section 117. Correspondence received by the Commission indicated that the local authority concerned routinely charged for Section 117 aftercare.

The Commission took the view that, although this matter fell within its complaints remit, it would be better dealt with by the Local Government Ombudsman, as he had greater powers to require the local authority to reverse its decision.

The patient's relative agreed with this view and the complaint was forwarded to the Local Government Ombudsman, on his behalf. The matter is still being investigated. (See 4.117 for further discussion of this issue)

7.8     The Commission now undertakes very few investigations itself. This is partly because fewer such requests are being received or judged to warrant investigation by the Commission, but mainly because hospital managers have developed more effective ways of implementing the NHS complaints procedures, more consistent ways of investigating complaints and better responses, often including an offer of a meeting. Hospitals now employ staff whose main or sole job is to deal with complaints. Many hospitals have introduced training in dealing with complaints for staff likely to be involved.

7.9     Some complaints are not accepted for investigation by the Commission because it is evident that the complaints have been fully considered at local level, any mistakes acknowledged and apologies offered where appropriate. In other cases the Commission decides not to investigate because it comes to the conclusion that nothing the Commission or anyone else could do would satisfy the complainant. A small number of very persistent complainants, sometimes patients who are suffering from illnesses which include persecutory elements, present a considerable difficulty to Trusts and the Commission in finding a appropriate way of seeking to resolve matters. It is the Commission's policy not to investigate complaints where litigation is pending or under way.

## Complaints about "Powers and Duties" Including Complaints from Third Parties.

7.10    Until a judicial review in May 1998, the Commission had taken the view that, in the case of complaints from relatives and people other than the detained patient, the Commission could only investigate such complaints if they were about defined powers and duties expressly referred to in the Act. The Commission's policy excluded investigation of complaints about care and treatment and was confined to matters relating to the correct legal implementation of such specific powers as for example, to detain or to grant leave. The Commission had sought legal advice on this interpretation on more than one occasion, including Counsel's opinion and, although the Commission felt constrained by this narrow interpretation of its remit, it was obliged to adhere to it.

7.11    This policy was challenged by the lawyers acting for the family of a patient who had committed suicide and about whose case relatives wished to make a number of complaints. The Commission's offer to investigate some, but not all complaints was declined and a judicial review took place in May 1998. Latham J. concluded that the Commission under the second limb of its complaints remit (Section 120 (1)(b)(ii) ) can investigate complaints about "all those rights and duties which flow necessarily and by implication from a Section 3 [and presumably other Sections'] detention" (i.e. complaints about "detention, management, control or treatment") and "such rights and duties as are expressly identified in the Act". The judgment also emphasised the broad discretion of the Commission under Section 120(2) not to investigate complaints. (See 2.23 et seq. for further discussion of this judgment).

7.12    The Commission welcomes this clarification and widening of its remit, which to all intents and purposes, allows it to investigate complaints from relatives about those aspects of patients' care and treatment which are of a serious nature (i.e. complaints about matters which materially affect the patient's quality of care in hospital). In many cases, the most clearly stated and well supported complaints are made by someone other than the detained patient who may not be well enough to complain, or even to give consent for this to be done on his or her behalf. Some complaints made by third parties are still outside the Commission's remit, such as complaints about food or bed linen.

7.13    Under this second part of its remit, the Commission can investigate complaints immediately and without reference to hospital managers. The Commission considers each complaint and exercises discretion about whether to ask hospital managers to investigate in the first instance, i.e. to follow the procedure laid down in the NHS Complaints Procedure. This is likely to be preferable in the majority of cases, thus giving an opportunity for local resolution.

7.14    As yet, complaints from third parties have not significantly increased in number and this may be because the Commission's extended remit is not widely known. Were it to lead to a large increase in complaints, it would have resource implications for the Commission.

## Liaison with the Health Service Commissioner

7.15    The Commission's role in investigating complaints from or on behalf of detained patients is not mentioned in the guidance issued in connection with the NHS complaints procedure which only refers to that of the Health Service Commissioner (HSC) (The Wilson Report, NHSE, 1996). However, the Commission has had an agreement with the HSC since 1991 that complaints from or on behalf of detained patients are dealt with by the Commission in the first instance. The HSC has discretion to investigate and ultimately, he can investigate any complaints dealt with by the Commission or indeed, complaints about the Mental Health Act Commission. This agreement has recently been revised in the light of the judicial review and other changes, including guidance about the HSC's power to require the Trusts' Complaints Convenors to reconsider a refusal to offer an IRP.

7.16    The Commission would welcome new guidance, which would clearly state the Commission's role as, at present, some Trusts do not mention the Commission in their complaints policies, which is liable to cause confusion to detained patients and their carers.

## Complaints in High Security Hospitals

7.17 Visits are paid regularly to each of the three High Security Hospitals in order to keep under review the operation of their respective complaints procedures and associated policies. This provides an opportunity to discuss policy developments and emerging trends in relation to the issues currently being complained about by individual patients.

7.18 A random selection of complaints files is routinely examined in detail in order to consider the adequacy of the investigation procedure for each complaint, the conclusions reached, the formal response to the patient, the timeliness of the response and the subsequent management action (if any) to address issues requiring attention. The results of this process are fed back orally to the designated Complaints Officer and subsequently confirmed in writing to the chief executive of the High Security Hospital concerned.

7.19 As a result of the constructive dialogue that has developed during the operation of the complaints monitoring process, a number of positive developments have emerged during the period under review in each of the three hospitals. Considerable efforts are made by staff in each complaints department to ensure that thorough and timely investigations are carried out and that follow up action takes place. A number of concerns have been identified and will be matters for further discussion and examination. Unacceptable delays in concluding investigations and formally responding to patients continue to be a cause for concern, although the complexity of many of the complaints made by patients in these hospitals is recognised. There appears to be a continuing need to reinforce in the minds of staff (particularly at clinical level) the right of individual patients to make complaints, the importance of effective, objective and timely investigation of complaints and the value of improving standards of care by acting upon issues identified in the investigation process. In a number of cases examined, there was clear evidence of inadequate or poor quality nursing records, often in relation to serious matters.

7.20 A series of training initiatives has been undertaken by staff with the purpose of achieving improved investigation procedures and more effective reports. These have been particularly targeted at nursing staff at ward manager and clinical nurse leader levels. Overall, with some exceptions, there was increasing evidence of detailed and rigorous investigations into individual complaints.

## Complaints from Black and Ethnic Minority Patients

7.21 Complaints from members of these groups have been routinely examined during complaints monitoring visits. The importance of auditing such complaints to identify matters requiring attention has been recognised by the hospitals. The appointment of an Ethnic Minority Project Co-ordinator at Rampton Hospital and the input of the Professional Development Advisor at Broadmoor have contributed to this process. There are still concerns about the need for staff to be culturally sensitive and to better address the needs of black and ethnic minority patients.

### Serious Allegations

7.22 A number of complaints concerned serious allegations of assaults upon patients by staff members, excessive use of force during restraint and inappropriate use of seclusion. In most cases, following investigation, they were not substantiated. However, two patients in one of the hospitals sustained fractures and as a result of the Commission expressing concern, control and restraint techniques were reviewed and modified. Complaints of this nature will continue to be closely monitored by the Commission.

7.23 Commission members on visits to Rampton have observed anxiety on the part of some patients when discussing their complaints, but have been frustrated from taking the issue further by the patient's refusal to make a written complaint. Patients have alleged coercion by ward staff or fellow patients acting on behalf of staff not to make complaints or to withdraw complaints they have made. Patients have reported that complaints concerning domestic, catering or general environmental matters appear to be processed with little difficulty, but also with little resultant action being taken. Complaints about improper behaviour of staff are regarded as being likely to result in adverse reaction for the patient's welfare or progress through the care and rehabilitation system.

### Staff Shortages

7.24 Staff shortages have adversely affected access by patients to a wide range of recreational and social activities and access to fresh air, which gave rise to a number of complaints.

## The Commission's Role in Investigating Complaints and the Review of Mental Health Legislation

7.25 It could be argued that, as NHS complaints handling has markedly improved, largely as a result of the NHS Complaints Procedure, the Commission now has little practical role in investigating complaints. Furthermore, the advisory and supportive role that it now increasingly plays in seeing complaints through the NHS procedure could conceivably be left to advocates and hospitals' complaints managers. However, if any future Mental Health Act removed the ability of either the Commission or any successor to investigate complaints from patients subject to detention (or other forms of compulsion), it would seriously weaken the statutory basis upon which such an organisation might intervene on behalf of those patients whose interests it should serve. Without the ability to take up investigations on behalf of patients, the Commission would have less to offer those patients whom it meets on its visits to hospitals and mental nursing homes, and would have less leverage with hospital managers when overseeing their handling of complaints. Thus the removal of the Commission's statutory authority to investigate patients' complaints would not only leave the organisation less able to intervene in cases where such intervention was warranted, but would also remove an important part of the organisation's statutory weight, with consequences in its perceived image amongst mental health services. The Commission considers that, in any new legislation, its complaints remit should be retained, with the discretionary element intact and that it should be extended to complaints about community-based powers, currently enjoyed by the Mental Welfare Commission for Scotland.

# Chapter 8

# Deaths

## Summary

*From February 1997 all hospitals and mental nursing homes registered to receive detained patients were asked to report to the Commission any deaths of detained patients with some details about the circumstances.*

*In the subsequent year, 374 deaths were reported, of which 81 were from unnatural causes.*

*In 33 cases there were issues of concern regarding risk assessment, observation levels, leave/absence without leave arrangements and ward security.*

# 8 Deaths

## The Commission's Procedure for Reviewing Deaths of Detained Patients

8.1    For some years the Commission has asked to be notified of the deaths of detained patients. Commissioners have attended inquests into such deaths to ascertain whether there are any matters of concern in relation to the care and treatment of detained patients that the Commission should follow up with the relevant hospitals.

8.2    In 1995 a review of Commission records on deaths of detained patients was published by the Mental Health Foundation (Banerjee et al, 1995). A year later, in line with the recommendations of this publication, the Commission undertook a major reorganisation of its activities, which resulted in centralisation of its work in reviewing the deaths of detained patients at its headquarters in Nottingham. A new policy for dealing with the deaths of detained patients was introduced, leading to the establishment of:

- a database for the recording of information on the deaths of detained patients;
- a team of Commissioners to specialise in reviews of deaths of detained patients; and
- a revised procedure for reviewing such deaths.

Under the revised procedure, deaths are reviewed by a Commissioner with special experience. A hospital visit may be undertaken to view records and interview staff, if considered appropriate. A Commissioner may also attend the inquest and may, in some cases, request Properly Interested Person (PIP) status, making it possible to ask questions of witnesses and make submissions to the Coroner on potential issues to be covered at the inquest.

8.3    In cases where issues of concern are identified, recommendations for action by the hospital may be made and these are either referred to hospital managers for comment and action, or referred to the relevant Commission Visiting Team for action on the next visit to the hospital concerned. Serious concerns may be referred to the health authority and/or other relevant bodies.

8.4    From 1 February 1997, all hospitals and registered mental nursing homes accommodating detained patients were asked to inform the Commission of deaths of detained patients, using a standard form, which calls for relevant information about the circumstances and causes of death.

## The Causes of Deaths

8.5    In the 12 month period between 1 February 97 and 31 January 98, 374 deaths were reported to the Commission. Deaths were divided into the following categories:

- **natural causes** – deaths which were a direct result of physical disorder, e.g. a cardio-vascular accident, aschaemic heart disease, or bronchopneumonia in an elderly patient.

- **suicide** – including probable suicide, taking into account all available information. This does not necessarily equate to the verdicts given at inquests, which require that the Coroner or jury is satisfied beyond reasonable doubt that the patient killed him or herself and intended to do so. Probable suicides include deaths from hanging from wardrobe and shower curtain rails and falls from high buildings.

- **accidental** – deaths where the circumstances indicated that an accident had occurred, eg. choking on food.

**Figure 6. Deaths Of Detained Patients - By Cause And Age Group (n=374)**

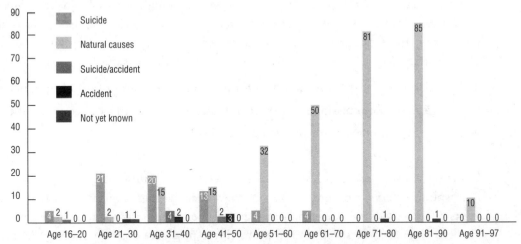

8.6    The majority of deaths notified were those of elderly patients, from natural causes. The Commission reviewed only those deaths which appeared to be from unnatural causes, i.e. suicides, suspected suicides, accidents and deaths where there might be cause for concern, eg. high dosage of medication, recent control and restraint or seclusion. Eighty-one deaths were from unnatural causes and they are examined in more detail below.

**Figure 7.  Unnatural Deaths - Apparent Cause of Death (n=81)**

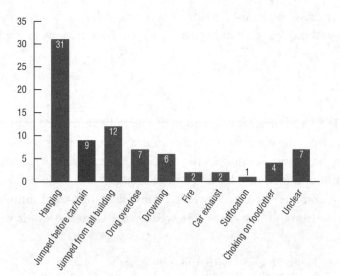

## Review of Deaths from Unnatural Causes

8.7  All unnatural deaths reported to the Commission were followed up by the Commission Complaints Unit (CCU), until sufficient information was available to enable a decision on the most appropriate action.

8.8  Where a review was considered necessary, copies of all relevant documents were passed to a reviewing Commissioner, who considered whether the review should be based on a scrutiny of documentary information held or requested by the Commission, or whether it was necessary to visit the hospital concerned for further information and/or to talk to staff. The Commissioner also recommended whether the Commission should be represented at the inquest and whether Properly Interested Person (PIP) status should be sought.

8.9  Of the 81 unnatural deaths reviewed by the Commission, there was sufficient concern in 35 cases to warrant a reviewing Commissioner visiting the hospital. A Commissioner attended the inquest in 33 cases, in three of which PIP status was requested and granted. There were 10 cases where the Commissioner both visited the hospital and attended the inquest.

8.10  Commissioners identified issues of concern and/or made recommendations for action regarding matters relating to the patient's death in 33 cases. These were all followed up by correspondence with the managers of the hospital concerned, or by the relevant Commission Visiting Team at the next visit. Five cases are on-going at the time of this report.

## Issues Raised

8.11   In the 33 cases where Commissioners raised issues of concern, risk assessment, observation levels, leave or absence without leave arrangements and ward security were identified as major factors.

### Safety Of Patients

8.12   The Mental Health Act 1983 authorises the detention of mentally disordered patients on the grounds that this is required in the interests of their own health or safety or for the safety of others. This places a duty on hospital managers to "detain", i.e. ensure that patients are not able to leave hospital without the knowledge and consent of staff and to keep them "safe", i.e. to protect them from coming to harm. However, some hospitals seem inhibited from exercising their powers to detain. In the cases reviewed by the Commission, it was found that:

- some patients were able to abscond with apparent ease;
- there were too many opportunities on the wards for patients to harm themselves;
- access to a means of committing suicide appeared to be freely available.

The Code of Practice gives clear and detailed guidance on the security of patients who may be at risk. It recommends that the management, security and safety of patients should, wherever practicable, be ensured by adequate staffing. When it is known that patients are likely to abscond, the Code gives advice on the temporary locking of ward doors.

8.13   Patients should not come to harm whilst detained in the safe environment of a hospital. The level of security needs to be commensurate with the risks posed by the patient's mental state. This is a matter of judgment for those engaged in providing care for detained patients. Nevertheless, the Commission acknowledges that it can be extremely difficult to prevent a determined individual from attempting suicide and is aware that he or she may succeed sooner or later. There is also the issue of how compatible an environment of total security is with human dignity. Nevertheless, it would seem reasonable to suggest that if suicidal intent is associated with patients' illnesses, it is imperative to keep them safe while they are being detained and treated.

### Hanging

8.14   The most frequent method of suicide used, for those which occurred on the hospital wards, was hanging. In a number of the cases reported, the patient had a known history of suicidal ideation or attempts and had indicated suicidal intent within a short period before the death. In 20 cases patients had access to belts, dressing gown cords, etc, and a load-bearing means of suspending themselves such as curtain, wardrobe and other rails (used in 9 cases). Lessons do not seem to have been learned from internal reviews of suicides, which examined the circumstances and the means employed. Not only does such information not seem to be shared between hospitals, but deaths by the same means (load bearing wardrobe and curtain rails) have occurred within the one hospital.

## Observation

8.15   Observation policies were often not clear and, in particular, observation level categories were not standardised. 'Level 3' observation, in some locations, meant that the patient was under constant visual supervision, whereas in other locations level 3 indicated normal ward observation.  This anomaly could lead to confusion amongst staff who work in more than one hospital. Even when policies were clear, they were not adhered to consistently and, in some instances, were not fully understood by staff.

## Risk Assessment

8.16   Finding the appropriate level of observation for each patient depends on the adequacy of the risk assessment. However, risk assessment is an inexact science and, with hindsight, factors will often be identified which were not given sufficient importance at the time. However, a risk assessment had not been carried out in some cases reviewed and in other cases, risk indicators had been ignored or not assessed for their potential importance. There were also instances where information was not shared between members of the multi-disciplinary team or where the action to be taken was not adequately recorded.

## Absence without Leave (AWOL)

8.17   AWOL policies did not always make it clear how staff should act when a patient had absconded, such as not giving a time-scale indicating when to inform the police. A speedy response can save lives. There were 22 cases where death occurred whilst the patient was AWOL. In 12 of these it was established that death took place within six hours, and a further four within 24 hours, of the patient's going absent.

## Authorised Leave

8.18   Five deaths occurred whilst patients were on authorised leave. Subsequent reviews showed that authorisation and documentation of leave had not always been in accordance with the Act and the Code of Practice.

## Staff Training

8.19   In some cases, where death occurred on a psychiatric ward, staff appeared to have been inadequately trained and/or were inexperienced in dealing with the emergencies they were faced with. There were examples of significant delays in cardio-pulmonary resuscitation being commenced and emergency equipment not being located quickly. In other cases, equipment was not in full working order or staff were not adequately trained in its use.

### Control and Restraint

8.20 Where death occurred during, or soon after, control and restraint, inadequate and non-standardised training are causes for concern, although numbers are too small to permit general conclusions (see 10.10 et seq.).

### Further Action

8.21 The Commission will undertake a further study when the data for the second year's work under the new policy is available, and intends to make its findings public.

# Chapter 9

# The Commission in Wales

## Summary

Between April 1997 and March 1999, the Commission made 11 Full Visits and 34 Patient Focused Visits to Trusts and social services departments in Wales. In addition, the three medium secure units in Wales have been visited, as have the nine mental nursing homes registered to take detained patients. The Commission has also held meetings with each of the five health authorities.

The opening of the new NHS Medium Secure Unit, Ty Llewelyn, Llanfairfechan, in North Wales will relieve the pressure on existing medium secure beds. However, there is still a requirement for more low secure units and community placements with 24 hour supervision. The significant increase in patients with drug and alcohol problems has exacerbated the difficulties in ward management.

There are continuing concerns about difficulties in accessing Section 12 approved doctors, and the failure of Responsible Medical Officers to comply with the requirements of the Code of Practice regarding the completion of consent to treatment forms.

The Commission has consulted upon and submitted its Welsh Language Scheme to the Welsh Language Board.

## 9 The Commission in Wales

## Structural Changes

9.1 The structural changes in Wales which came into force in April 1996, reducing the number of health authorities from nine to five and increasing the number of social services departments from eight to 22, have not resulted in any serious problems in the delivery of mental health services during the last two years. Operational policies and procedures were quickly established, allowing good relationships to develop between the new authorities and the Trusts.

9.2 Now it is the Trusts that are to undergo change. The White Paper "Putting Patients First" (Welsh Office, 1998) has set out a framework for replacing the internal market in NHS Wales with a system of integrated care which is accountable to the National Assembly for Wales. At the heart of the new service are Local Health Groups, working in close collaboration with the NHS Trusts. The number and shape of the Welsh NHS Trusts have been subject to a major review. The impact of these management changes on mental health care in Wales will need to be carefully monitored.

## Visiting Activity in Wales

9.3 Between April 1997 and March 1999 a total of 11 full visits, involving Trusts and social service departments and 34 patient focused visits took place. In addition, Caswell Clinic, an NHS medium secure unit at Bridgend and Llanarth Court, a private medium secure unit near Abergavenny, were each visited on four occasions. The new NHS medium secure unit, Ty Llewelyn, Llanfairfechan, was visited on one occasion. There are nine mental nursing homes in Wales registered to take detained patients, all of which were visited at least once during the reporting period. Since the visit one of the nursing homes has withdrawn from registration to take detained patients, but another new nursing home is to be so registered and will be included in the Commission's visiting schedule.

9.4 Meetings have been held with each of the five health authorities. Issues relating to the Act and services for detained patients were discussed. It was encouraging to learn that the Commission's Guidance Notes to Health Authorities (GN1) and GPs (GN2) on the Mental Health Act have been widely distributed since their issue in December 1996. A meeting was also held with the Chief Nursing Officer at the Welsh Office. It was agreed that issues relating to nursing practice that are highlighted in Commission reports to Trusts in Wales will be made the subject of specific feedback to the Chief Nursing Officer. This would enable such issues to be the basis of further training in nursing seminars.

# Concerns regarding service provision

## Forensic Service

9.5     The opening of the new medium secure unit, Ty Llewellyn on the Bryn y Neuadd site, Llanfairfechan in North Wales, is a most welcome facility and will certainly help relieve the pressure on the existing medium secure beds in Wales.

9.6     However, it may be necessary to give consideration to the establishment of a small regional medium secure forensic unit for female patients. Their numbers are small, but their needs require a highly specialised service.

## Low Secure Units

9.7     Medium secure units, to function efficiently, require the support of an adequate number of low secure beds which need to be placed in strategic localities. Trusts across Wales have developed business cases for the development of small low secure units; many of these proposals are awaiting approval from the relevant health authority and/or the Welsh Office.

## Community Placements with 24 Hour Supervision

9.8     Many patients, who may have had a forensic background or who may have presented challenging behaviour, are detained in hospital longer than necessary because of a serious shortage of community placements with 24 hour supervision. Such patients are blocking hospital beds which could be more appropriately used for patients requiring acute treatment or active rehabilitation.

## Drug and Alcohol Service

9.9     There appears to have been a significant increase in admissions of patients with drug and alcohol problems into the acute wards during the last two years. Difficulties in ward management have thus been exacerbated. Drug and alcohol services throughout Wales welcome the promise of increased resources recently made by Central Government to help develop their services.

# Concerns regarding in-patient care

### Nurse Staffing Levels

9.10 In the majority of Trusts in Wales, nurse staffing levels are reported to be adequate and in line with patient dependency levels, with a skill mix ratio of 60% trained and 40% untrained being achieved. While many Trusts have been successful in recruiting and retaining nursing staff, other Trusts continue to experience difficulties and are often forced to employ either bank or agency nurses, or resort to the practice of regular staff being required to work excessively long hours. This is a dangerous practice in that nurses become tired and overworked, with a consequent increase in sickness levels.

### Admission Policies and Acute Psychiatric Wards

9.11 Operational policies relating to admissions to acute wards appear to be underdeveloped in a number of Trusts. Hence, acute wards in these Trusts frequently find themselves having to cope with serious management problems – having to meet the needs of patients who are acutely ill, patients requiring rehabilitation, men and women of widely differing age groups and patients suffering from alcohol and drug misuse. A more dynamic approach to developing rational admission policies would help reduce this problem.

### Violence on the Wards

9.12 A number of Trusts report an increase in violent behaviour on the acute wards and in intensive care units. One incident was so serious as to necessitate calling in the police who decided to use CS spray (see 10.26 for further discussion). When a Trust finds itself in such a situation, it is imperative that decisions are based on a multi-disciplinary consensus. It would also seem appropriate, as one Trust has already done, to develop a joint policy with the police for dealing with criminal or potentially criminal behaviour by psychiatric patients.

### Training in Control and Restraint

9.13 Training is well established in most psychiatric services with the appropriate policy and procedural guidelines in place (see 10.10). Nevertheless, there are still a number of concerns which need to be addressed. The use of control and restraint should always be carefully recorded and when used frequently, it should be evaluated, such evaluation forming part of clinical audit. Further, there should be sufficient number of staff trained, with their training regularly updated. This is not always the case.

### Single Sex Facilities

9.14 The availability of single gender accommodation is slowly increasing. It is encouraging to note the excellent facilities which have been incorporated into the new psychiatric unit at the Bronglais Hospital, Aberystwyth. Wards in the older psychiatric hospitals are gradually being improved but there is still much to be done to ensure the safety of vulnerable female patients and the privacy and dignity of all psychiatric patients, as outlined in the Welsh Office letter (DGM/97/98) of October 1997.

## Mental Health Act Issues

9.15 Table 16 gives the number of admissions and changes in legal status following admission, for private mental nursing homes and NHS facilities in Wales. It shows a substantial increase from 1996/7 to 1997/8 in both informal and formal admissions. The Court of Appeal judgment in L v Bournewood could have resulted in more detentions in the last quarter of 1997/8 and may account for some of the increase in formal admissions.

9.16 The pattern of admissions is similar to England (see 4.1). About 40 % of admissions are under Section 3 and 43% of all admissions under the Act for both England and Wales occur after the patient has been admitted to hospital informally. The proportion of emergency admissions under Section 4 in Wales is now down to 4.4% of formal admissions at the point of entry to hospital, which is lower than in England, which was 6.7% in 1997/8.

Table 16. Mental Health Act Admissions for Wales (Welsh Office, 1998 and 1999)

| | 1996/7 | 1997/8* |
|---|---|---|
| Informal admissions | 15,417 | 17,840 |
| Admissions under Part 11 | | |
| Section 2 | 619 | 793 |
| Section 3 | 430 | 603 |
| Section 4 | 57 | 64 |
| Total | 1,106 | 1,460 |
| From informal to: | | |
| Section 5 (2) | 514 | 536 |
| Section 5 (4) | 38 | 46 |
| Section 2 | 131 | 234 |
| Section 3 | 254 | 289 |
| Total | 937 | 1105 |
| Court and Prison Disposals | | |
| Sections 35-38 | 66 | 59 |
| Sections 47 and 48 | 17 | 15 |
| Total | 83 | 74 |
| Supervised Discharge | 28 | 11 |

9.17   During Commission visits, legal documents were carefully examined and, for the most part, they were in good order, with evidence of medical and administrative scrutinies in place in most, if not all, Trusts. There were, however, areas which caused concern.

### Section 12(2) Doctors

9.18   Difficulties in accessing Section 12(2) approved doctors were widespread. In some areas, these difficulties arose from the low number of doctors with such approval; in other areas difficulties arose not because the approved doctors were few in number but because of their lack of availability. This is a national problem and may require action on a national scale for its resolution (see 4.31 et seq.).

### Section 17 Leave

9.19   The need to complete Section 17 leave forms appeared to be increasingly recognised. The forms, however, did not always give sufficient detail as to leave conditions; they were not always signed by the RMO and they did not always indicate a date when the leave arrangements should be reviewed.

### Section 58

9.20   Commissioners found that a significant number of Forms 38 relating to consent to treatment did not comply with Chapters 15 and 16 of the Code of Practice. In some cases, treatment appeared to be unlawful. The Commission is deeply concerned that there continues to be a lack of care in completing these forms by RMOs and a failure on the part of nursing staff to check them as a matter of routine before administering medication.

### Section 136

9.21   Joint policies for the implementation of this Section were available in nearly all areas of Wales. Representatives of the respective police forces often expressed a wish for on-going training in Mental Health Act issues.

### Training in Mental Health Act issues

9.22   Training in Mental Health Act issues is not only important for police officers but also for hospital staff and staff of the social service departments. Much training in the early part of 1998 was directed at implementing the Bournewood judgment and training courses scheduled for 1999 were targeting the revised Code of Practice.

## Welsh Language Policy

9.23   The Commission's Welsh Language Scheme is awaiting the statutory approval of the Welsh Language Board. It has been submitted to a public consultation process. Ten written responses were received mainly from Trusts, health authorities and social services departments and all were either complimentary or congratulatory. Copies of the scheme are available from Commission headquarters.

9.24 The Commission is committed to fulfilling its obligations under the Welsh Language Act 1993. It will do this by ensuring that the principles of equality with regard to the Welsh and English speaking people in Wales will be applied in service planning and delivery, in dealing with the public and in the Commission's public profile.

9.25 The Commission recognises that, for many people with mental health problems, being given a service in their language of choice, may be one of several factors which help them to feel valued and listened to at a time when they are particularly vulnerable.

# Pennod 9

# Y Comisiwn Yng Nghymru

## Crynodeb

Rhwng Ebrill 1997 a Mawrth 1999, fe wnaeth y Comisiwn 11 Ymweliad Llawn a 34 Ymweliad Canolbwyntio ar Gleifion ag Ymddiriedolaethau ac Adrannau Gwasanaethau Cymdeithasol. Yn ychwanegol at hyn, fe ymwelwyd â'r tair Uned Ddiogelwch Ganolig yng Nghymru, yn ogystal â'r naw cartref ymgeledd meddwl a gofrestrwyd i gymeryd cleifion dan orchymyn. Y mae'r Comisiwn yn ogystal wedi cynnal cyfarfodydd gyda phob un o'r pum awdurdod iechyd.

Fe fydd agoriad Uned Ddiogelwch Ganolig GIG newydd, T Llewelyn, Llanfairfechan, yng Ngogledd Cymru yn lliniaru'r pwysau ar y gwelyau diogelwch canolig presennol. Fodd bynnag, y mae gofyniad o hyd am unedau diogelwch isel a lleoliadau cymunedol gyda goruchwyliaeth 24 awr. Y mae'r cynnydd arwyddocaol mewn cleifion sydd â phroblemau cyffuriau ac alcohol wedi dwysau'r anawsterau mewn rheolaeth wardiau.

Y mae'r Comisiwn yn pryderu yngln â'r anawsterau sy'n parhau mewn rhai Ymddiriedolaethau mewn recriwtio a dal gafael ar staff nyrsio a'r cynnydd sydd yn yr enghreifftiau mewn ymddygiad treisiol ar wardiau salwch difrifol ac mewn unedau gofal dwys. Fe fydd angen i rai Ymddiriedolaethau ddatblygu eu polisïau ar dderbyn er mwyn ymdopi ag anghenion y grp amrywiol o gleifion a dderbynnir i unedau gofal difrifol. Y mae'r Comisiwn wedi nodi cynnydd yn argaeledd llety un rhyw.

Y mae pryder yn parhau i fod yngl$ln$ â'r anawsterau sy'n deillio mewn cael mynediad at ddoctoriaid cymeradwyedig Adran 12, a methiant y Swyddogion Meddygol Cyfrifol i gydymffurfio â gofynion y Côd Ymarfer parthed cwblhau'r ffurflenni Caniatâd Triniaeth.

Y mae'r Comisiwn wedi ymgynghori ynglyn â'i Gynllun Iaith Gymraegac wedi ei gyflwyno i Fwrdd yr Iaith Gymraeg.

# Y Comisiwn yng Nghymru

## Newidiadau Strwythurol

Nid yw'r newidiadau strwythurol a ddaeth i rym yn Ebrill 1996, a oedd yn gostwng y nifer o Awdurdodau Iechyd o naw i bump ac yn cynyddu'r nifer o Adrannau Gwasanaethau Cymdeithasol o wyth i 22, wedi achosi i unrhyw broblemau difrifol ddigwydd mewn cyflenwi gwasanaethau iechyd meddwl yn ystod y ddwy flynedd diwethaf. Fe sefydlwyd polisïau a gweithdrefnau gweithredol yn gyflym, gan ganiatáu datblygu perthynas dda rhwng yr awdurdodau newydd a'r Ymddiriedolaethau.

Yn awr yr Ymddiriedolaethau a fydd yn mynd drwy newidiadau. Y mae'r Papur Gwyn "Putting Patients First" (Y Swyddfa Gymreig, 1998) yn gosod fframwaith ar gyfer disodli'r farchnad newydd yn GIG Cymru gyda system o ofal integredig a fydd yn Atebol i Gynulliad Cenedlaethol Cymru. Yn ganolog i'r gwasanaeth newydd fe fydd y Grwpiau Iechyd Lleol, a fyddant yn gweithio mewn cydweithrediad clòs gyda Ymddiriedolaethau GIG. Y mae nifer a siâp yr Ymddiriedolaethau GIG Cymreig wedi bod yn wrthrych adolygu mawr. Fe fydd angen monitro'n ofalus effaith y newidiadau hyn ar reolaeth gofal iechyd meddwl yng Nghymru.

## Gweithgarwch Ymweld yng Nghymru

Rhwng Ebrill 1997 a Mawrth 1999 fc gynhaliwyd cyfanswm o 11 ymweliad llawn, a oedd yn ymwneud ag Ymddiriedolaethau ac Adrannau Gwasanaethau Cymdeithasol a 34 ymweliad a oedd yn canolbwyntio ar gleifion. Yn ychwanegol at hyn, fe ymwelwyd â Chlinig Caswell, uned ddiogelwch ganolig ym Mhen-y-bont ar Ogwr a Chwrt Llanarth, uned ddiogelwch ganolig breifat ger Abergafenni, y ddwy ohonynt ar bedwar achlysur. Fe ymwelwyd â'r uned ddiogelwch ganolig GIG, T Llewelyn, Llanfairfechan ar un achlysur. Y mae naw o gartrefi ymgeledd meddwl yng Nghymru sydd wedi eu cofrestru i gymerwyd cleifion dan orchymyn, ac fe ymwelwyd â phob un ohonynt o leiaf unwaith yn ystod y cyfnod adrodd yn ôl. Ers yr ymweliad fe dynnodd un o'r cartrefi ymgeledd yn ôl o gofrestriad i dderbyn cleifion dan orchymyn, ond y mae cartref ymgeledd newydd arall i'w gofrestru yn unol â hyn ac fe fydd yn cael ei gynnwys yn rhestr ymweld y Comisiwn.

Fe gynhaliwyd cyfarfodydd gyda phob un o'r pump Awdurdod Iechyd. Fe drafodwyd materion a oedd yn ymwneud â'r Ddeddf a gwasanaethau ar gyfer cleifion dan orchymyn. Yr oedd hi'n galonogol deall bod Nodiadau Cyfarwyddyd y Comisiwn i Awdurdodau

Iechyd (GN1) ac i Feddygon Teulu (GN2) ar y Ddeddf Iechyd Meddwl wedi cael eu dosbarthu'n eang ers eu cyflwyno yn Rhagfyr 1996. Fe gynhaliwyd cyfarfod hefyd gyda'r Prif Swyddog Nyrsio yn y Swyddfa Gymreig. Fe gytunwyd y bydd y materion sy'n ymwneud ag arfer nyrsio sy'n cael eu hamlygu yn adroddiadau'r Comisiwn i Ymddiriedolaethau yng Nghymru'n cael eu gwneud yn destun adrodd yn ôl penodol i'r Prif Swyddog Nyrsio. Fe fyddai hyn yn ei gwneud yn bosibl i faterion o'r fath fod yn sylfaen hyfforddiant pellach yn y seminarau nyrsio.

## Pryderon parthed darpariaeth y gwasanaeth

### Y Gwasanaeth Fforensig

Y mae agoriad yr uned ddiogelwch ganolig newydd, T Llewelyn ar safle Bryn y Neuadd, Llanfairfechan yng Ngogledd Cymru, yn gyfleuster a groesewir yn fawr ac fe fydd yn sicr yn cynorthwyo i liniaru'r pwysau ar y gwelyau diogelwch canolig yng Nghymru.

Fodd bynnag, fe all y bydd angen rhoi ystyriaeth i sefydlu uned fechan fforensig ddiogelwch ganolig ranbarthol ar gyfer cleifion benywaidd. Y mae eu niferoedd yn fychan, ond y mae eu hanghenion yn gofyn am wasanaeth arbenigol uchel.

### Unedau Diogelwch Isel

Y mae unedau diogelwch canolig, er mwyn iddynt weithredu'n effeithiol, angen cynhaliaeth nifer digonol o welyau diogelwch isel sydd wedi eu lleoli mewn lleoliadau strategol. Y mae Ymddiriedolaethau ledled Cymru wedi datblygu achosion busnes ar gyfer datblygiad unedau diogelwch isel bychain; y mae llawer o'r cynigion hyn yn disgwyl am gymeradwyaeth gan yr Awdurdod Iechyd perthnasol a/neu y Swyddfa Gymreig.

### Lleoliadau Cymunedol gyda Goruchwyliaeth 24 awr

Y mae llawer o gleifion, a all fod wedi cael cefndir fforensig neu a all fod wedi dangos ymddygiad herfeiddiol, yn cael eu cadw yn yr ysbyty yn hirach nag sy'n angenrheidiol oherwydd y prinder difrifol sydd o leoliadau cymunedol gyda goruchwyliaeth 24 awr. Y mae cleifion o'r fath yn blocio gwelyau ysbyty y gellid eu defnyddio'n fwy priodol ar gyfer cleifion sydd angen triniaeth gofal difrifol neu ailsefydlu gweithredol.

### Y Gwasanaeth Cyffuriau ac Alcohol

Y mae'n ymddangos bod cynnydd arwyddocaol wedi digwydd mewn derbyniadau o gleifion gyda phroblemau cyffuriau neu alcohol yn y wardiau gofal difrifol yn ystod y ddwy flynedd diwethaf. Y mae anawsterau mewn rheolaeth wardiau felly wedi dwysáu. Y mae'r Gwasanaethau Cyffuriau ac Alcohol drwy Gymru gyfan yn croesawu'r addewid o gynnydd mewn adnoddau a wnaed yn ddiweddar gan y Llywodraeth Ganolog i gynorthwyo i ddatblygu eu gwasanaethau.

# Pryderon ynghylch gofal cleifion mewnol

### Lefelau Staffio Nyrsio

Yn y rhan fwyaf o Ymddiriedolaethau yng Nghymru, fe adroddir bod y lefelau staffio nyrsys yn ddigonol ac yn unol â lefelau dibyniaeth y cleifion, gyda chymhareb cymysgedd sgiliau yn cyrraedd 60% wedi eu hyfforddi a 40% heb hyfforddiant. Tra bod llawer o'r Ymddiriedolaethau wedi bod yn llwyddiannus mewn recriwtio ac ail hyfforddi staff nyrsio, y mae Ymddiriedolaethau eraill yn profi anawsterau ac yn aml yn cael eu gorfodi i gyflogi naill ai nyrsys 'banc' neu nyrsys asiantaeth, neu orfod troi at yr arfer ble mae'r staff rheolaidd yn cael gofyn iddynt weithio am oriau gormodol o faith. Y mae hwn yn arfer peryglus gan fod y nyrsys yn mynd yn flincdig ac yn cael eu gorweithio, gyda chynnydd o ganlyniad yn y lefelau gwaeledd.

### Polisïau Derbyn a Wardiau Seiciatrig Gofal Difrifol

Y mae'r polisïau gweithredol sy'n berthnasol i dderbyniadau i wardiau dwys yn ymddangos fel eu bod yn danddatblygiedig mewn nifer o Ymddiriedolaethau. Gan hynny, y mae'r wardiau dwys yn yr Ymddiriedolaethau hyn yn eu cael eu hunain yn gorfod ymdopi â phroblemau rheolaeth difrifol - gorfod diwallu anghenion cleifion sydd yn ddifrifol wael, cleifion sydd ag angen ailsefydlu, dynion a merched o wahanol grwpiau oedran eang a chleifion sy'n dioddef o gamddefnyddio alcohol a chyffuriau. Fe fyddai dull gweithredu mwy deinamig tuag at ddatblygu polisïau derbyn o gymorth mewn lleihau'r broblem hon.

### Trais ar y Wardiau

Y mae nifer o Ymddiriedolaethau'n adrodd bod cynnydd mewn ymddygiad treisgar ar y wardiau gofal difrifol ac mewn unedau gofal dwys. Yr oedd un amgylchiad mor ddrwg nes ei gwneud hi'n angenrheidiol galw'r heddlu i mewn ac fe benderfynasant ddefnyddio chwistrell CS (gweler 10.1.6 am drafodaeth bellach). Pan fo Ymddiriedolaeth yn ei chael ei hun mewn sefyllfa o'r fath, y mae'n hanfodol i'r penderfyniadau gael eu sylfaenu ar gonsensws aml ddisgyblaethol. Fe fyddai'n ymddangos yn briodol hefyd, fel y mae un Ymddiriedolaeth wedi ei wneud eisoes, datblygu polisi ar y cyd gyda'r heddlu ar gyfer trin ymddygiad troseddol neu ymddygiad â photensial troseddol gan gleifion seiciatrig.

### Hyfforddiant mewn Rheoli ac Atal

Y mae hyfforddiant wedi'i sefydlu'n dda yn y rhan fwyaf o'r gwasanaethau seiciatrig gyda'r polisïau a'r canllawiau gweithdrefn mewn bod. Fodd bynnag, y mae nifer o bryderon yn parhau sydd angen talu sylw iddynt. Fe ddylai'r defnydd o reoli ac atal gael ei gofnodi'n ofalus bob amser a phan ddefnyddir ef yn aml, fe ddylai gael ei werthuso, gyda'r cyfryw werthuso yn ffurfio rhan o awdit clinigol. Yn ychwanegol at hyn, fe ddylasid bod digon o staff sydd wedi cael eu hyfforddi'n briodol, gyda'u hyfforddiant yn cael ei ddiweddaru'n rheolaidd (gweler 10.1.3). Nid dyma sy'n digwydd bob amser.

### Cyfleusterau Un Rhyw

Y mae argaeledd llety ar gyfer un rhyw yn cynyddu'n araf. Y mae'n galonogol nodi'r cyfleusterau ardderchog sydd wedi cael eu hymgorffori i'r uned seiciatrig newydd yn Ysbyty Bronglais, Aberystwyth. Y mae'r wardiau yn yr ysbytai seiciatrig hynaf yn araf bach yn cael eu gwella ond y mae angen gwneud llawer mwy i sicrhau diogelwch cleifion benywaidd hawdd eu niweidio a phreifatrwydd ac urddas cleifion seiciatrig, fel yr amlinellir yn llythyr y Swyddfa Gymreig (DGM/97/98) yn Hydref 1997.

## Materion y Ddeddf Iechyd Meddwl

Mae Tabl 16 yn rhoi nifer y derbyniadau a newidiadau yn y statws cyfreithiol yn dilyn derbyniadau ar gyfer cartrefi ymgeledd iechyd meddwl preifat a chyfleusterau GIG yng Nghymru. Y mae'n dangos cynnydd sylweddol o 1996/7 i 1997/8 mewn derbyniadau anffurfiol a ffurfiol fel ei gilydd. Fe allasai'r dyfarniad Llys Apêl yn L v Bournewood fod wedi golygu mwy o ataliadau yn chwarter olaf 1997/98 ac fe all gyfrif am beth o'r cynnydd mewn derbyniadau ffurfiol.

Y mae'r patrwm derbyniadau'n debyg yn Lloegr (gweler 4.1). Y mae tua 40% o'r derbyniadau'n unol ag Adran 3 ac y mae 43% o'r holl dderbyniadau sy'n unol â'r Ddeddf ar gyfer Lloegr a Chymru'n digwydd ar ôl i'r claf gael ei dderbyn i'r ysbyty'n anffurfiol. Y mae cydran y derbyniadau argyfwng o dan Adran 4 yng Nghymru bellach i lawr i 4.4% o'r derbyniadau ffurfiol ar adeg derbyniad i'r ysbyty, sydd yn is nag yn Lloegr, a oedd yn 6.7% ym 1997/98.

**Tabl 16. Derbyniadau Deddf Iechyd Meddwl ar gyfer Cymru (Y Swyddfa Gymreig, 1998 a 1999)**

|  | 1996/97 | 1997/8* |
|---|---|---|
| **Derbyniadau anffurfiol** | 15,417 | 17,840 |
| **Derbyniadau o dan Rhan 11** | | |
| Adran 2 | 619 | 793 |
| Adran 3 | 430 | 603 |
| Adran 4 | 57 | 64 |
| **Cyfanswm** | 1,106 | 1,460 |
| **O anffurfiol i:** | | |
| Adran 5 (2) | 514 | 536 |
| Adran 5 (4) | 38 | 46 |
| Adran 2 | 131 | 234 |
| Adran 3 | 254 | 289 |
| **Cyfanswm** | 937 | 1105 |
| **Defnydd Llys a Charchar** | | |
| Adrannau 35-38 | 66 | 59 |
| Adrannau 47 a 48 | 17 | 15 |
| **Cyfanswm** | 83 | 74 |
| **Rhyddhau Gorchwyledig** | 28 | 11 |

Yn ystod ymweliadau'r Comisiwn, fe archwiliwyd y dogfennau cyfreithiol yn ofalus a, chan mwyaf, yr oeddynt mewn trefn dda, gyda thystiolaeth o archwiliadau meddygol a gweinyddol yn bodoli yn y rhan fwyaf, os nad ym mhob, Ymddiriedolaeth. Yr oedd, fodd bynnag, feysydd a oedd yn achosi pryder.

## Adran 12(2) Doctoriaid

Yr oedd yr anawsterau mewn cael mynediad at ddoctoriaid cymeradwyedig Adran 12(2) yn gyffredin. Mewn rhai ardaloedd, yr oedd yr anawsterau hyn yn deillio o'r nifer isel o ddoctoriaid a oedd â chymeradwyaeth o'r fath; mewn ardaloedd eraill yr oedd yr anawsterau'n codi nid oherwydd bod y doctoriaid cymeradwyedig yn fach mewn nifer ond oherwydd diffyg eu hargaeledd. Y mae hon yn broblem genedlaethol ac fe all y bydd angen gweithredu ar raddfa genedlaethol ar gyfer ei datrys (gweler 4.6).

## Adran 17 Seibiant

Yr oedd yn ymddangos bod yr angen i gwblhau ffurflenni Seibiant Adran 17 yn cael ei gydnabod yn gynyddol. Nid oedd y ffurflenni, fodd bynnag, yn rhoi digon o fanylion bob amser yngln ag amodau'r seibiant; nid oeddynt yn cael eu harwyddo bob amser gan y Swyddog meddygol Cyfrifol ac nid oeddynt bob amser yn dynodi dyddiad pryd y dylid adolygu'r trefniadau seibiant.

## Adran 58

Fe ganfyddodd y Comisiynwyr nad oedd nifer arwyddocaol o'r Ffurflenni 38 a oedd yn berthnasol i ganiatâd ar gyfer triniaeth yn cydymffurfio â Phennod 15 ac 16 y Côd Ymarfer. Mewn rhai achosion, yr oedd yn ymddangos bod y driniaeth yn anghyfreithlon. Y mae'r Comisiwn yn pryderu'n arw bod diffyg gofal yn parhau wrth gwblhau'r ffurflenni hyn gan yr Swyddog Meddygol Cyfrifol a methiant ar ran y staff nyrsio i'w gwirio fel mater o drefn cyn rhoi moddion.

## Adran 136

Yr oedd polisïau ar y cyd ar gyfer gweithredu'r Adran hon ar gael mewn ymron i'r holl ardaloedd yng Nghymru. Yr oedd cynrychiolwyr o'r heddlu priodol yn aml yn datgan dymuniad am hyfforddiant parhaus mewn materion y Ddeddf Iechyd Meddwl.

### Hyfforddiant mewn materion y Ddeddf Iechyd Meddwl

Y mae hyfforddiant parhaus mewn materion y Ddeddf Iechyd Meddwl nid yn unig yn bwysig ar gyfer swyddogion yr heddlu ond hefyd ar gyfer staff ysbytai a staff yr Adrannau Gwasanaethau Cymdeithasol. Fe gyfeiriwyd llawer o'r hyfforddiant yn nechrau 1998 at roi'r dyfarniad Bournewood mewn grym ac fe restrwyd cyrsiau hyfforddiant ar gyfer rhan olaf 1999 at y Côd Ymarfer newydd.

## Y Polisi Iaith Gymraeg

Y mae Cynllun Iaith Gymraeg y Comisiwn yn aros cymeradwyaeth statudol Bwrdd yr Iaith Gymraeg. Fe gafodd ei gyflwyno ar gyfer proses ymgynghori cyhoeddus. Fe dderbyniwyd deg ymateb ysgrifenedig gan mwyaf gan Ymddiriedolaethau, Awdurdodau Iechyd ac Adrannau Gwasanaethau Cymdeithasol ac yr oeddynt i gyd naill ai yn ganmoliaethus neu yn ein llongyfarch. Y mae copïau o'r cynllun ar gael o bencadlys y Comisiwn.

Y mae'r Comisiwn wedi ymrwymo i gyflawni ei oblygiadau yn ôl Deddf yr Iaith Gymraeg 1993. Fe fydd yn gwneud hyn drwy wneud yn sir bod egwyddorion cyfartaledd parthed siaradwyr Cymraeg a Saesneg Cymru yn cael ei gymhwyso at gynllunio a chyflenwi gwasanaethau, mewn delio â'r cyhoedd ac ym mhroffil cyhoeddus y Comisiwn.

Y mae'r Comisiwn yn cydnabod, ar gyfer llawer o bobl gyda phroblemau iechyd meddwl, bod cael gwasanaeth yn eu dewis iaith, yn un o nifer o ffactorau sydd o gymorth iddynt deimlo'u bod yn cael eu gwerthfawrogi ac yn cael gwrando arnynt ar adeg pryd y maent yn neilltuol o hawdd eu niweidio.

# Chapter 10

# Special Issues

## Summary

*There is great uncertainty about the extent of the powers of staff to impose rules and enforce sanctions with regard to the behaviour of patients.*

*Both qualified and unqualified health care staff likely to face situations of patient aggression and violence must be given comprehensive training, which is updated at regular intervals.*

*A considerable number of units have policies on seclusion that are either inadequate or not kept updated and where the guidance in the Code of Practice is not followed.*

*Additional guidance on the use of seclusion is given (see 10.16), which supplements the Code of Practice.*

*Patients confined alone in a restrictive situation should be subject to rigorous control and audit, whether or not it is defined as seclusion.*

*The police should consult with mental health professionals before deciding to use CS spray.*

*There is an urgent need for central guidance on policies and procedures to deal with the widespread problem of substance misuse within mental health units.*

*Ward staff should have accurate information on ethnicity so that the everyday care of the patient is responsive to cultural preferences, but only 62% of ward notes checked recorded ethnicity.*

*The use of the Act for black ethnic groups is over six times greater than the proportion of such groups in the population.*

*The National Visit of 11 May 1999 examined policies and practice with regard to ethnic monitoring, racial harassment and the use of interpreters.*

*In addition to the need for separate facilities for women, the Commission has identified some key factors to help safeguard the safety, dignity and privacy of women patients (see 10.69).*

*A model of how to meet the specific needs of adolescents, where admission to adult wards is unavoidable, is put forward (see 10.78).*

*The Code of Practice now contains more extensive guidance on the choice between using the Children Act 1989 or the Mental Health Act 1983.*

*There are a few units for patients with learning disabilities, where the Commission found very poor environments.*

*Mental Health Act assessments for patients with learning disability should be done by practitioners with specialist expertise, but this should not result in a delay in the provision of a service.*

*Where the patient is not capable of giving informed consent to treatment and the conditions for admission under the Act can be satisfied, detention under the Act should be considered.*

# 10 Special Issues

## Control and Discipline

### The Issues in General

10.1 The management of dangerous or disruptive behaviour in hospital settings continues to present professionals and managers with significant anxiety and challenge. Incidents of obscene or threatening language, assaults on patients or staff, abuse of alcohol or drugs, sexually inappropriate behaviour and racial and sexual harassment all have to be controlled. However there is great uncertainty about the extent of the powers of staff to impose rules and enforce sanctions with regard to the behaviour of patients. The position of detained patients is even more problematic. Informal patients can be asked for an undertaking to abide by the rules or ultimately be told to leave. However for detained patients, whose behaviour is disruptive, discharge is not an option. Detained patients are, by definition, unwilling patients and, either because of their illness or their personality, they may resist control, behave badly and break rules. Indeed, certain patients may be so detained in order to protect the public and, in these circumstances, a risk of their behaving dangerously is a significant reality. This gives rise to some difficult and unresolved questions. What measures are the institution entitled to take to maintain order? What is the legal, ethical or therapeutic justification for these measures? How are the entitlements and interests of individual patients safeguarded? How can the risk of problem behaviour be minimised?

10.2 There are indications that problem behaviour on wards is a growing concern. As mentioned earlier (see 5.23), a one week census of acute and intensive care in-patient wards in inner London found that, in the average ward, there was one assault and just under one other untoward incident every three days. Violence against staff was twice as common as violence perpetrated by one patient on another (Gourney et al, 1998). Aggression and violence is not confined to the inner city areas, as is shown in the following example of a hospital in Bangor, North Wales.

**Visit to Gwynedd Community Health NHS Trust; 21 November 1997**

Medical and nursing staff expressed deep concern about the increase in violent behaviour on the wards in the Hergest Unit. Some members of staff have been, it would seem, seriously assaulted and much damage has been caused to hospital property. Clarification was required as to when people with mental disorder should be prosecuted for criminal offences and as to when people presenting extreme violence should be transferred to units with facilities to control such behaviour. It was felt that further discussions on these issues should take place between the Trust, the Police, the Crown Prosecution Service (CPS) and the forensic services.

An incident in which CS spray was used had caused much heart-searching among medical and nursing staff, with a number of differing views being held as to the appropriateness of police action. It was put to Commissioners that a study into the use of CS spray in incidents involving mentally ill patients might helpfully lead to the production of guidelines as to the circumstances in which this form of restraint should or should not be used and as to who should take the final decision as to its use in hospitals. It was also suggested that research into the interaction of medication for mental illness and the toxicity of CS spray should be initiated.

(See discussion of CS spray in 10.26 et seq.)

10.3 These problems are not new. Over 200 years ago, Philippe Pinel, writing during the period of the French Revolution in 1794, spoke of the need to balance safety requirements with the rights of patients, of the importance of non-punitive approaches and of non-retaliation when staff were assaulted by patients. But he also pointed to the importance of adequate supervision of patients and of sensitive management of any disturbed behaviour. These principles are equally relevant today. The quality of the therapeutic environment has a significant impact on reducing the risk of problem behaviour. How patients spend their day, the ward environment, the type and level of patient contact with staff and the consistency of staff responses are key factors.

10.4 This section explores issues surrounding the management of patients whose behaviour presents particular problems. It focuses on the use of measures such as searching of patients, control and restraint, seclusion and segregation, CS spray and other emerging practices. While there is much that can and should be done to obviate the need to apply these measures, it is not always possible, without recourse to unacceptable levels of medication, to completely rule out the use of such procedures. Where used, they should be on limited occasions and for the shortest possible duration for the effective management of severely symptomatic patients.

10.5 The revised Code of Practice includes new and expanded guidance on the handling of patients who present particular management problems, which covers the use of physical restraint, seclusion and the locking of doors (chapter 19) and on searching of patients and their belongings (chapter 25). It also emphasises that methods aimed at reducing or eliminating unacceptable behaviour should take account of:

- the need for individual care planning;
- the physical condition of the patient;
- the physical environment of the ward or unit; and
- the need to maintain adequate staffing levels.

The guidance points to the need for continuing risk assessment and management where there is a risk of problem behaviour, for training by qualified trainers and for clear written policies.

10.6    The Code now more clearly states that "Other than in exceptional circumstances, the control of behaviour by medication should only be used after careful consideration, and as part of a treatment plan" (19.15). It also states that if the patient is not detained and restraint has been deemed necessary (19.8) or seclusion has been used (19.16) consideration should be given to whether formal detention under the Act is appropriate.

**The Legal Perspective**

10.7    What is the extent of staff powers to exercise control and discipline? The Mental Health Act 1983 confers the power to detain and treat for mental disorder but nowhere explicitly refers to the control of patients; no reference appears in the Act about the power to restrain patients, to keep them in seclusion, to deprive them of their personal possessions or to regulate the frequency and manner of visits to them. Apart from the duty of care that staff owe patients and common law powers to act in emergency situations, the case of *Poutney v Griffiths [1975] 2 All E.R, 888* does give some legal justification for the control and discipline of detained patients. The House of Lords held that treatment necessarily involves the exercise of discipline and control and that, in this case, a nurse was justified in imposing restrictions on the visit of family and friends to the patient, as this was seen as being a necessary part of the patient's treatment. The Broadmoor Case (see 2.20) may have extended the powers of the institution to take measures to maintain order beyond that needed for the treatment of the individual patient. The case concerned a challenge by three patients of the hospital's policy to introduce random and routine searches. Previous policy had been to search patients and their belongings only when there had been reason to do so, as indeed was recommended in the 1993 edition of the Code of Practice. The change of policy had been prompted by a patient who had secreted a heavy drinking mug used for attacking a hospital chaplain. The Court of Appeal held that "... it is obvious that in the interests of all in particular the need to ensure a safe therapeutic environment for patients and staff that the express power of detention must carry with it a power of control and discipline, including, where necessary, of search with or without cause and despite individual medical objection". The judge, Lord Justice Auld, added that "it is plain common sense that, on occasion, an individual patient's treatment may have to give way to the wider interest." The justification, then, for the hospital's exercise of its power of control and discipline, in this case, was not in terms of the patient's treatment, but because of the need to maintain order for the safety of all. However, this case has been interpreted narrowly and, as is now stated in the Code of Practice (25.3), a policy of routine and random searching without cause should only be applied in exceptional circumstances, for example, where the dangerous or violent criminal propensities of patients create a self evident and pressing need for additional security.

10.8 In discussing the Broadmoor case, Davenport (1999) is concerned that if the interests of security and safety were to override the interests of the patient in every case, it would be difficult to escape the conclusion that the patient's treatment is an irrelevancy. But, it is difficult to draw a dividing line between what is permitted in the name of treatment and what can only be justified in the name of detention; often measures to control behaviour involve a mixture of both. Eldergill (1997, pp.59 – 61) points out that it is important not to lose sight of the purpose of the statutory powers, which is that they enable necessary treatment to be given to a patient whose behaviour is putting himself or others at risk, the aim being to eliminate the risk of harm, or further harm, being done. This is the statutory objective, not the imposition of discipline, control and force for their own sake. It is not possible to complete a necessary programme of hospital treatment unless a disturbed patient can be restrained from leaving the ward or from behaving violently towards himself or others. The patient's recovery, like that of any other patient, depends on the maintenance of a safe, calm, therapeutic environment, and this is only possible if medical and nursing staff can control violent behaviour. However, there must be no malice, no ill treatment or wilful neglect and any force used must be reasonable in the circumstances.

10.9 The Commission has submitted to the Mental Health Legislation Review Team an argument for greater regulation of the powers to exercise control and discipline in the interests of staff and patients alike. Where the Act specifically deals with a control and discipline issue – the withholding of mail (Section 134) – it is quite exacting about when the use of such a power is justifiable and, therefore, gives a clear direction as to what remains outside the legal powers of service providers. In the formulation of new mental health legislation similar attention could be given to:

- powers to search patients;
- powers to withhold property;
- powers to refuse leave or access to hospital activities; and
- the whole raft of measures considered or taken by service providers to maintain control and discipline in hospitals.

Equally important is the provision for patients of a form of appeal and redress when they feel they have been subjected to unnecessary, arbitrary or extreme measures. Such an appeal could be directed, in the first instance, to a body analogous to the current Mental Health Act managers. There could also be statutory rights to advocacy for patients making such appeals. The Commission is pleased to note that, at the time of going to press, these suggestions have been taken on board in the draft outline proposals of the Review Team.

## Control and Restraint

10.10 In some hospitals the term 'control and restraint', with its connotations of the exercise of power over patients, has been replaced by reference to 'care and reassurance' or 'care and responsibility'. It is understandable that staff, as clinicians whose raison d'être is to care and treat, may be uneasy about using methods of control and restraint and consequently tend to justify any action is this area in therapeutic terms. Such terminology also rightly serves to emphasise the importance of understanding why people behave violently, but the majority of patients subject to such controls will still see them as the exercise of power by those in authority. They may also be subject to the additional frustration of it being more difficult to challenge the staff version of events and the response to them, when these are cloaked in therapeutic terms.

10.11 The Code of Practice emphasises that, in addition to individual care plans, there is much which can be done to prevent the need for restraint and provides a list of general measures (19.5). These might include the availability of adequate activity space, pleasant décor and surroundings, a staff to staff call system, access to fresh air and light, good eating facilities, distinction of smoking and non-smoking areas, individualised patient control of room lighting, access to a quiet area, recreation rooms and visitors' rooms, access to a telephone, availability of defined personal space and a secure locker for each patient.

10.12 All of this points to the use of physical restraint as a last resort when other interventions have failed. It should only be used where the patient is engaged in actual physical assault, deliberate or accidental self-harm, or, in certain circumstances, the destruction of property (such as where the debris may be used as a weapon, or where patients' property is being damaged). Where physical restraint is necessary, a trained three-person team should usually deal with the situation, with each team member having a defined role to play in the intervention. A higher number of staff may result in the situation becoming further inflamed, increase the possibility of injury to either the patient or staff members, and could severely limit space in which to manoeuvre effectively. Physical interventions should not rely on the infliction of pain to restrain a patient and should not be seen by staff as an automatic precursor to the seclusion of the patient. The evidence that, following episodes of violence, the rate of absorption of anti-psychotic medication administered by intra-muscular injection is greatly increased, should be clearly borne in mind by mental health practitioners involved in the restraint of violent patients.

10.13 The National Association of Control and Restraint Trainers advocates the need for a range of techniques which can be adapted to suit different circumstances. For example, there has been a move, particularly within learning disability services, from large institutions to community units with smaller staff teams and it may not be possible to engage a three person team when controlling violent behaviour. There are techniques for two members of staff to use low level restraint. This can be effective with patients with learning disabilities to ensure control without discomfort.

10.14 Other patients may also be traumatised by witnessing methods of control and restraint and there is a risk that their relationship with and confidence in the clinical team may be undermined. Patients in the vicinity of the incident should be reassured by other staff members and quickly moved from the immediate area. Post-incident reviews should be carried out after every incident in which physical restraint has been applied and lessons learned documented and acted upon. Counselling and support should be provided for all patients and staff involved in episodes of physical restraint and records should confirm that this has occurred. These records should be subject to regular audit and review by senior managers.

10.15 It is essential that managers of mental health units ensure that both qualified and unqualified health care staff likely to face situations of patient aggression and violence are given comprehensive training and updating. In the last Biennial Report, the Commission commented on the proliferation of courses of instruction in this area (Seventh Biennial Report, p. 168). These were not regulated by any statutory awarding body, which led to a divergence of practices which in some instances have been found to be contradictory. The Department of Health has responded to this problem by including guidance in the Code of Practice (19.9), which states that courses should be taught by a qualified trainer and that the trainer "should have completed an appropriate course of preparation designed for health care settings and preferably validated by one of the health care bodies (English National Board or Royal College of Nursing Institute)".

## Seclusion

10.16 Seclusion, as with control and restraint, poses significant ethical and practical dilemmas, awareness of which is essential to good practice. Doctors and nurses should be cognisant of the adverse effects on patients and be aware of the conflicts between the rights of a secluded patient to freedom, choice and autonomy and the rights of others to protection from harm. It is an emergency measure, which should be imposed only where there is a significant risk of harm to the patient and others. It should be used as infrequently as possible, only for so long as it takes for the patient to return to a calmer frame of mind and never for suicidal or self harming patients. Its use is clearly open to abuse and therefore requires the most rigorous control, monitoring and evaluation.

10.17 The Commission collects annual statistics on the use of seclusion via the hospital profile sheets (see 3.39). The data for 1996/7 and 1997/8 is consistent in showing that nearly 120 hospitals (excluding high security hospitals) are using seclusion for up to 2000 patients on about 5000 occasions.

**Table 17. The Use of Seclusion**

| Year | Hospitals using seclusion | Episodes of seclusion | Patients secluded |
|---|---|---|---|
| 1996/7 | 114 | 5373 | 1952 |
| 1997/8 | 119 | 4934 | 1993 |

10.18 Seclusion was also one of the items in the Commission's 'Matters Requiring Particular Attention' procedure (see 3.36 et seq). There were 299 wards where seclusion was found to be used, including 48 wards in High Security Hospitals, of which 277 were able to show Commissioners a policy, but only 60% of these policies had been reviewed within the previous 2 years. The Code of Practice specifies that there should be a special seclusion book or forms which should contain a step-by-step account of the seclusion procedure in every instance and that the record should be countersigned by a doctor (19.23). Where seclusion needs to continue, there should be reviews every two hours by nurses and every four hours by a doctor. Commissioners examined records for 236 patients where seclusion had been used within the previous 12 months to monitor compliance with the Code. It was found from these 236 records:

- seclusion is most often initiated by a nurse (185 episodes);

- doctors had signed the record form in most cases (34 were without a signature);

- there was no record of the time of a doctor's attendance in 45 instances; of the remainder, there was a delay in the doctor's attendance of over 30 minutes and sometimes over 60 minutes in more than 42% of cases;

- seclusion lasted for more than 2 hours on 141 occasions, of which 114 had a record of being reviewed within 2 hours; and

- 81 episodes lasted for more than 4 hours, of which 56 had a record of a second review within that time period.

While many hospitals in both the NHS and independent sector have excellent policies and procedures that adhere to the guidance in the Code of Practice, these findings indicate that there is also a considerable number of units where policies are either inadequate or out-of-date and the guidance in the Code is not followed.

10.19 There are some points for which the Code of Practice does not offer detailed guidance and which therefore may not be addressed in local policies. The Code does not specify, for example, any details about the content of periodic reviews, when decisions are made concerning the continuation or termination of seclusion. These reviews should include an assessment of both the mental and physical state of the patient. Staff should be clearly aware of the potentially harmful psychological consequences of seclusion, notably feelings of increased despair and isolation, anger, worsening of delusions and hallucinations and the effects of sensory deprivation. Equally important to note is the potential for the physical condition of a secluded patient to deteriorate. Nursing staff should carefully observe, assess and record the patient's level of consciousness, pulse and respiration rates, noting any physical symptoms or abnormalities. It may also be necessary, if practicable, to record both blood pressure and temperature levels of a secluded patient, if he or she has been given psychoactive drugs. Other physical health points relate to ensuring adequate fluid and food intake (particularly in terms of avoidance of dehydration) and monitoring urinary output, and maintaining records of these.

10.20 To maintain dignity and comfort, patients should retain as much of their personal clothing as is compatible with their safety. Indeed, the Code of Practice specifies that a secluded patient should always be clothed (19.22). There is, however, a need for particular vigilance on the part of nursing staff in relation to what clothing is retained and worn by a secluded patient both in terms of possible self-harm or harm to others. Certain item such as shoes and boots (including laces), belts and ties, dressing gown cords and jewellery can present particular dangers. For a very small minority of patients (in medium or high secure settings) it may be necessary to provide a secluded patient with protective clothing and/or bedding which is almost indestructible. On the rare occasions where such items are needed, authorisation should be given in writing by a doctor.

10.21 The Code of Practice now states that hospital guidelines should ensure that the patient receives the necessary care and support both during and after the seclusion. At the earliest possible safe moment following the cessation of an episode of seclusion, patients should be given every opportunity by the clinical team to talk about the incident which led to their seclusion and about the seclusion itself. The aims of such interventions will vary according to the individual patient, but they should generally seek to assess any adverse effects, confirm recognition by staff that seclusion can be traumatic, explain why it was necessary to institute seclusion, seek the patient's views (particularly in terms of possible alternatives to seclusion), jointly consider future alternative means by which the patient might express anger (without recourse to violence) and record any complaints or comments which the patient may wish to make.

## De Facto Seclusion

10.22 Seclusion is defined in the Code of Practice as "the supervised confinement of a patient in a room, which may be locked to protect others from significant harm" (19.16). Certain strategies for managing problem behaviour fall outside this definition, although they amount to what is, to all intent and purposes, 'de facto' seclusion. In some units, patients will be nursed in a room not specifically designated for seclusion, with the door unlocked (and possibly ajar) and with nursing staff observing from the corridor. However, the patient will not be allowed to leave the room unsupervised and is, therefore, effectively in a situation of seclusion. A few patients may present such disturbed and disruptive behaviour that it is necessary for staff to keep them segregated from fellow patients for periods in excess of 'time out' as described in the Code of Practice (18.9) and which again may be little different from seclusion.

**Visit to an NHS Trust; May 1997**

Commissioners were extremely concerned to note the high incidence of extended periods of restraint. Commissioners were told that a 16 year old woman had frequently been restrained for periods of an hour but, because SCIP (strategies in crisis intervention and prevention) rather than control and restraint procedures were used, these incidents were not recorded separately. In the six months prior to the visit, on one unit, there were over 30 occasions on which patients had been restrained for ten minutes or more and on one occasion for two hours. Often restraint was accompanied by the use of anti-psychotic medication. In view of the possible side effects of such medication when patients are highly aroused, Commissioners queried whether the hospital managers were satisfied that these procedures were the safest way of managing such patients.

In addition, patients were frequently nursed in their rooms. The young woman referred to above had spent periods of several days in her room. Although the Commission was aware that this was only a temporary management strategy while a more appropriate placement was found, they undertook to raise the issue of suitable provision for difficult to manage adolescents with the NHSE Regional Office.

On Runis Unit there were incidents of patients being restrained if they tried to leave their rooms during a 15 minute period when they were required to calm down. At times this period was referred to as "Time Out" but there was no evidence of time out being used as part of a programme where the achievement of positive goals is as much part of the treatment plan as reducing unwanted behaviour (Code of Practice, 18.9). In view of the very limited use of seclusion, Commissioners wondered whether these procedures were being used as an alternative, but were concerned that the monitoring and involvement of other professionals, which is required for the protection of the patient in the use of seclusion, was not taking place.

It was suggested that clear procedures be adopted to record the consent of patients to behavioural treatments.

In a subsequent visit in May, 1998, Commissioners noted that restraint techniques were generally well recorded and were never applied for more than 15 minutes.

10.23 According to the definition in the Code of Practice, if a patient is not being supervised or is in solitary confinement as part of a behaviour modification programme, he or she is not being secluded. The issue is whether the patient is being confined to a particular room, not the length of time or whether the room within which the patient is being isolated is also a bedroom. Nor is it helpful to distinguish between seclusion and 'time-out'. The element of deprivation of liberty is the same and both may involve the detention and restraint of an individual. Indeed short term seclusion is sometimes referred to as 'time out' or 'cooling down' (Gostin, 1986).

10.24 Where a serious incident cannot be managed by talking with and calming the patient, the Commission recognises that procedures which remove a patient from the environment contributing to the disturbance can, in certain circumstances, have advantages over other methods of restraint, such as emergency medication (Rangecroft et al, 1997). But such restrictive situations should be subject to rigorous control and audit, whether or not they are defined as seclusion, and should have similar requirements in terms of documentation and both clinical and managerial supervision as for seclusion itself. To avoid confusion in the use of terms, the Commission suggests that consideration be given to restoring the term "solitary confinement" to describe all situations in which a patient is isolated in a room at any time of day or night so that he or she is unable to leave that room at will.

10.25 The Commission has suggested as part of its submission for the review of the legislation that the practice of seclusion and related procedures (i.e. solitary confinement) and also the use of physical restraint, including the locking of doors, should be subject to greater statutory regulation. Whatever the outcome of the review, these procedures should be regularly reviewed and audited by senior management and subsequent reports considered by Trust Boards.

## The Use of CS Spray

10.26 There are occasions when mental health practitioners cannot manage a disturbance without the assistance of the police. Among the tools of control which the police have at their disposal is CS spray. There are a number of concerns which have been raised with the Commission about the use of CS spray in relation to those with mental health problems (see 10.2, Gwynned example and also in the Seventh Biennial Report, pp. 50/51). Some issues that require further exploration are:

- the possibility of adverse reactions between CS spray and psychiatric medication;

- the different effects on patients with different psychiatric disorders (there is anecdotal evidence that CS spray may be less effective on patients in a manic state);

- the need for guidance on the mental health assessment of persons who have been sprayed (how long do the effects last?);

- whether there are any longer term effects, including psychological as well as physical problems;

- the use in enclosed spaces and possible cross-contamination, for example of ward staff and other patients;

- the nursing procedures which should be used to mitigate the immediate after-effects of the spray; and

- variations in use between different police forces and the reasons.

10.27 It is understandable that when the police are called in to deal with potentially dangerous situations on psychiatric wards or in the community, they will expect to be able to adopt what they regard as the most practical and safest methods of control. On the other hand, because of its ease of use, there is a concern that police may be inclined to use CS spray not as a last resort and in place of other less potentially harmful techniques to de-escalate and defuse potential violence. While the decision to use CS spray ultimately lies with the police, consultation should take place with mental health professionals when police are called in to mental health units. In the case of ASWs calling for intervention by the police, the ASW has the overall professional responsibility for co-ordinating the process of assessment under the Act and CS spray should, therefore, be used only after consultation with the ASW.

10.28 There is a need for policies agreed between the police and mental health services about how to handle contingencies involving the possible use of CS spray, when police are called both to in-patient units and to assist in Mental Health Act assessments and conveying to hospital. A survey on the use of CS spray on NHS premises revealed that, out of 35 Trusts with experience of patients having been sprayed either before admission or while an in-patient, only one Trust had produced guidelines on the use of CS spray on NHS premises and two on the handling of patients on whom the spray had been used (Bell and Thomas, 1998).

10.29 The formulation of local policies is handicapped by the apparent lack of consensus about what amounts to good practice. The Commission welcomes, therefore, the convening by the Royal College of Psychiatrists of a series of meetings in which the Association of Chief Police Officers (ACPO) and various mental health organisations, including the Commission, are represented. ACPO reported to this group that it intends to update the existing guidelines on CS spray and include mental health issues as a component.

## Substance Misuse

10.30 The use and misuse of drugs and alcohol is a growing problem for all mental health services, but poses particularly difficult clinical and managerial problems for inpatient psychiatric services. Given that the population of psychiatric wards is disproportionately young, male and socially disadvantaged, one might expect that drug misuse in them would equal, if not outstrip, the general trend. In addition, there is a significant and apparently increasing association between substance misuse and psychiatric disorders, especially schizophrenia, and there is also an increased risk of relapse because the rate of non-compliance with treatment increases greatly in patients who use illicit drugs and alcohol (NHS Health Advisory Service, 1996, Gourney et al, 1997, Weaver, 1999). In a Royal College of Nursing survey of mental health nurses, 68% of 187 respondents reported illicit drug use in their unit and the problem seemed to be as widespread in rural as in urban areas (Sandford, 1995). It is not surprising that the Commission is finding that it has become common for drug misuse to be raised as a concern in units visited.

> Visit to Dudley Priority Health; 24 October 1997
>
> On one ward staff reported their concern about the impact of the substance misuse patients on the running of the ward with regard to crowding, clinical responsibility when dedicated staff are not available and the effects of intoxicated behaviour on their patients. The Commissioners recommended that the Trust consider reviewing whether these beds were appropriately located.

Visit to Tameside and Glossop Community and Priority Services NHS Trust; 11 December 1997

Commissioners pointed to the urgent need for the managers to complete their review of the Trust's observation policy in light of the identified difficulties in managing patients with dual diagnosis. Commissioners were informed by staff of the current difficulties experienced in maintaining a therapeutic environment when illicit drugs were being brought to the ward. Although the Commission learned after the visit that an illicit drugs policy had been in place for some months, Commissioners on the visit had pointed to a need for clear guidelines for staff on this issue. The Trust agreed to address the staff's understanding and personal responsibilities in respect of this policy.

10.31 These and other reports testify to the risks posed by the integration of patients with substance misuse problems (both drugs and alcohol) with other mentally disordered patients. Apart from the potentially harmful effects for the individual patients, substance misuse can have an unsettling effect on the ward regime and lead to conflict between staff and patients and amongst the patients themselves. In extreme circumstances, there may be concerns about the actual physical safety of staff and patients arising from the effects of intoxication, possibly worsened when combined with psychiatric symptoms and medication and the aggressive and anti-social behaviour associated with certain aspects of substance abuse. Furthermore, there may be limited access to substance misuse services for mentally ill patients and advice and consultation for staff about how to manage the problems. If anything, there may be even greater non-availability of specialist substance misuse services for mentally ill people who are already in the care of the generic mental health services. It is almost as if treatment in one setting by one part of a mental health service reduces rather than enhances the prospect of gaining access to other service elements (Cohen et al, 1999).

10.32 One imaginative approach that has been adopted in some units, as part of their strategy to address the consumption of alcohol and illegal drugs by patients, is the introduction of a treatment contract. Each patient is asked to sign a treatment contract or declaration, giving an undertaking not to use alcohol or illegal drugs on the ward, consenting to staff searching possessions on suspicion that the patient has brought alcohol or drugs on the ward and agreeing to provide blood, urine and breath samples when asked by staff. Successful implementation of this approach requires measures to be taken to ensure that both staff and patients fully understand the policy. There would also need to be a range of options which could be considered if there is evidence of substance misuse, such as an increase in observation levels, restrictions on leave, more frequent property searches, limits on visits and discharge or, for detained patients, transfer to higher security wards.

10.33 Where a treatment contract has been introduced, patients are reported to accept the policy as part of the admission process and tend to adhere to it during their hospital stay. But such contracts lack legal force and their success depends on the patient's co-operation, which may not always be forthcoming. Even allowing for the ruling in the Broadmoor case, the personal search of a patient or his possessions (including urine screening) without consent and without lawful authority would constitute a trespass to the person. However, Jones (1996, 6-241) submits that "a search would be lawful if there were reasonable grounds for suspecting that the patient was in the possession of substances or articles that could be used to harm himself or other people .... or was in possession of a controlled drug in contravention of the Misuse of Drugs Act 1971". Furthermore, where it is suspected that a patient may be under the influence of illicit drugs, the obvious dangers – such as the possibility of such substances reacting with prescribed medication or the possibility of other deleterious consequences of drug use – would justify the Responsible Medical Officer, under the common law duty of care to the patient, considering carrying out some investigation such as urine sampling.

10.34 The RCN survey cited earlier (see 10.30) showed that, of the 68% of respondents who reported incidents of illicit drug and alcohol use in their units, almost half had no policy guidelines to assist them in dealing with the problem. The Commission frequently recommends that hospitals should consider the production of a policy with well defined rules governing the management and control of substance misuse. Where policies and guidelines do exist, they may be unclear or not adhered to consistently and patients or even staff may be unaware of their existence. The following are examples of common failings.

- It is not clear whether the policy applies equally to alcohol, the hidden use of which can pose as many risks to mentally disordered patients as illicit drugs.

- It is not clear how patients will be informed of the policy of not allowing illegal drugs on the premises and the position with regard to alcohol use. Should not all patients be informed of the policy, in writing, before or on admission to the ward? This might also be extended to visitors.

- No advice is given to staff on what action they should take in the event of a refusal by the patient to be searched or to provide a urine test. It should also be noted that a positive urine test may identify drugs which could have been used prior to admission to hospital; traces of cannabis, for example, can be detected in samples up to 28 days after the drug was initially taken.

- There has been no consultation with the local police. The issue of how far confidentiality can and should be protected is subject to wide variations in practice. On Merseyside, guidelines establishing partnership with the police on substance misuse, have been in existence since 1995 and offer a high degree of protection for patient confidentiality at the same time as active police support and presence when required.

- There is widespread confusion about the 'misuse of drugs' legislation and especially about the rights of staff to seize hold and destroy substances. It is understood that Section 5 of the Misuse of Drugs Act 1971 provides protection in law for nurses, pharmacists and those responsible for the destruction of drugs to handle the substances.

- The differences in the application of the policy to informal and detained patients are not addressed; in particular whether treatment contracts can be used for detained patients when the ultimate sanction for breach of the rules, discharge, is not available.

10.35 Many units are struggling with the same difficulties and policies are being developed in a piecemeal way. The fact that many psychiatric wards have the characteristics of both closed and open institutions in that they contain voluntary and detained patients (some of whom are also forensic patients) increases the complexity of the problems raised by such control measures as searching, compulsory drug testing, the exclusion of visitors, confidentiality and cooperation with the police.

10.36 The Commission has suggested before (Seventh Biennial Report, p. 167) that there is an urgent need for central guidance to help the many incomplete and disparate efforts that are being made by providers to develop policies and procedures and to achieve consistency and greater effectiveness. One way forward could be to use the opportunities presented by the development and implementation of the National Service Framework and the inception of Clinical Governance to produce national guidelines for good practice in dealing with substance misuse in psychiatric units both for the institutions and the professions involved.

# Race and Culture

## Introduction

10.37 From the first Biennial Report onwards, the Commission has drawn attention to the inadequacy of the service response to the needs of detained patients from black and ethnic minority groups. A sample of points made is reprinted here.

### RACE AND CULTURE STATEMENTS FROM BIENNIAL REPORTS

**First Biennial Report 1983 - 85**
- suffered disadvantages additional to those commonly experienced by mentally ill people
- are detained disproportionately and in some cases inappropriately
- the lack of Commissioners from ethnic minority backgrounds

**Second Biennial Report 1985 - 87**
- alienation of Black staff
- no ethnic monitoring
- poor interpretation services

**Fifth Biennial Report 1991 - 93**
"The Commission view with concern the disadvantages that continue to be experienced by people from black and minority ethnic communities who come into contact with the mental health services."

**Sixth Biennial Report 1993 - 95**

"Black and minority ethnic groups continue to experience considerable disadvantages in the provision of mental health services because of the difficulty in obtaining treatment which is appropriate to their need."

**Seventh Biennial Report 1995 - 97**

Provision for patients from ethnic minority communities often remain basic, insensitive and piecemeal, leading to patients feeling alienated and isolated. It is dispiriting that the serious issues of inappropriate care and treatment of patients from black and ethnic minority communities, which were raised in previous Biennial Reports, continue to cause concern and to be noted in reports of Commission Visits.

10.38 It is clearly not enough merely to comment on these issues, and so the Commission Management Board decided on a more pro-active strategy within the context of the Commission's Equal Opportunities Policy (see 1.13 et seq.). In the last Biennial Report, the Commission announced that it was undertaking a phased programme of action on equal opportunities issues. For the first phase, three target areas were identified as a focus during visits. These were ethnic monitoring, racial harassment and the use of interpreters and all Commission members were to be given training to deal with these issues.

10.39 On May 11th 1999, the Commission conducted a National Visit (see 1.33), which included a systematic investigation of the three target areas to find out:

- whether services monitor the ethnicity, religion and language of detained patients and use this information for both clinical care and service planning

- whether patients whose first language is not English have access to appropriate interpreting facilities

- how incidents of racial harassment are recorded and responded to by staff and, where a policy on racial harassment is in place, how it is implemented.

## Ethnic monitoring

10.40 The collection of ethnic group data for all in-patients was made mandatory from April 1995 (EL (94) 77) and the Code of Practice (1.13) now states that there should be a system to monitor compulsory admissions by race and sex. Besides being examined as a theme in the National Visit, ethnic monitoring was also included as one of the items in the Commission 'Matters Requiring Particular Attention' (MRPA) procedure (see 3.36 et seq).

10.41 According to the information from the MRPA procedure, most Trusts collected ethnic data at unit level, but only 62% of ward notes scrutinised (n = 1276) recorded ethnicity. It is important for ward staff to have accurate information on ethnicity so that the everyday care of the patient is responsive to cultural preferences. Ethnicity cannot be assumed from appearance; staff must never record what they judge to be a person's ethnic group. This can result in inconsistent recording of ethnic data. For example the ethnic origin of one patient, who had an Irish mother and Jamaican father was described at different times as 'mixed race', 'white British' and 'British'. The identification must be based on the patient's perception of ethnicity, but no pressure must be put on patients to answer. On admission, the patient's mental state may prevent staff collecting the information about his or her ethnicity. There was evidence in the notes that this was the case for 69 (14%) patients where no ethnic category was recorded. While the patient may be approached at a more suitable time following admission, ethnic data should be collected once only per hospital episode of patient care.

10.42 The ONS categories (taken from the 1991 census) are to be used for ethnic monitoring with the two additional categories 'patient refused' and 'not collected'. Units have discretion on the type and degree of additional detail to be collected and used locally, provided that they are also able to report the data in the ONS format – so that national comparisons can be made. The Commission found in the MRPA procedure that about 75% of hospitals comply with ONS categories.

10.43 Ethnic monitoring is no more than a statistical exercise that by itself can achieve nothing. However, it is an essential tool to 'root out' discrimination, which is often covert and unintentional. Without ethnic monitoring, it is difficult to establish the nature and extent of inequality, the areas where action is most needed and whether measures aimed at reducing inequality are succeeding. The Commission is exploring through its National Visit II how hospitals are using ethnic monitoring to expose possible discriminatory or inappropriate services in a number of areas, including the number of informal and formal admissions, ECT, use of therapies and activities, seclusion, secure facilities, self harm, violent incidents, deaths, complaints and employment policies.

10.44 It is equally important to monitor rigorously in areas with a low ethnic minority population. Where there is less familiarity with the needs of ethnic minorities, there could be a greater risk of responding inappropriately. *Norfolk Mental Health Care NHS Trust* is an example of determined efforts being made to ensure good monitoring, although the black and Asian population is relatively low at 0.9 %. The Trust copied to the Commission an Ethnicity Project Report to the Trust Board meeting of 26th November 1998, which clearly outlined what had been achieved and the gaps which remained. It recognised that the small size of the ethnic population and the relative inexperience and lack of understanding of staff, despite the best intentions, might cause some practical problems in responding to the diverse needs of the patient population.

10.45 For the past two years, the Commission has included in the 'Hospital Profile Sheet' an item on ethnicity and the use of the Mental Health Act. It is the first time that such information had been collected on a national scale. Hospitals were asked to record the number of patients who had been made subject to a Section of the Mental Health Act during 1996/7 and 1997/8. However, there may be some inconsistencies in the data, as some hospitals have returned the number of Mental Health Act admissions rather than the number of patients admitted in any one year. Consequently, the data needs to be interpreted with caution. At best, it gives an indication of trends in the use of the Act between different ethnic groups.

10.46 Hospital profile sheets were received from 437 hospitals in the first year and 363 in the following year. Of these, 350 (82%) and 314 (87%) respectively were able to provide ethnic data. The following table gives the breakdown of the figures where ethnicity is known compared to the 1991 census data on ethnicity in England and Wales.

**Table 18. Mental Health Act by Ethnicity in England and Wales**

| Ethnic Group | Mental Health Act data 1996/7 (n= 29,426)* % | Mental Health Act data 1997/8 (n= 33,552)** % | Census data % |
|---|---|---|---|
| White | 84.0 | 83.3 | 94.5 |
| Black Caribbean | 5.4 | 6.2 | 0.9 |
| Black African | 2.7 | 2.5 | 0.4 |
| Black other | 1.8 | 2.0 | 0.3 |
| Indian | 1.7 | 1.6 | 1.5 |
| Pakistani | 1.3 | 1.0 | 0.9 |
| Bangladeshi | 0.4 | 0.6 | 0.3 |
| Chinese | 0.3 | 0.3 | 0.3 |
| Other groups | 2.4 | 2.5 | 0.9 |

\* ethnicity not known (1996/7) = 2,102 – not included in table
\*\* ethnicity not known (1997/8) = 1,505 – not included in table

10.47 The use of the Act for black ethnic groups is over six times greater than the proportion of such groups in the population, while the use for Asian groups is roughly in line with the census. It should be noted that the detained patient and census population are not strictly comparable. There are a number of intervening demographic and socio-economic factors which could partly account for the over-representation of black ethnic groups. For example, allowance needs to be made for the younger age structure of ethnic minority populations and the fact that a greater proportion of detained patients are from younger age groups. However, there are a number of research studies which confirm the high use of the Act among African-Caribbean people and suggest that they are more likely to be seen by junior staff, be assessed as violent, and to be given 'physical treatments' with higher doses of medication with a greater likelihood of its being administered intramuscularly (Christie and Smith, 1997). A long-term follow-up study comparing African-Caribbean and White patients admitted to hospital with functional psychosis found that the African-Caribbean patients diagnosed with schizophrenia received more frequent and longer hospitalisations and more compulsory treatment than their white counterparts (Takei et al, 1998). It is also well documented that there is a disproportionate number of patients from some black and ethnic minority communities currently being treated in secure services. Black people, predominantly African-Caribbean, constitute 30% of the patient group in medium secure and 16% in high secure services[1].

10.48 The Commission welcomes an initiative by the Social Services Inspectorate to examine the role of Approved Social Workers with particular reference to the incidence of compulsory admissions of people from black and ethnic minority backgrounds. There will be a total of nine inspections planned to take place between December 1999 and March 2000. The findings, alongside the data being gathered by the Royal College of Psychiatrists' Research Unit's study on the way the Act is used (Marriott et al, 1998), should provide valuable background information for the mental health legislative review process.

## Racial Harassment

10.49 Racial harassment not only includes physical attacks on people but also verbal abuse and any other form of behaviour that deters people from using or participating in a particular service. Racial harassment can be deliberate and conscious, but it can also be unintentional such as banter which is insensitive to another person's feelings and is racially or culturally offensive.

10.50 The Department of Health has drawn up a plan to end racial harassment in the NHS by embarking on a zero tolerance campaign which would challenge racial harassment of both staff and patients with perpetrators facing the threat of prosecution (Dept. of Health 1999b). The Commission is contributing to this campaign by investigating, as part of the second National Visit, whether hospitals have a written policy dealing with racial harassment of patients from minority ethnic groups by other patients and any policies relating to ant-racist and anti-discriminatory practice for staff. The Commission is examining whether the policies are kept up to date and whether staff and patients are aware of them. Information has also been collected on any incidents of racial harassment and successes and difficulties which were experienced in dealing with them.

10.51 Both patients and staff may experience racial harassment. Patients may be harassed by other patients or by staff and staff by patients and other members of staff. A Trust may have policies which cover harassment in connection with employment practices, but not in relation to the care and treatment of patients. This was found to be the case in the following example, which also illustrates the Commission's concerns about ethnic monitoring procedures.

---

[1] The Future Provision of Secure Psychiatric Services for Black People: A consultation event held by the HSPCB on 4th September, 1997

Visit to Huddersfield NHS Trust - Mental Health Services Directorate at St Luke's Hospital; 22 December 1997

Staff assured Commissioners that any form of harassment would be dealt with as a matter of urgency. Commissioners were given a copy of a "Harassment Policy" in respect of staff. However, the Trust did not appear to have a written policy or procedures to deal with such issues pertaining to patients. Commissioners suggested that the Trust should consider developing a specific policy to address these important issues.

The old psychiatric in-patient identification sheets did not have a space for recording a patient's ethnicity (many were also badly photocopied which made reading difficult).

Commissioners suggested that the Patient Profile sheet should be amended to include an accurate recording of a patient's language, i.e. mother tongue.

Commissioners also suggested that staff should consistently and accurately record a patient's ethnic group e.g. Pakistani, Indian, Bangladeshi and not simply state "Asian".

## Use of Interpreters

10.52 It is always preferable for patients to communicate to a mental health professional who is able to understand their culture and language and providers, and indeed the Commission, should seek to recruit staff from relevant backgrounds. However, there is likely to be a continuing need for interpreters, who should be given training in mental health situations, as should staff in the use of interpreters.

10.53 The principle of ensuring effective communication with the patient is enshrined in Section 13(2) of the Act:

"Before making an application for the admission of a patient to hospital an approved social worker shall interview the patient in a suitable manner ..."

Prominence is given to issues of communication in the first chapter of the revised Code of Practice, where it is stated:

"Local and Health Authorities and Trusts should ensure that ASWs, doctors nurses and others receive sufficient guidance in the use of interpreters and should make arrangements for there to be an easily accessible pool of trained interpreters. Authorities and Trusts should consider cooperating in making this provision." (1.4)

The lack of interpreters has sometimes created difficulties on Commission visits.

Visit to Newham Community Health NHS Trust (East Ham Memorial Hospital); 10 And 23 July 1998

The Commission was concerned that one patient who wished to see the Commission on the date of its first visit was unable to do so because no interpreter was available. This raised issues wider than the Mental Health Act Commission visit, including the question of her ability to communicate with staff and for staff to communicate with her on a day to day basis. The Commission advised against relying on a family member to interpret and asked that consideration be given to the provision of regular interpreters for those patients for whom there is no staff member who is able to communicate with them directly. Due to the lack of an interpreter on the day of their visit, the Commission had to arrange a further visit to the unit to see the patient. The Trust informed the Commission that it was "dismayed...by the plight of" the patient concerned and that interpreters were usually available. The managers informed the Commission that the acute services manager would look into the matter.

10.54 The Commission explored a wide range of issues on the use of interpreters on National Visit II, which included questions on:

- policies on accessing and using interpreters and staff awareness of them;

- the availability of interpreters for all staff, including social workers, doctors nurses, therapists and advocates and whether they can be called upon out-of-hours i.e. at night and weekends;

- the familiarity of interpreters with mental health issues and the ward;

- whether staff are trained to use interpreters effectively; and

- the adequacy of the budget and access to it.

## Commission Visiting

10.55 The Commission undertook two pilot visits during 1998 focussing on issues affecting the care and of black and minority ethnic patients with a view to improving the way it addresses the needs of such patients during the course of its regular visiting programme. The following are illustrations of the successes and difficulties found in a medium secure unit. The unit is not identified in this example as the visit was intended as much as an exercise to help the Commission consider how to address race and cultural issues on Commission visits as it was to provide feedback to the Trust on the service. In fact, Commissioners found many aspects of the service to be positive and creative and commended the staff on the initiatives taken.

Resources were allocated to enhance the service provided to patients from black and ethnic minority groups, most notably in the development of menus, the display of culturally specific and positive images on the walls of the wards, the occupational therapy and activity programme and in the provision of interpreters. However, it was noted, as the following points testify, that there were discrepancies between what was intended and what was actually achieved.

- Weekly newspapers and magazines were purchased for particular ethnic groups but patients might only see them if they attended the 'Current Affairs Group', as they were not found to be generally available on the ward.

- Zee T.V for Asian patients was introduced in the video room, but there was a lack of awareness among ward managers about its availability.

- Halal and African-Caribbean food was being introduced on the menu, but the Trust also needed to prepare for an increased demand for such food from patients from all ethnic groups, increasing catering costs.

- The Trust had asked the shop run by independent contractors to stock cosmetic / toiletry products for African-Caribbean patients, but there had been no response from the shop.

- Much effort had been taken to organise a programme of multi-faith worship, but there were no notices displaying the arrangements for multi-faith worship on any of the wards visited.

- There was no black hairdresser and so patients using the existing hairdressing service had to "tell her what to do".

- It was agreed that monthly telephone contact could be made by one patient, whose parents had returned to the West Indies, but the patient had not been encouraged to make full use of this opportunity.

- The recording of ethnicity on the wards was not consistent in the categories used and did not always match the data held centrally.

- The use of seclusion had been ethnically monitored over a three year period but more detailed analysis of the findings to identify how percentages related to the patient population in general was needed. Ethnicity was not routinely recorded in other matters such as untoward incidents.

- The training programmes did not clearly indicate how race and culture issues were incorporated into training sessions, such as whether training on risk assessment included considerations of the perceptions of certain groups in society as being violent and aggressive.

- The establishment of an Ethnic Development Group was a positive initiative, but there was a lack of clarity about the remit of the group and the commitment to it from senior levels in the Trust.

- Racial and cultural needs were not routinely identified at the level of individual care planning. This was because care planning was problem-led, which meant that social and cultural needs were only recorded when they were a problem area.

10.56 The above points were made in the spirit of constructive criticism in a Trust where there was an impressive development of culturally sensitive services. The Chief Executive of the Trust also expressed a commitment to address the matters raised. They are outlined here to demonstrate the range of issues and the rigour needed in ensuring that not only are race and culture policies in place but that they are implemented and monitored in all areas of the hospital.

# Women's Issues

## Declining Proportion of Detained Women Patients

10.57 The proportion of women detained under Part II of the Act has declined from 57% to 46% over the past ten years. The number of women detained under Part III has always been relatively low; currently 13% of all admissions from court disposals are of women. On any one day, according to the Department of Health census on 31st March 1998, out of 11,350 detained patients in NHS Trust and private hospitals (excluding High Security Hospitals), 4,394 (39%) were women (Dept. of Health 1998b). Possible explanations for the declining proportion of women is that priority for scarce in-patient beds is being given to patients assessed as dangerous, who are more likely to be men, or there may be a reluctance to admit women to a ward environment where they may not feel safe. Whatever the reason, women will normally be in the minority on psychiatric wards as the vast majority of wards are of mixed gender. This has a number of consequences for the privacy, safety and care of women patients.

## The Physical Environment

10.58 The physical environment on mixed wards often does not help women feel safe. The Department of Health, in accordance with the Patient's Charter Standards, has set objectives for the provision of segregated washing and toilet facilities and good physical separation of sleeping accommodation, including safe facilities for men and women who are mentally ill (EL (97)3). An audit tool was introduced to assist Trusts in evaluating progress on delivering the objectives (HSC 1998/143). The Commission has also focused on these standards by including them in its 'Matters Requiring Particular Attention' procedure (see 3.36 et seq). The following table shows the responses to the questionnaire from visits made to 1128 wards with women assigned to them.

**Table 19. Ward arrangements/facilities for women**

| Arrangements/Facilities | n (%) |
| --- | --- |
| Wards with female nursing staff working at the time of the visit | 1113 (99%) |
| Wards with separately labelled facilities for the use of women:<br>Toilets<br>Bathroom(s) and/or Showers<br>Lounges | <br>750 (66%)<br>411 (48%)<br>120 (11%) |
| Wards with toilet cubicles with locks for the patients' use. | 1019 (90%) |
| Wards with bathrooms with locks for the patients' use. | 1005 (89%) |

10.59 Female staff were working on the shift during the time of the visit on nearly all the wards with women patients. About 90% of toilets and bathrooms have locks, but in 1998, when the procedure was completed, there were still one third of wards without gender specific toilets and half without gender specific bathrooms. Occasionally Commissioners have noted a complete absence of facilities for proper disposal of sanitary items in toilets used by women, which raises issues regarding dignity (do women have to ask for disposal facilities?) and hygiene.

10.60 The distress caused to women patients about the lack of privacy is illustrated in the following example.

> Visit to Camden & Islington Community Health Services NHS Trust (The Huntley Centre & St Pancras Hospital); 6 March 1998
>
> The Commission had raised the issue of gender-designated toilets and bathrooms on previous visits. They were told that the paper signs are torn down by patients; there were no signs on Laffan, New and Archway Wards. Signs were seen on some toilets on Cedar House, and there was one female toilet on Tredgold.
>
> On one ward, a patient complained to Commissioners about the lack of privacy in the bath and shower rooms, which were not gender designated. She was particularly distressed when men patients banged on the door when she was washing. She was also concerned that the only female designated toilet was at the other end of the ward from the female dormitory. She described her distress and embarrassment at having to walk through the communal areas and past the male dormitories in her nightdress in the evening and at night. Commissioners suggested that a staff toilet close to the female dormitory could be opened for womens' use during the night.
>
> Commissioners stressed the importance of this issue, especially as the toilet areas were not visible to nursing staff in the main ward areas. They reminded the Trust of the Patients' Charter and the Department of Health's Circular EL 97(3), stressing the importance of women patients' safety and privacy especially where a high proportion of psychiatric patients might have experienced abuse and harassment in the past. Plastic or wooden signs that cannot easily be removed by patients were suggested as a practical solution to the problem.
>
> Following the Visit, staff acted on the Commissioners' suggestion of allowing women patients access to the staff toilet at night and, on the next visit in September 1998, Commissioners were pleased to note that permanent signs were in place on many wards.

10.61 Older women tend to have less privacy, as it is easy for their dignity to be forgotten. Lakeside Mental Health Unit is an example of good practice in a new unit, but which is not extended to the ward for older patients (Dove Ward). Staff argue that there is no point in labelling toilets, as patients cannot understand because of their level of confusion and would not use gender specific facilities. But they can be helped by being given clear aids and prompts. This example also points to the problem for women patients on wards where they are in a small minority.

> **Visit to Lakeside Mental Health Centre, Hounslow and Spelthorne NHS Trust; 20 November 1997**
>
> Womens' toilet and bathroom facilities were designated in all the psychiatric wards but there were no separate bathrooms on Dove Ward. Commissioners were concerned at the lack of privacy for patients on Dove Ward where men's and women's sleeping areas were only separated by curtains.
>
> A woman on Finch Ward told Commissioners that she felt uncomfortable in the company of so many male patients but was only able to separate herself by staying in her bedroom. It was again suggested that some consideration be given to a women's sitting area.

10.62 There are problems in adapting some purpose built wards, which have been poorly designed from the point of view of women patients, but imaginative solutions can be found. Commissioners suggested that the poor environment at Ashford Hospital, for example, could be greatly improved by floor to ceiling partitions with doors.

> **Visit to Ashford Hospital, Hounslow & Spelthorne Community and Mental Health NHS Trust; 21 November 1997**
>
> Commissioners were gravely concerned that there had been no changes to the environment to provide privacy for women patients. On all wards women slept in dormitories that were separated from main thoroughfares only by curtains, providing no privacy. Women patients and a patient's relative complained vociferously about noise and the lack of privacy. Although bathrooms and toilets on Charlton and Grosvenor were designated for men and women, Commissioners were told that these designations were disregarded. There were no designated bathrooms on Halliford and no ward provided separate sitting areas for women. There were short term plans to provide some screening on Halliford but no firm dates could be given at the time of the visit, even for this very temporary solution. Commissioners commented that the presently planned screens might not preclude individuals standing on chairs to see over. There were no plans for locks to provide privacy and security.

10.63 Since this report, Hounslow and Spelthorne NHS Trust has made significant improvements and has shown that much can be achieved on a shoestring budget. Weller Wing, Bedford General Hospital is an example of an older site where imaginative use has been made of limited space. For example, particular lounges are designated for women only in the evenings, enabling women patients the opportunity to relax in dressing gowns, watch TV and socialise without male company.

10.64 Improvements made for women can also serve to highlight deficiencies in facilities for men patients.

> **Visit to Tower Hamlets Healthcare NHS Trust; 4 & 5 June 1998**
>
> Despite the difficulties in working within the structure of an old hospital, all wards have attempted to segregate sleeping areas for men and women with some success. This is to be commended. Access for women to bathrooms was still problematic on many wards, often involving either a long walk or movement through male areas.
>
> There was particularly good refurbishment of the female wing on Pinhey Ward which served to highlight the extremely poor physical state of the male sleeping areas on the same ward.

## Safety

10.65 Concerns about privacy and safety are even greater when there are few women patients on the ward. Women may prefer to stay in their bedroom, where they feel safer (see Lakeside Mental Health Centre example at 10.61). It is also a matter of special concern for Asian women, who may be particularly reluctant to be admitted to mixed accommodation. Gender issues are important when considering the needs of patients in secure units where women are in a minority and do not feel safe mixing with men whose behaviour is disturbed and possibly violent.

> **Visit to West London Healthcare NHS Trust and Ealing Social Services Department; 7, 13 & 14 November 1997**
>
> Commissioners were concerned at the numbers of wards in the Trust that have only one or two women residents. Patients (both men and women) raised concerns about the safety of women and the inappropriate sexual behaviour of some men.
>
> The Limes, Beverley and Campion Wards had no designated male and female facilities. Commissioners were informed that Campion had a largely Asian catchment area and that Asian women were generally unhappy to be admitted into the mixed sex facilities on the ward. Bevan Ward had no sanitary towel disposal and the womens' sleeping area was accessed through the day area. Not all the patients' rooms had locks. Three patients on one ward complained about other patients intruding into their bedrooms at night. The Trust has undertaken a pilot and Commissioners were told that locks would shortly be installed in all rooms.
>
> The care and safety of women at West London was a serious concern and the Commission urged that more appropriate facilities should be provided in advance of the planned separate secure facilities.
>
> The Commission raised these concerns with the Health Authority at a meeting on 13th February 1998 and asked for details and time scales within which improvements might be made.

10.66 There is a lack of awareness among some staff about the problems of placing women in vulnerable positions. The findings of the first National Visit highlighted a dissonance between views about sexual harassment and the evidence. Over 70 % of staff did not perceive sexual harassment to be much of a problem, but it was also found that problems of sexual harassment had occurred on over half the wards (Sainsbury Centre, 1996).

10.67 Insensitive handling of women patients by staff may heighten feelings of vulnerability. For example, men staff members will generally attend disturbances, but women patients, particularly those with experience of abuse, may find the experience of being restrained by men traumatising.

10.68 There is an under-reporting of these problems, because women tend not to use the complaints system. Staff may devalue incidents and dismiss complaints. If staff themselves are abused they are usually encouraged to report the incident, but patients are not given the same encouragement. Incidents should be recorded whether or not there has been a complaint. The *Reaside Unit, Birmingham* is to be commended for adopting the practice of recording verbal comments as well as more obvious harassment. The complaints system should be monitored to identify problems over the care and treatment of women patients.

### What Is Needed

10.69 In addition to the need for separate facilities for women, the Commission has identified some key factors as being of particular importance in the care and treatment of detained women patients.

10.70 Women should be able to:

- lock doors;
- have the choice of a female keyworker;
- be in contact with other women;
- have the opportunity to take part in women-only therapy groups and social activities;
- engage safely in the full range of activities, even when their number may be small;
- have physical health checks on admission;
- have access to a female doctor for medical care;
- have access to a female member of staff at all times; and
- be reassured that there is adequate staff supervision at night.

10.71 Mother and baby units need to be self-contained and separate from general psychiatric wards, although care should be taken that the mother does not feel isolated. There should be facilities available for children to visit. Bearing in mind the importance of the father bonding with the baby, it is good practice for there also to be facilities for the partner to stay over, if practicable – otherwise there may be problems when mother and baby return home. Health visiting staff should come into hospital and nursing staff should be trained and have skills in child care.

10.72 Specific policies or guidelines which relate to the safety of women patients should be available on every ward and be subject to review every two years. There should be identification and appropriate observation of women patients at risk or vulnerable to sexual exploitation and also of men who have a history of harassment or violence towards women. Complaints should be monitored to identify problems over the care and treatment of women patients and, whether or not there has been a complaint, all incidents of women patients being pestered or harassed should be recorded, including verbal comments. Restraint procedures on women should be carried out by female nursing staff, where possible. Staff training should cover the safety and special needs of women patients and a designated officer appointed to have oversight over womens' issues.

10.73 These suggestions were forwarded to the Department of Health for consideration as part of further guidance being issued on the provision of safe facilities for patients in hospital who are mentally ill which safeguard their privacy and dignity.

## Services for Children and Adolescents

### Gaps in Provision

10.74 The Commission's Seventh Biennial Report (p. 187-8) highlighted its concern over the uneven provision of services for the relatively few children and adolescents who are detained under the Act, which had sometimes led to the inappropriate placement of adolescents in adult facilities. The Government has acknowledged, in its response to the Health Committee on Health Services for Children and Young People's Report on Child and Adolescent Health Services, that child and adolescent mental health services (CAMHS) had been historically neglected[1] and has pointed to initiatives to remedy this. The National CAMHS Audit will identify the extent to which authorities commission and purchase comprehensive mental health services for children and adolescents and will report in Summer 1999 (Shaw, 1999). The third of four mental health objectives set in the National Priorities Guidance for 1999/00-2001/02 (Dept. of Health, 1998e), which for the first time combines guidance for the NHS and social services, is for the improved provision of appropriate, high-quality care and treatment for children and young people by building up locally based CAMHS. The objectives also include the aim that users of such services should be able to expect in-patient care in a specialist setting, appropriate to their age and clinical need.

---

[1] Dept. of Health (1997) Government Response to the Reports of the Health Committee on Services for Children and Young People, Session 1996-97: "The Specific Health Needs for Children and Young People" (307-1); "Health Services for Children and Young People in the Community, Home and School" (314-1); "Hospital Services for Children and Young People" (128-1); "Child and Adolescent Mental Health Services" (26-1). p.60

10.75 Whilst the Commission welcomes the action being taken to improve CAMHS provision, its experience in visiting hospitals in this reporting period demonstrates that much needs to be done.

---

### Visit to an NHS Trust in February 1998

The Commission expressed concerns about the detention of a 16 year old in an adult ward. Alongside the general inappropriateness of this placement, which was acknowledged by the hospital managers, Commissioners were concerned that the patient was not receiving appropriate education in accordance with the Code of Practice and had not received a visit from a priest, although it was understood that he was a practising Catholic. It was not clear from the patient records whether the parents had been informed of their rights in relation to discharge and appealing to the Mental Health Review Tribunal. Attention also needed to be paid to the hospital's handling of the patient's monies to ensure that he was not treated differently from other patients.

---

### Visit to an NHS Trust in October 1998

At the time of the Commission visit three adolescent patients (aged 16-18) were detained on adult acute wards. The managers and the Clinical Director agreed that these placements were unsatisfactory, both because of the unsuitability of the environment in which the adolescents were detained and because, in an acute ward with a bed occupancy that was running at up to 136%, their placement was blocking beds badly needed for other patients. The nearest adolescent unit was unable to deal with the demand for places from the hospitals in its surrounding area.

---

10.76 The Commission has also raised the issue of CAMHS provision at its meetings with social services departments.

---

### Visit to a Social Services Department in January 1998

Commissioners were very concerned to hear of the lack of an in-patient facility for young people detained under the Act. Local in-patient facilities were rarely able to admit detained patients, even in emergencies. On the day of the visit a bed was being sought for an 11 year-old.

The Commission has discussed the problems with Anglia and Oxford NHSE and North Thames NHSE at its annual meetings and learnt that a strategic review of CAMHS in the Anglia and Oxford Region had been completed in February 1998. The Commission will continue to closely monitor service provision for this group of patients.

---

10.77 It is apparent that independent healthcare providers are stepping in to fill some of the gaps in NHS services for children and adolescents:

Visit to Priory Healthcare (Grovelands Priory Hospital); 4 December 1998

On their visit in June 1998 Commissioners were pleased to hear that the unit had increased its facilities for adolescents, with the appointment of a new specialist consultant and the specification of a wing in one of the wards for adolescent services. Commissioners noted that the adolescent service provision was continuing to develop when they visited in December 1998. The wing was then being reconfigured to provide separate facilities for adolescents, including a teaching room, recreation room and separate living room with a non-smoking area. An adolescent co-ordinator had been appointed, who had responsibilities for contact with the local authority education and children's Services. The appointment of a teacher to provide three educational sessions per week was planned.

10.78 The Commission is also aware of some encouraging strategies aimed at ensuring that, where the admission of adolescents to adult wards is unavoidable, the best possible care is made available to them. *The Talygarn Unit, Gwent Healthcare NHS Trust*, has operated a joint procedure with Child and Adolescent Mental Health Services from May 1998. The Talygarn Unit has been identified as the chosen link ward for the emergency admission of adolescents due to the suitability of its environment, central position within Gwent and staff profile. The Unit has access to a designated pool of child and adolescent bank nurses for whom training, including training in the Children Act, is provided. Upon the request of any Gwent child psychiatrist, a bed and specialist nurse cover is arranged and the adolescent is assigned a nursing key-worker from the ward. Daily assessment by the child psychiatrist or a designated junior is provided to the patient and is recorded. All nursing staff working with the adolescent are treated as a part of the ward team and cover for observations is rotated, so as to reduce the stress to staff from being with a patient for long periods of time and to prevent the isolation of either the patient or nursing staff. An on-call child psychiatrist is available for queries and advice out-of-hours and an identified clinical services manager provides the same at other times. A discharge summary is placed in the patient's CAMHS notes on discharge from the unit. While the aim must be to provide treatment in a more appropriate setting as soon as is practically possible, the joint procedure between the Talygarn Unit and Gwent CAMHS would seem to be a useful model of how adult wards may attempt to meet the specific needs of children and adolescents.

## The Mental Health Act 1983 and the Children Act 1989

10.79 In its last Biennial Report (pp. 46-7) the Commission recommended more extensive Code of Practice guidance on the choice between using the Children Act 1989 or the Mental Health Act 1983 as a means of providing secure accommodation and/or compulsory treatment for children and adolescents. The revised Code of Practice (31.3) now contains such guidance, although it acknowledges the complexity of the legal framework for the admission to hospital of children and adolescents and recommends that professional staff who address this question should have access not only to the relevant information and statutory provisions, but also to competent legal advice. The revised Code of Practice also highlights the importance of the role of those with parental responsibility in making decisions on the care and treatment of children and adolescents.

### Children and Adolescents in Future Mental Health Legislation.

10.80 In its submission to the Mental Health Legislation Review, the Commission argued that future mental health legislation should contain specific provisions for children and adolescents. New mental health legislation could enshrine general principles of care analogous to those in the Children Act 1989, such as a principle that children should be treated in environments that are developmentally appropriate and managed by staff with relevant training. Further principles within which such legislation could be framed could promote the expectation that professionals take account of the position of children within their families, including the nature and role of parental responsibilities. The Commission also welcomed the opportunity given by the review of mental health legislation to recommend that selected parts of extant case-law should be brought into statute and thus consolidate the legal position of the ability of minors to consent, or refuse consent, to admission to and treatment in hospital.

## Services for Patients with Learning Disabilities

### Environmental Standards

10.81 Generally, the Commission has found good quality provision in units for people with learning disabilities detained under the Act, some examples of which are given below. There is a need for flexible staffing arrangements to respond to the needs of individual patients who require high levels of observation.

> Visit to East Surrey Priority Care NHS Trust; 30 September 1997
>
> The Trust's various in-patient facilities for people with learning disabilities provide a good environment for patients, a varied programme of activities utilising local community resources where available, good individual care plans for patients, constructive links with a specialist advocacy service and good staff training. Overall, patients are being provided with a high standard of care in pleasant surroundings.

> Visit to The Pembrokeshire & Derwen NHS Trust; 3, 4, 5 September 1997
>
> Bro Myrddin Assessment and Treatment Unit
> This newly built four bedded locked unit for patients with learning disability and challenging behaviour had two patients in the unit at the time of the visit, one of whom was cared for in a special suite of rooms. The unit appeared to be well staffed and the member of staff in charge was well versed in the requirements of the Mental Health Act.

West Wales Hospital
Teilo Ward, a 28 bedded acute unit for adults includes a four bedded dual diagnosis unit (Mental Illness and Learning Disability). The ward operates at a high bed occupancy. It appears to provide a high standard of care, and several patients spoke highly of the care they received. On the dual diagnosis unit, there can be problems with nurse staffing levels when the need for nursing observation and care is high.

10.82 However, in a few units for patients with learning disabilities, Commissioners have found very poor environments. There were grave concerns at the conditions in the *Coleridge Road Assessment and Treatment Unit at Forest Healthcare Trust*, which was described in the Commission report of an unannounced visit of 18th September, 1997 as "*totally unsuitable for detained patients*". There were problems with regard to fire safety, kitchen hygiene, a discarded fridge and dishwasher and other rubbish dumped in the hallway, broken light fittings with exposed live wires, no toilet seats or toilet rolls (patients have to request toilet paper), broken furniture, dining room walls being extremely dirty, piles of accumulated rubbish in the garden and only one trained nurse on duty during the night with two untrained nurses. Following this and a subsequent unannounced visit in January 1998, the Trust was commended for extensive improvements at Coleridge Road.

10.83 There are some individuals who present exceptional challenges to services because of their behaviour. It has been estimated that over the whole country about 20 adults with a learning disability per 100,000 total population present a significant challenge. Only a few of these will present such a challenge more or less all of the time. Most challenging behaviour will be intermittent depending on changes in circumstances and how well services meet associated needs (Mansell, 1993). The implications for services are that care and treatment should be highly individualised to meet the widely differing needs of people in this group. It is alarming that some specialist in-patient units do not have adequate policies and procedures to cope with behaviour of an exceptionally challenging nature. One Trust, for example, lacked any clear guidance on matters relating to patients' sexuality and was unable to provide suitable facilities for two patients, who had to be separated from other patients because of their inappropriate and unpredictable sexual behaviour. The Trust resorted to re-opening a disused and most unsuitable villa to accommodate them.

Visit to an NHS Trust in July 1997
On visiting one particular villa Commissioners were shocked by the poor environment. The villa was shabby and in a serious state of disrepair, plaster having fallen off internal walls. There were no curtains in the villa either in the patients' bedrooms, bathroom or lounge and there was minimal furniture. At the time of the visit, patients' files were being kept on the table in the patient's lounge, thus raising issues of confidentiality. Staff informed Commissioners that when they had moved into the villa it was extremely dirty and that they had worked very hard to make the villa habitable for the patients.

> The use of the villa raised the following serious issues:-
>
> At the time of the visit, the environment provided by the villa was not of an acceptable standard for patients or for staff to work in. It was the Commissioners' view that alternative accommodation should be found for the patients.
>
> The villa did not have any permanent nursing staff, as these are drawn from other parts of the hospital on an ad hoc basis. Commissioners seriously questioned whether the hospital could properly assess the patients under such conditions. It was their view that the only treatment the patients were receiving was containment.
>
> At the subsequent Commission visit, one patient still remained in the villa, but alternative accommodation was being arranged through an extra contractual referral and then the villa would not be used again because of its poor environment. This could mean that the patient may be placed at considerable distance from home, which, in turn, may present a new set of problems.

10.84 The monitoring of standards in units which take patients from a wide geographical area can be complex, because of the number of authorities purchasing services. Furthermore, there is no systematic inspection system for NHS units as there is for independent nursing homes. *Calderstones NHS Trust* can have upwards of 100 purchasing authorities and it emerged at a Commission meeting with the Trust on 10th February 1998 that a service specification had not been produced by purchasers nor did they undertake routine quality monitoring visits. This meeting, which included representatives from the NHS Executive and East Lancashire and Manchester Health Authorities, had been called to discuss emerging themes of concern arising from recent Commission reports from visits to the Trust. These included:

- *the need for adequate completion of patients' legal documentation;*
- *the need for individual care and treatment plans to be agreed by a multi-disciplinary team and properly recorded;*
- *the requirement of appropriate discharge planning; and*
- *the requirement that patients have regular contact with their RMO.*

*It was noted that the senior hospital management team were committed to the provision of an extended service at Calderstones Hospital and making it into a centre of excellence. The plan was to concentrate on increasing the bed numbers for the forensic service and for people with challenging behaviour with up to 70 beds on Chestnut Drive and 70 beds on West Drive. These would be supported by additional facilities in the community. The latter was particularly important, as there currently appeared to be a gap between being cared for in the community and medium secure type provision. Patients were being referred to specialist units, whether or not they needed that level of security.*

## Advocacy and the Giving of Information

10.85 The Calderstones meeting also highlighted the need for an independent advocacy service. An assertive advocacy service is all the more important for this group of patients, who, because of the nature of their disabilities, have a less powerful user voice. Advocates can support patients in the formulation of complaints that they wish to make and may also be present at, or prepare users, for Commission visits.

10.86 The legal position and rights under the Act need to be explained in a way that patients can understand. The Commission has distributed a poster using Makaton signs for display in learning disability units to notify patients of forthcoming Commission visits. On a visit to Stallington Hall, the Commission commended *North Staffordshire Trust* on its plans to develop leaflets explaining patients' rights under Section 132 of the Act in language that would be easily understood by people with learning disability.

10.87 Attention also needs to be paid to the giving of information to patients who cannot read, often older patients. However, there is a limit to the number of attempts which should be made to explain rights to patients who have severe learning disabilities and are not considered to have the capacity to understand. The attempts should be clearly recorded but the Commission has advised, in such cases, that they may be discontinued after two attempts have been made.

10.88 Good practice was noted at Rockingham Forest NHS Trust, which has made leaflets in braille available.

> Visit to Rockingham Forest NHS Trust  Adult Mental Illness Directorate; 16 May 1997
>
> Commissioners commended the Trust on making available a Braille copy of the rights leaflet. They drew attention to a partially sighted patient with learning disability who was very persistent in expressing her wish to leave and asked that she be helped to make an appropriate appeal against her detention. The Trust was reminded of the importance of providing assistance and, where appropriate, advocacy support for patients who wish to be discharged but who cannot pursue their rights of appeal without help.

## Specialist Expertise in Learning Disability

10.89 The revised Code of Practice has strengthened the recommendation that patients should not be classified as mentally impaired without an assessment by a consultant psychiatrist in learning disabilities and a formal psychological assessment. ASWs should also have experience of working with people with learning disabilities or be able to call upon someone who has. Finding the appropriate specialist can present difficulties, as is shown in the following example, about which the Commission was informed via correspondence. The patient was held under Section 136 for 45 hours waiting for an assessment and then a hospital bed. The patient had mild learning difficulties and a diagnosis of autism. He was arrested after an attack with a screwdriver on a social worker. At the time of the incident, the patient was also having hallucinatory experiences.

| | | |
|---|---|---|
| *Day one:* | *12.26* | *Detention authorised* |
| | *13.50* | *Seen by forensic medical examiner who made the assessment that it was appropriate for him to be detained.* |
| | *18.45* | *Review of detention. Patient no longer held in custody for an offence but held under Section 136.* |
| | *19.10* | *On-call psychiatrist telephoned and requested to make a Mental Health Act assessment. He refused and said he would try to find a psychiatrist with appropriate specialisation in learning disabilities. This did not materialise.* |
| *Day two:* | *02.00* | *Custody Sergeant decided that there was no other option to the patient remaining in the custody block overnight.* |
| | *18.00* | *Psychiatrist and ASW attended the police station to undertake a Mental Health Act assessment.* |
| | *20.32* | *Psychiatrist finally found a bed but could not be admitted until following day.* |
| *Day three:* | *09.30* | *Patient left police station for hospital.* |

10.90 The inability of the on-call psychiatric service to provide a speedy assessment for patients with learning disability, is discriminatory. The onus of finding a suitable placement, in the context of a bed shortage for patients who combine mental illness with learning disability and who pose a risk to staff and the public, is another reason which may have been deterring psychiatrists from responding to the referral. While the Code of Practice states that a specialist assessment should also be carried out where it is proposed that a mentally impaired patient is to be admitted under Section 2 on the grounds of mental disorder, it is recognised that there are emergency situations which would preclude this.

10.91 Skilled multi-disciplinary input is required in specialist units for the treatment of behavioural problems. Patients are placed in specialist nursing homes, often at a considerable distance from their home and family, because the local service has been unable to offer a suitable programme. However, when called to some mental nursing homes, Second Opinion Appointed Doctors have encountered difficulty in finding a professional from a discipline other than nursing or medicine, with whom to consult (Code of Practice, 16.31b). This begs the question where the specialist input comes from if there is no clinical psychologist, occupational therapist or other suitable professional.

## De Facto Detention

10.92 The Bournewood case (see 2.12 et seq.) has served to highlight the position of informal patients who lack capacity but are not allowed to leave the unit because of their vulnerability. It is not unusual for units which cater for residents with severe learning disabilities and challenging behaviours to keep the door to the accommodation permanently locked. The residents in these units are not usually detained under the Act, despite their freedom of movement being curtailed and their receiving medication for mental disorder. The Commission advises that where the patient is not capable of giving informed consent and the conditions for admission under the Act can be satisfied, detention under the Act should be considered. This would provide the safeguards of regular independent review by the Mental Health Review Tribunal and for a Second Opinion where required under the provisions of Section 58. These safeguards were regarded as being of considerable benefit to Mr L, the patient concerned in the Bournewood case, by his carers, Mr and Mrs E., who wrote to the Guardian on 30 June 1998, as follows:

*"Had it not been for ... the Appeal Court, L would never have been allowed home. However, the rights afforded him under the Mental Health Act when the hospital 'legalised their position' allowed him to achieve his discharge from the hospital back to his home with us where, in just a few days, he made the most remarkable recovery".*

# References

Banerjee, S., Bingley, W. & Murphy, E. (1995) *Deaths of Detained Patients: A Review of Reports of the Mental Health Act Commission.* London: Mental Health Foundation.

Beck, A., Croudace, T., Singh, S. & Harrison G. (1997) "The Nottingham Acute Bed Study: Alternatives to acute psychiatric care". *British Journal of Psychiatry*, 170, pp. 247-252.

Bell, F. & Thomas, B (1998) "Police use of CS spray: Implications for NHS mental health services". *Mental Health Care* 1 no. 12. pp. 402-4.

Bhatti, V., Kenney-Herbert, J., Cope, R. & Humphreys, M. "Knowledge of current mental health legislation among medical practitioners approved under section 12(2) of the Mental Health Act 1983 in the West Midlands." *Health Trends*, 30 no. 4 pp 106-8.

Blom-Cooper, L. et al (1995) *The Falling Shadow: One Patient's Mental Health Care.* London: Duckworth.

Brugha T S., Wing J K. & Smith B L. (1989) "Physical Health of the Long-term Mentally Ill in the Community. Is there unmet need?" *British Journal of Psychiatry*, 155, pp. 777-781.

Clements, L (1999) "Where does duty begin?" *Community Care* 21-27th January, p 26.

Cohen, J., Runciman, R. & Williams, R. (1999) "Substance Use and Misuse in Psychiatric Wards". *Drugs: education, prevention and policy*, vol 6, no.2.

Christie, Y. & Smith, H. (1997) "Mental Health and Its Impact on Britain's Black Communities". *The Mental Health Review*, 2 issue1 pp. 5-18.

Davenport, A. (1999) "Random Searches of Detained Patients". *Journal of Mental Health Law*, 1, pp. 59-61

Department of Health (1990) *The Care Programme Approach for People with a Mental Illness Referred to the Specialist Psychiatric Services.* HC(90) 23/LASSL(90)11. London: HMSO.

Department of Health (1993) *Legal Powers on the Care of Mentally Ill People in the Community. Report of the Internal Review.*

Department of Health (1995) *Building Bridges: A Guide to Arrangements for Inter-Agency Working for the Care and Protection of Severely Mentally Ill People.* London: HMSO

Department of Health (1998a) *In-Patients Formally Detained in Hospitals under the Mental Health Act 1983 and other Legislation, England: 1991-92 to 1996-97.* Statistical Bulletin 1998/01.

Department of Health (1998b) *In-Patients Formally Detained in Hospitals under the Mental Health Act 1983 and other Legislation, England: 1987-88 and 1992-93 to 1997-8.* Statistical Bulletin 1998/34.

Department of Health (1998c) *Modernising Mental Health Services: Safe, Sound and Supportive.* London: Stationery Office.

Department of Health (1998d) *Information for Health - An Information Strategy for the Modern NHS 1998-2005.* NHS Executive.

Department of Health (1998e) *Modernising Health and Social Services: National Priorities Guidance 1999/00-2001/02.* LAC(98)22

Department of Health: Local Authority Personal Social Services Statistics (1998) *Guardianship under the Mental Health Act 1983: England 1998.*

Department of Health (January 1999a) *Press Release: 'Nurses Make a Difference' Recruitment Campaign Launched.*

Department of Health (1999b) *Tacking Racial Harassment in the NHS - A Plan for Action.* HSC 1999/060

Department of Health (1999c) *Effective Care Co-ordination in Mental Health: Modernising the Care Programme Approach. A Policy Booklet. NHS Executive Consultation Paper.*

Eldergill A. (1997) *Mental Health Review Tribunals. Law and Practice.* Sweet and Maxwell.

Fallon, P. et al (1999) *Report of the Committee of Inquiry into the Personality Disorder Unit, Ashworth Special Hospital.* London: The Stationery Office.

Fulford, K.M. (1998) "Invited commentaries on: Mental health legislation is now a harmful anachronism". *Psychiatric Bulletin* 22 no. 11 pp.666-8.

Ford, R., Duncan, G., Warner, L., Hardy, P. & Muijen, M. (1998) "One day survey by the Mental Health Act Commission of acute adult psychiatric wards in England and Wales". *British Medical Journal*, 317, 1279-1283.

Freeman C P. (1995) "ECT in those under 18 years old". In C. P. Freeman (Ed.) *The ECT Handbook.* (Council Report CR 39) London: Royal College of Psychiatrists.

Geddes, J. R., Game, D., Jenkins, N E., Peterson, L A., Pottinger, G R. & Sackett D. L. (1996). "What proportion of primary psychiatric interventions are based on evidence from randomised control trials?" *Quality in Health Care*, 5, 215-217.

Gostin L., 1986 - *Mental Health Services Law and Practice*. London: Shaw and Sons.

Gourney, K., Sandford, T., Johnson, S. & Thornicroft, G. (1997) "Dual diagnosis of severe mental health problems and substance abuse / dependence: a major priority for mental health nursing". *Journal of Psychiatric and Mental health Nursing*, 4, pp. 89-95

Gourney K., Ward M., Thornicroft G. & Wright S. (1998) "Crisis in the capital: inpatient care in inner London". *Mental Health Practice*, 1, 5, pp. 10-18.

Greenwood, N. (1999) "Satisfaction with inpatient psychiatric services' relationship to patients and treatment factors". *British Journal of Psychiatry*, 174, pp. 159-63

Harris, E C. & Barraclough, B. (1998) "Excess Mortality of Mental Disorder". *British Journal of Psychiatry*, 173, pp. 11-53.

Harris, J. (1999) *Evaluation Report: MHAC Race and Culture Training. The Ethnicity and Health Unit*, University of Central Lancashire. Unpublished: MHAC internal report.

Higgins, R., Hurst, K. & Wistow, G. (1998) *The Mental Health Nursing Care Provided for Acute Psychiatric Patients*. Research Bulletin, June. Leeds: The Nuffield Institute for Health.

Hoggett, B. (1996) *Mental Health Law*. London: Sweet and Maxwell

Hurst K. (1993) *Nursing Workforces Planning*. Longman.

Hurst K. (1995) "Promotions and relegations: the psychiatric nursing league". *Journal of Nursing Management*, 3, pp. 43-46

Johnson, S., et al. (1997) *London's Mental Health: Report to the King's Fund London Commission*. London: King's Fund.

Jones, R. (1996) *Mental Health Act Manual (5th ed)*. London: Sweet and Maxwell.

Kaye, C. (1998) "Hallmarks of a Secure Psychiatric Service for Women". *Psychiatric Bulletin* 22 no. 3 pp. 137-9

Kluiter, H. (1997). "Inpatient treatment and care arrangements to replace or avoid it - searching for an evidence-based practice". *Current Opinion in Psychiatry*, 10, 160-167.

McDermott G. (1998) "The Care Programme Approach: A patient perspective". *Nursing Times Research*, 3, 1, 47-63.

Mackay, R., and Machin, D, (1998) "Transfers from Prison to Hospital - the Operation of Section 48 of the Mental Health Act". *Research Findings No. 84*. London: Home Office

Macpherson, W. (1999) *The Stephen Lawrence Inquiry*. London: The Stationery Office

Marriott, S., Audini, B., Webb. Y., Duffett, R. & Lelliott, P. (1998) *Research into the Mental Health Act. Phase 1*. Royal College of Psychiatrists Research Unit: unpublished.

Munshi, S. (1999) "Registered Nursing Homes and the Mental Health Act 1983". *Journal of Mental Health Law*, no. 1. pp. 33-40

Meltzer H., Gill B., Petticrew M. & Hinds K. (1996) "Physical complaints, service use and treatment of adults with psychiatric disorders". *OPCS Surveys of Psychiatric Morbidity in Great Britain. Report 2.* London: HMSO.

MILMIS Project Group. (1995) "Monitoring Inner London Mental Illness Services". *Psychiatric Bulletin,* **19**, 276-280.

NHS Executive (1996) *Complaints: Listening, Acting and Improving. Guidance on the Implementation of the NHS Complaints Procedure* (EL(96)19)

NHS Health Advisory Service (1996) *The Substance of Young Needs.* London: HMSO.

Penal Affairs Consortium (1998) *An Unsuitable Place for Treatment.*

Percy, Lord (1957) *Report of the Royal Commission on the Law Relating to Mental Illness and Mental Deficiency 1954 - 57*, Cmd. 169. London: HMSO.

Pinfold, V., Bindman, J., Friedl, K., Beck, A., & Thornicroft, G., (1999) "Supervised discharge orders in England. Compulsory care in the community". *Psychiatric Bulletin,* 23 pp. 199-203

Rangecroft, M. E. H., Tyrer, S. P. & Berney T.P. (1997) "The use of seclusion and emergency medication in a hospital for people with learning disability". *British Journal of Psychiatry* 170: 273-7

Robertson C. & Freeman C P. (1995) "Scottish survey of ECT clinics". *In Clinical Research & Audit Group of the Scottish Office Consensus Report on ECT* (ed. C. Freeman). Scotland: CRAG.

Royal College of Psychiatrists (1997) *Standards of Places of safety under Section 136 of the Mental health Act (1983)* - Council Report CR61

Royal College of Psychiatrists (1998) *Not Just Bricks and Mortar. Report of the Royal College of Psychiatrists Working Party on the size, staffing, structure, siting and security of new adult psychiatric in-patient units.* Council Report CR62. London: Royal College of Psychiatrists.

Sandford T., (1995) "Drug Use is Increasing". *Nursing Standard* 9: 38, pp. 16-17

Sainsbury Centre for Mental Health (1998) *Acute Problems: A survey of the quality of care in acute psychiatric wards.* London: The Sainsbury Centre for Mental Health.

Shaw, M. (1999) The National CAMHS Audit. *Mental Health Review,* 4 issue 1, pp. 22-3

Street, R. (1998) *The restricted hospital order: from court to the community.* Home Office Research Study 186.

Social Services Inspectorate (1998) *A Matter of Choice for Carers.* Inspection of local authority supports for carers. Department of Health.

Social Services Inspectorate (1999) *Still Building Bridges. The Report of a National Inspection of Arrangements for the Integration of the Care Programme Approach with Care Management.* Department of Health.

Takei, N., Persaud, R., Woodruff, I., Brockington, I., & Murray, R. M. (1998) "First episodes of psychosis in Afro-Caribbean and White People". *British Journal of Psychiatry* 172, pp. 147-153

Taylor, P.J., Goldberg, E., Leese, M., Butwell, M. & Reed, A. (1999) "Limits to the value of mental health review tribunals for offender patients". *British Journal of Psychiatry* 174 164-9.

Welsh Office (1998) Putting Patients First. Stationery Office

Welsh Office (1998) Admission of Patients to mental health facilities in Wales 1996-97. Report No: HAS/98/02.

Welsh Office (1999) Admission of Patients to mental health facilities in Wales 1997-98.

Weaver, T., Renton, A., Stimson, G. & Tyrer, P. (1999) "Editorial: Severe mental illness and substance misuse". *British Medical Journal*, 318, pp. 137-8.

# 1 The Mental Health Act Commission Policy on Openness

1. The Mental Health Act Commission was established in 1983 as a Special Health Authority. The Commission's headquarters is **Maid Marian House, 56 Hounds Gate, Nottingham NG1 6BG**. Its essential role is to keep under review the implementation of the 1983 Mental Health Act (the Act) as it relates to patients detained under its provisions; its various functions are set out in the following sections of this policy statement.

2. This policy document is published as a result of the Government's intention to secure greater access of information to the public about services provided under the National Health Service and takes account of the Code of Practice on Openness in the NHS issued by the NHS Executive in 1995 and the Code of Practice on Access to Government Information issued in January 1997. The Commission also subscribes to the Public Bodies (Admission to Meetings) Act 1960.

3. In respect of each of the functions described in paragraph 6 to 15 below the Commission will, to such extent as may be appropriate and practicable, provide information about:

   3.1 its general polices concerning the discharge of each function;

   3.2 its guidance as to the manner in which patients and other interested parties should be interviewed;

   3.3 the cost of the discharge of the function;

   3.4 such conclusions as can properly be derived from patients or others as to the value or effectiveness of the discharge of the function;

   3.5 general issues of concern which may become apparent from the discharge of the function;

   3.6 the manner in which the Commission draws to the notice of those concerned such examples of good and bad practice as may be identifiable.

4. In respect of each of the functions described, the Commission will not normally provide information which may be withheld under one or more of 15 exemptions in Part 11 of the Code of Practice on Access to Government Information. Exemptions which are likely to be of relevance are:

   4.1 the disclosure of internal policy advice or opinion which has been given to Ministers leading up to a policy decision;

   4.2 the release of information which might undermine the efficient running of the Department of Health or some other public body or authority;

4.3  information which has been given in confidence (including where individual patients can be identified).

Where requests for information have been refused in whole or part, applicants will be told which exemptions were considered relevant and why.

The various functions of the Commission are now considered in detail.

5.  The function imposed by Section 120(1) of the Act of keeping under review the exercise of the powers and the discharge of the duties conferred or imposed by the Act so far as they relate to the detention of patients or to patients liable to be detained under the Act.

    5.1  The Commission will provide information concerning:

        5.1.1  the scope and nature of the information collected by the Commission;

        5.1.2  the sources from which it is collected;

        5.1.3  the method by which it is collated, edited and made available to those wishing to see it;

        5.1.4  the arrangements for the systematic study of the information.

6.  The function imposed by Section 120(1)(a) of visiting and interviewing detained patients.

    6.1  The Commission will provide information concerning:

        6.1.1  visiting programmes (except for unannounced visits);

        6.1.2  the results of visits and the nature of any subsequent correspondence with the managers of the hospital or mental nursing home but not so as to disclose the identities of individual patients visited or of any persons (whether or not officers or members of the staff of the hospital or mental nursing home) referred to by patients[1]

7.  The function imposed by Section 120(1)(b)(I) and Section 120(1)(b)(ii) of investigating complaints.

    7.1  The Commission will provide information concerning:

        7.1.1  its guidance as to how interviews with complainants should be conducted and recorded and as to the action (if any) properly to be taken following investigation;

        7.1.2  the numbers and types of complaints received;

        7.1.3  the numbers of complaints received but not investigated, with the reasons for non-investigation.

    7.2  The Commission will not provide details of individual complaints.

---

[1] The Commission's normal action is to refer the enquirer to the unit visited initially and only if the request for information is refused will the Commission respond directly.

8.   The function imposed by Section 121(2)(a) of appointing registered medical practitioners to give second opinions for the purpose of Part IV of the Act or certificates for the purposes of Section 118(2) of the Act.

  8.1  The Commission will provide information concerning:

    8.1.1  the criteria which it applies in considering appointments;

    8.1.2  the numbers and names of the registered medical practitioners holding appointment at any time;

    8.1.3  the number of second opinions provided in any given period and their cost;

    8.1.4  the number of certificates provided pursuant to Section 118(2) and their cost.

9.   The function imposed by Section 121(2)(a) of appointing other persons for the purposes of Section 57(2)(a) of the Act.

  9.1  The Commission will provide information concerning:

    9.1.1  the criteria which it applies in considering appointments;

    9.1.2  the numbers and names and professional addresses of the persons holding appointment at any time;

    9.1.3  the number of certificates provided for the purposes of Section 57(2) in any given period and their cost.

10.  The function imposed by Section 121(2)(b) of receiving reports on patients' treatment and condition pursuant to Section 61 of the Act.

  10.1 The Commission will provide information concerning:

    10.1.1 its procedures for ensuring that the reports required under Section 61 are given at the specified times and contain such information as is reasonably required by the Commission;

    10.1.2 its policy in respect of the evaluation of the reports and any further action required to be taken;

    10.1.3 the cost of receiving and evaluating the reports and of taking such further action in regard to those reports as may be necessary;

    10.1.4 the number of occasions on which the Commission gives notice for the purposes of Section 61(3).

11.  The function of monitoring the implementation of the Code of Practice referred to in Section 118 of the Act and of advising on appropriate changes.

11.1 The Commission will provide information as to:

11.1.1 its procedures for identifying from reports and other sources matters which might usefully alter or amplify the Code of Practice as it exists from time to time;

11.1.2 its procedures for inviting proposals from other persons or bodies concerning the Code of Practice and for collating and evaluating any such proposals.

11.2 The Commission, except with the approval of the Secretary of State, will not provide information as to the nature of any recommendations which it may make to the Secretary of State.

12.    The function of advising the Secretary of State about additional forms of medical treatment giving rise to special concern, pursuant to Section 118(2) of the Act.

12.1 The Commission will provide information about:

12.1.1 any proposals received from Commissioners or others as to any such medical treatments;

12.1.2 its arrangements for evaluating such proposals.

13.    The function imposed by Section 121(7) of the Act of reviewing decision to withhold postal packages pursuant to the provisions of Section 134.

13.1 The Commission will provide information concerning:

13.1.1 its interpretation of the provisions of Section 134 of the Act;

13.1.2  its policy for dealing with applications to review any decision by the Mangers of a hospital to withhold a postal package;

13.1.3 the number of applications received, the number investigated and the outcome (ie. whether or not the decision to withhold a postal package was upheld);

13.1.4 patterns of withholding as between different hospitals if they can be identified from the cases investigated by the Commission.

13.2 The Commission will not give details of individual instances of the withholding of patient's postal packages or any associated correspondence.

14.    The function imposed by Section 121(10) of publishing a Biennial Report.

14.1 The Commission will provide information about its arrangements for obtaining, collating and processing information on its activities relevant to the Biennial Report.

14.2 The Commission will not disclose details of a Biennial Report prior to its publication, except that units may be notified when an example of practice in the Report is drawn from their service.

15.    The Senior Officer of the Commission responsible for the operation of this policy and for ensuring that the Commission complies with the Code is the Office Manager (hereinafter called "The Responsible Officer"). He/she will report directly to the Chief Executive. He/she works from Maid Marian House (see paragraph 2) and his/her telephone number is 0115 9437100.

16. Requests for information from the Commission should be addressed to the Responsible Officer.

17. Requests for information will be acknowledged within 4 working days and in most cases the information requested should follow within 20 working days.

18. Information will normally be provided free of charge, but if its collection seems likely to prove difficult or expensive, the person requesting it will be advised of the probable cost and asked whether he or she wishes to withdraw his application.

19. Complaints about failure to provide information, or the cost of its provision, or about delay should be made within 3 months to the Responsible Officer. If the complainant remains dissatisfied, the matter in issue should be raised with the Chief Executive of the Commission. If, in the opinion of the complainant, the Chief Executive does not deal with the matter satisfactorily, reference may be made to the Health Service Ombudsman whose address is Church House, Great Smith Street, London SW1P 3BW.

Reviewed and updated November 1997

# Mental Health Act Commission Members 1997-1999

| | | |
|---|---|---|
| **Chairman** | Dame Ruth Runciman OBE (until 30 Nov 1999) | |
| **Acting Chairman** | Mr Gordon Lakes | |
| **Vice Chairman** | Professor Richard Williams | |

**Lay Members**

| | | |
|---|---|---|
| Mrs J Rogers | Mrs J Spencer | Ms C Bamber |
| Mrs A Anderson | Mrs B Stroll | |

**Lay Visit Members**

| | | |
|---|---|---|
| Ms M Nettle | Mrs A Cooney | Mr S Hedges |
| Mr B Burke | Mrs J Gossage | Mr M Wilce |
| Mrs F Eliot | Miss I Reinbach | Mr E Wong |
| Ms J Hesmondhalgh | MS H Burke | |

**Legal Members**

| | | |
|---|---|---|
| Ms J Tweedie | Mr A Eaton | Ms N Rickman |
| Mrs J Olsen | Mr R Robinson | Mrs J Patterson |
| Mrs M Lloyd | Ms C Grimshaw | Ms A Henry |
| Mr J Horne | Mrs C Bond | Mr A Eldergill |
| Professor M Gunn | Mrs S Breach | Ms G McMorrow |
| Mr H Chapman | | |

**Legal Visit Members**

| | | |
|---|---|---|
| Mr T Wrigglesworth | Mr M Frost | Mr D Hewitt |
| Mr J Sedgman | Miss L Marriott | Mrs A McKenna |
| Ms A Lawrence | Ms C Parker | Ms D Johnson |
| Ms J Burton | Mr C Inyama | Ms G Downham |

**Medical Members**

| | | |
|---|---|---|
| Dr S Bannerjee | Dr D Black | DR O Daniels |
| Dr J Holiday | Dr N Fisher | Dr C Davies |
| Dr D Dick | Dr J MacKenzie | Dr M Swan |
| Dr C Berry | Dr S Francis | Dr D Black |
| Dr T Jerram | Dr R Mather | Professor M Weller |
| Dr T Zigmond | Professor J Scott | Dr P Hettiaratchy |
| Dr S Soni | Dr G Pryce | Dr E Miller |
| Dr T O'Hare | | |

**Medical Visit Members**

| | | |
|---|---|---|
| Dr C Foster | Dr I Mian | Dr S Manjubhashini |

**Nursing Members**

| | | |
|---|---|---|
| Mr D Hill | Mrs R Riddle | Mr H Field |
| Miss C Harvey | Mr D McCarthy | Mr C Aggett |

Mr A Persaud
Mr C McCarthy
Mr S Gannon
**Nursing Visit Members**
Mr M Naylor
Ms P McKenzie
Mr M Dodds
Mrs C Baptiste-Cyrus
Mr R Southern
Mr A Best
Mr R Dosoo
**Psychology Members**
Ms E Rassaby
Ms P Spinks
**Psychology Visit Members**
Mrs A Sayal-Bennett
**Social Work Members**
Mr E Prtak
Mr S Klein
Mr P Howes
Mr J Walker
Mr R Lingham
Ms L Jones
Mr B Windle
**Social Work Visit Members**
Mr M Follows
Mrs M Madden
Ms M Napier
Mrs J Healy
Mr R Nichol
Mr R Bamlett
Mr A Wright
Ms G Heath
**Specialist Members**
Mr G Lakes
Ms P Letts
Mr K Patel
Professor D West
**Specialist Visit Members**
Mr P Lee
Mrs A Navarro
Mrs S Ramprogrus
Canon F Longbottom
Mr T Wright
Ms B Allwood

Mr A Morley
Mr S Pierre
Mr N Lees

Ms M Caswell
Ms S McKeever
Mr A Deery
Mr H Davis
Ms L Ndoro
Ms J Turnball

Ms H Roberts
Dr B Ashcroft

Mrs S Ledwith

Mr J Cohen
Ms H Lewis
Mr R Brown
Mrs E Frost
Mr W Morgan
Mrs S McMillan

Mrs B Sensky
Ms P Heslop
Mr J Moran
Mrs C Hewitt
Mrs J Lewis
Mr M Beebe
Mr M Hefferman
Mrs P McCaig

Dr R Ryall
Dr D Brandford
Mr C Curran
Mrs J Prior

Mr Y Marsen-Luther
Ms G Gower
Mr T Wishart
Ms N Chesworth
Mr R Mason

Mr R Earle
Mr M Hill

Mrs M Dos Anjos
Mr J Marlow
Mrs K Berry
Miss M McCann
Mr N Khan
Mr S Ramrecha

Mr R Webster
Mr J Sharich (deceased)

Mrs A Anderson
Mr A Williamson
Mrs H Ross
Mr G Holliday
Mr R Plumb
Ms L Bolter

Mr A Drew
Mrs R Williams-Flew
Mr M Golightley
Ms B Howard
Mrs H Thomas
Mr D Lee
Mrs C Sheehy

Ms M Purcell
Inspector N North
Ms L Ingham
Mr A Milligan

Mrs K Sheldon
Mrs J Meredith
Mr J Woolmore
Ms M Garner
Mrs E Meade

# Sections 58 and 57 Appointees 1997-1999

## Section 58 Appointed Doctors

Dr M Abdurahman
Dr R Abed
Dr P Abraham
Dr M Alldrick
Dr S Ananthakopan
Dr T Ananthanarayanan
Dr D Atapattu
Dr D Battin
Dr S Benbow
Dr L Berraondo
Dr K Bergman
Dr C Berry
Dr J Besson
Dr M Bethell
Dr D J Bevington
Dr K Bhakta
Dr E Birchall
Dr N Bishay
Dr R N Bloor
Prof R S Bluglass
Dr J Bolton
Dr N Bouras
Dr C E Boyd
Dr C Brook
Dr A C Brown
Dr N Brown
Dr M Browne
Dr A Burke
Dr C Calvert
Dr M Cashman
Dr R Chitty
Dr M Cleary
Dr J Cockburn
Dr J Conway
Dr M Conway
Dr M Courtney

Dr S Craske
Dr R Davenport
Dr I Davidson
Dr C Davies
Dr J Davies
Dr M Davies
Dr N Davies
Dr K Davison
Dr K Day
Dr V Deacon
Dr N Desai
Dr M Devakumar
Dr R Devine
Dr D Dick
Dr A Drummond
Dr G Dubourg
Dr K Dudleston
Dr D Dunleavy
Dr J Dunlop
Dr A Easton
Dr H Edwards
Dr S Edwards
Dr V Evans
Dr A Fairbairn
Dr G Feggetter
Dr T Fenton
Dr S Fernando
Dr J Fisher
Dr M Forth
Dr R Gall
Dr E Gallagher
Dr G Gallimore
Dr C Ghosh
Dr N Gittleson
Dr M Goonatilleke
Dr E Gordon

Dr H Gordon
Dr C Green
Dr E Gregg
Dr G Grewal
Dr J Grimshaw
Dr K Gupta
Dr J Hailstone
Dr M Harper
Dr T Harrison
Dr F Harrop
Dr B Harwin
Dr M Hession
Dr P Hettiaratchy
Dr S Hettiaratchy
Dr O Hill
Dr R Hughes
Dr G Hughes
Dr M Humphreys
Dr M Hussain
Dr J Hutchinson
Dr G Ibrahimi
Dr S Iles
Dr H James
Dr S James
Dr P Jefferys
Dr J Jenkins
Dr B John
Dr D Jones
Dr R Jones
Dr F Judelsohn
Dr A Kaeser
Dr G Kanakaratnam
Dr I Keitch
Dr D Kellam
Dr T Kerr
Dr K Khan

Dr D Kohen
Dr L Kremer
Dr G Langley
Dr L Liebling
Dr N Lockhart
Dr B Lowe
Dr J Lyon
Dr S Malik
Dr B Mann
Dr P Marshall
Dr G Mathur
Dr F McKenzie
Dr D McVitie
Dr L Measey
Dr G Mehta
Dr I Mian
Dr G Milner
Dr A Minto
Dr N Minton
Dr B Moore
Dr J Mumford
Dr D Myers
Dr G Nanayakkara
Dr C Narayana
Dr T Nelson
Dr H Nissenbaum
Dr J Noble
Dr M O'Brien

Dr S Olivieri
Dr R Orr
Dr S Palia
Dr A Patel
Dr I Pennell
Dr A Perini
Dr J Phillips
Dr R Philpott
Dr W Prothero
Dr I Pryce
Dr Raj-manickam
Dr D Rajapakse
Dr D Ramster
Dr S Rastogi
Dr N Renton
Dr E Richards
Dr J Robertson
Dr J Rucinski
Dr A Rugg
Dr R Sagovsky
Dr M Salih
Dr G Sampson
Dr Sarkar
Dr P Sebaratnam
Dr A Sheikh
Dr G Shetty
Dr A Silverman
Dr I Singh

Dr M Smith
Dr S Soni
Dr V Spotswood
Dr C Staley
Dr D Stephens
Dr M Swan
Dr R Symonds
Dr L Tarlo
Dr R Thavasothy
Dr R Thaya-paran
Dr J Thomas
Dr I Thomson
Dr R Toms
Dr N Tyre
Dr P Urwin
Dr H Verma
Dr G Vincenti
Dr J Waite
Dr G Wallen
Dr A Walsh
Dr D Ward
Dr B Weerakoon
Dr Y Wiley
Dr A Wilson
Dr S Wood
Dr A Yonace
Dr T Zigmond

## Section 57 Panel Members

### Appointed Doctors

Dr E Carr
Dr C Davies
Dr K Day
Dr D Dunleavy

Dr E Gordon
Dr J Grimshaw
Dr M Harper
Dr P Jefferys

Dr G Langley
Dr F Oyebode
Dr L Tarlo

### Appointed Persons

Mr A Ball
Mrs C Bennett
Dr A Blowers
Mr E Chitty
Mr H Davis
Prof B Dimond
Mr M Edwardes-Evans
Mrs J Hanham
Archdeacon A Hawes

Mr G Lakes
Mrs R Lewis
Rev B Lillington
Mr R Lingham
Ms G Linton
Mr C McCarthy
Mr A Milligan
Mrs M Morris
Ms M Nettle

Ms C Parker
Mr A Parkin
Mr T Peel
Ms J Pinschof
Dr R Ryall
Mr G Smith
Mr H Teaney
Mr D Torpy
Mr L Wilson

**APPENDIX**

## Summary of Finances

## STATEMENT OF THE CHIEF EXECUTIVE'S RESPONSIBILITIES AS THE ACCOUNTABLE OFFICER OF THE ORGANISATION

The Secretary of State has directed that the Chief Executive should be the Accountable Officer to the organisation. The relevant responsibilities of Accountable Officers, including their responsibility for the property and regularity of the public finances for which they are answerable, and for the keeping of proper records, are set out in Accountable Officer's Memorandum issued by the NHS Executive.

To the best of my knowledge and belief, I have properly discharged the responsibilities set out in my letter of appointment as an Accountable Officer.

Dated:   3/8/98                  Signed:   _William Bingley_

                                               Chief Executive

## STATEMENT OF DIRECTORS' RESPONSIBILITIES IN RESPECT OF THE ACCOUNTS

The Directors are required under the National Health Service Act 1977 to prepare accounts for each financial year. The Secretary of State, with the approval of the Treasury, directs that these accounts give a true and fair view of the state of affairs of the organisation and of the income and expenditure of the organisation for that period. In preparing those accounts, Directors are required to:

◆  Apply on a consistent basis accounting policies laid down by the Secretary of State with the approval of the Treasury

◆  Make judgements and estimates which are reasonable and prudent

◆  State whether applicable accounting standards have been followed, subject to any material departures disclosed and explained in the account

The Directors confirm that they have complied with the above requirements in preparing the accounts.

The Directors are responsible for keeping proper accounting records which disclose with reasonable accuracy at any time the financial position of the organisation and to enable them to ensure that the accounts comply with the requirements outlined in the above mentioned direction by the Secretary of State.

By Order of the Board

Dated:    3/8/98                       Signed:    *Willer Bingly*

                                                            Chief Executive

Dated:    3/8/98

                                                          Director of Finance

## STATEMENT OF DIRECTOR'S RESPONSIBILITY IN RESPECT OF INTERNAL FINANCIAL CONTROL

The Chief Executive as Accountable Officer, together with the other Directors, has responsibility for ensuring that there is an appropriate[1] system of internal financial control within the organisation. This system must provide reasonable assurance of:

◆    The safeguarding of assets against unauthorised use or disposal

◆    The maintenance of proper accounting records; and

◆    The reliability of financial information used within the organisation or for external publication.

No system can provide absolute assurance against material mis-statement or loss but the system should provide reasonable assurance that material errors, irregularities or fraud are either prevented or would be detected within a timely period.

The Chief Executive as Accountable Officer, together with the other Directors, has responsibility for reviewing the organisation's system of internal control as required in HSG(97)17.

In carrying out the review, as set out in EL(97)55, the Directors are required to confirm that:

◆    The organisation has an appropriate system of internal financial control

◆    The 'minimum control standards' laid down by the NHS Executive have been in existence within the organisation throughout the financial year.

◆    The Directors confirm that they have undertaken the review and the above requirements have been met.

◆    The Commission did not have in place for the 1997/98 financial year a Fraud and Corruption policy.

---

[1]  Appropriate is defined in EL(97)55 as 'fit for the purpose for which they were intended'

◆   The Commission does not have an Audit Committee, instead there is a Finance Sub-Committee of the Management Board.

By Order of the Board

Dated:   3/8/98

Signed:   *Willer Bingly*

Chief Executive

# AUDITORS' REPORT

We certify that we have completed the audit of the financial statements on pages 8 to 16, which have been prepared in accordance with the accounting policies relevant to the National Health Service as set out on page 10.

## Respective Responsibilities of Directors and Auditors

As described above the Directors are responsible for the preparation of financial statements. It is our responsibly to form an independent opinion, based on our audit on those statements, and to report our opinion to you.

## Basis of Opinion

We carried out our audit in accordance with part 1 of the National Health Service and Community Care Act 1990 and the Code of Audit Practice issued by the Audit Commission, which requires compliance with relevant auditing standards.

Our audit included examination, on a test basis, of evidence relevant to the amounts and disclosures in the financial statements. It also included an assessment of the significant estimates and judgements made by the authority in the preparation of the financial statements, and of whether the accounting policies are appropriate to the authority's circumstances, consistently applied and adequately disclosed.

We planned and performed our audit so as to obtain all the information and explanations which we considered necessary in order to provide us with sufficient evidence to give reasonable assurance that the financial statements are free from material misstatement, whether caused by fraud or other irregularity or error. In forming our opinion we also evaluated the overall adequacy of the presentation of information in the financial statements.

## Opinion

In our opinion the financial statements give a true and fair view of the state of affairs of the Mental Health Act Commission at 31 March 1998 and its income and expenditure for the year then ended.

Dated:   5/8/98

Signed:   *C B WILSON*

Name:     C B Wilson

## REPORT BY AUDITORS TO THE MENTAL HEALTH ACT COMMISSION ON INTERNAL FINANCIAL CONTROL

In addition to our audit work on the financial statements, we have reviewed the statement of directors' responsibilities in respect of internal financial control set out on page 4 in compliance with the NHS Executive's directions set out in EL(97)55.

We carried out our review in accordance with the approach set out in the Audit Commission's Technical Release 37/97 relating to internal financial control. This does not require us to perform the additional work necessary to, and we do not, express any opinion on the effectiveness of the Commission's system of internal financial control.

Our review was not performed for any purpose connected with any specific transaction and should not be relied upon for any such purpose.

### Opinion

With respect o the directors' statements on internal financial control on page 4, in our opinion the directors have provided the disclosures required by EL(97)55 and the statement is not inconsistent with the information of which we are aware from our audit carried out under the Code of Practice.

Dated:    5/8/98                              Signed:    C B WILSON

                                             Name:      C B Wilson

## INCOME AND EXPENDITURE FOR THE YEAR ENDING 31 MARCH 1998

|  | Notes | 1997/98 £000 | 1996/97 £000 |
|---|---|---|---|
| **INCOME** |  |  |  |
| Advances from the Department of Health and Welsh Office | 2 | 2665 | 2567 |
| **EXPENDITURE** |  |  |  |
| Members' fees and expenses | 3 | 1809 | 1839 |
| Administrative support staff salaries | 4.1 | 547 | 503 |
| Other Operating Expenses | 5 | 343 | 293 |
| Total Expenditure |  | 2699 | 2635 |
| DEFICIT FOR THE FINANCIAL YEAR |  | (34) | (68) |

The Commission has no recognised gains or losses other than the surplus for the year.

## BALANCE SHEET AS AT 31 MARCH 1998

| Notes | | 31 March 1998 £000 | 31 March 1997 £000 |
|---|---|---|---|
| **CURRENT ASSETS** |  |  |  |
| Debtors 6 |  | 29 | 38 |
| Cash in hand |  | 5 | 8 |
| **CURRENT LIABILITIES** |  |  |  |
| Creditors : falling due within one year | 7 | (212) | (190) |
| TOTAL ASSETS LESS CURRENT LIABILITIES |  | (178) | (144) |
| **FINANCED BY:** |  |  |  |
| Income and Expenditure Reserve |  | (178) | (144) |

## CASH FLOW STATEMENT AS AT 31 MARCH 1998

|  | 31 March 1998 £000 | 31 March 1997 £000 |
|---|---|---|
| Net cash inflow from operating activities | (3) | 0 |
| Increase/(Decrease) in cash | (3) | 0 |

## NOTES TO THE ACCOUNTS

1. Accounting Policies

1.1 Accounting Conventions

This account has been prepared in accordance with the standard accounting practice for NHS approved by the Secretary of State and accounts directions issued by the Secretary of State with approval by Treasury.

1.2 Income Allocations

The Department of Health make payments on behalf of the Commission within an approved cash limit; a recharge is made to the Welsh Office. These payments on the Commission's behalf are recorded as income in the Commission's accounts on a cash basis.

1.3 Leases

Rentals under operating leases are charged on a straight-line basis over the terms of the leases.

1.4 Public Sector Payment Policy

The Department of Health pays all invoices on behalf of the Commission and therefore information on adherence to Public Sector Payment Policy is not readily available.

1.5 Pension Costs

The Commission participates in the Principal Civil Service Pension Scheme (PCSPS), the Civil Service Compensation Scheme (CSCS) and other statutory schemes made under the Superannuation Act 1972.

Expenditure on the Civil Superannuation Vote covers the payment of pensions and other superannuation benefits and injury benefits to civil servants and staff of certain fringe bodies, to former civil servants or to their dependants. It also covers the payment of annual compensation arising from early retirements that are funded by lump sum payments made by departments and agencies in a previous financial year. In common with most other public service schemes the PCSPS is unfunded. The Civil Service Pensions Division of the Cabinet Office manages the Civil Service Superannuation Vote.

Individual members bear a share of the pension costs in two ways; through making an explicit contribution of 1.5% of salary, and by pay being set at levels lower than would be appropriate if the value of pension benefits we not taken into account. The balance of costs is met by departments and agencies through accruing superannuation liability charges, which are the equivalent of the contributions made by employers in the private sector to an occupational pension arrangement. The charges are based on the principle of meeting pension costs as they are accrued by members rather than when expenditure on benefits is incurred. The balance of pension costs is met on a pay-as-you-go basis from the Civil Superannuation Vote.

The Civil Service Additional Voluntary Contribution Scheme is a money purchase arrangement linked to the Equitable Life Assurance Society and/or the Scottish Widows' Fund and Life Assurance Society. Members can choose to pay contributions, which can either be used to provide additional life cover, or be paid into an individual fund where they build up until retirement when the fund is used to purchase a pension.

Expenditure on the Civil Superannuation Vote for the payment of pensions and other benefits to or in respect of former staff is not directly related to the current staff costs of each departmental programme. Departments, agencies and other bodies meet the cost of the pension cover provided through the PCSPS for their staff by payment of charges calculated on an accrual basis, the rates of which are reassessed every three years by the Government Actuary. Charges are specified for different groups of civil servants according to their grade. The costs of early retirement are met by the last employing Department under the CSCS.

## 1.6  Tax Liability

The Commission meets its tax liability by way of the Agreed Voluntary Settlement. All funds allocated for this purpose are transferred by the Department of Health who make the necessary arrangements with the Inland Revenue. Funds cannot be utilised for operational purposes. These accounts do not show the amount received or transferred.

| | Note | 31 March 1998 £000 | 31 March 1997 £000 |
|---|---|---|---|
| 2 | **Receipts** | | |
| | Advances from the Department of Health | 2590 | 2493 |
| | Advances from the Welsh Office | 65 | 65 |
| | Other Receipt | 10 | 9 |
| | **Total** | 2665 | 2567 |
| 3 | **Members' fees and expenses** | | |
| | Commission members' fees | 765 | 749 |
| | Commission members' expenses | 231 | 337 |
| | Second Opinion Appointed Doctors' fees | 711 | 657 |
| | Second Opinion Appointed Doctors' expenses | 102 | 96 |
| | **Total** | 1809 | 1839 |
| 4.1 | **Staff Costs** | | |
| | Salaries | 462 | 421 |
| | Social Security Payments | 85 | 81 |
| | Agency costs | 0 | 1 |
| | **Total** | 547 | 503 |

## Average number of staff

4.2 The average number of employees (excluding agency staff) in 1997/98 was 35. (1996/97 - 29staff)

4.3 Members Remuneration

Executive members of the Management Board are civil service staff seconded from the Department of Health. The total remuneration paid to executive members is £74,000. (1996/97 - £69,000).

The Chairman's emoluments, excluding employer's pension contributions was £17,370. (1996/97 - £16,000).

The remuneration of other Board members fell within the following ranges

| Range £ | 1997/98 Number | 1996/97 Number |
|---|---|---|
| Up to 5,000 | 4 | 1 |

4.4 The Chief Executive's total remuneration including the employer's contribution to the Civil Service Pension Scheme, was £54,000. He was the only employee who received in excess of £40,000. (1996/97 - £45,000).

| | Note | 31 March 1998 £000 | 31 March 1997 £000 |
|---|---|---|---|
| 5 | **Other Operating Expenses** | | |
| | Non Executive Management Board Members | 18 | 21 |
| | Premises and fixed plant | 170 | 114 |
| | Establishment expenses | 106 | 121 |
| | Appointed auditor's remuneration | 9 | 8 |
| | Transport and moveable plant | 40 | 29 |
| | **Total** | 343 | 293 |

5.1 Hire and operating lease rentals include £4,000 in respect of hire of plant and machinery. (1996/97 - £2,000)

| | Note | 31 March 1998 | 31 March 1997 |
|---|---|---|---|
| 6 | **Debtors** | | |
| | VAT recoverable | 4 | 12 |
| | Prepayments | 25 | 26 |
| | **Total** | 29 | 38 |
| 7 | **Creditors: falling due within 1 year** | | |
| | Income Tax and Social Security | 22 | 21 |
| | Staff Salaries | 120 | 109 |
| | Other Creditors | 70 | 60 |
| | **Total** | 212 | 190 |
| 8 | **Net Cash inflow/(outflow) from operating activities** | | |
| | Operating deficit | (34) | (68) |
| | Decrease in debtors | 9 | 40 |
| | Increase in creditors | 22 | 28 |
| | **Total** | (3) | 0 |

9. Analysis of changes in debt

|  | 31 March 1997 £000 | Cash Flows | 31 March 1998 £000 |
|---|---|---|---|
| **Cash in hand** | 8 | 3 | 5 |

10. Related Party Transactions

The Mental Health Act Commission is a body corporate established by order of the Secretary of State for Health.

The Department of Health is regarded as a related party. During the year the Commission has had significant numbers of material transactions with the Department, and with other entities for which the Department is regarded as the parent Department viz:

|  | Income £000 | Expenditure £000 |
|---|---|---|
| Department of Health | 2665 | 2671 |
| Oxfordshire Learning Disabilities NHS Trust | 0 | 10 |

During the year none of the Board Members or members of the key management staff or other related parties has undertaken any material transactions with the Mental Health Act Commission.

# MENTAL HEALTH ACT COMMISSION PUBLICATIONS

## GENERAL INFORMATION

The Commission publishes Guidance Notes (formerly called Practice Notes) which give advice on particular issues drawn to its attention. The Guidance Notes will generally refer to matters not included in the Mental Health Act Code of Practice. Occasionally they will provide amplification or explanation by the Commission of the Code. The Commission will, from time to time, also publish Position Papers and Discussion Papers containing its views on particular issues drawn to its attention.

Any authoritative interpretation of the law can be given only by the courts. In the absence of any judicial decision, the Commission's view of any interpretation can at best only be informed opinion and must not be treated as, or substituted for, professional legal advice.

In order to maintain relevance, Guidance Notes will be reviewed no later than two years following the date of issue.

In March 1999, the Practice and Guidance Notes were updated to accord with the third edition of the Code of Practice..

## COMMISSION PRACTICE / GUIDANCE NOTES AND OTHER PAPERS CURRENTLY AVAILABLE

PRACTICE NOTE 1:      *Guidance on the administration of Clozapine and other treatments requiring blood tests under the provision of Part IV of the Mental Health Act 1983*

PRACTICE NOTE 2:      *Nurses; the administration of medicines for mental disorder and the Mental Health Act*

PRACTICE NOTE 5:      *Guidance on issues relating to the administration of the Mental Health Act in nursing homes registered to receive detained patients (currently subject to review)*

GUIDANCE NOTE 1:      *Guidance to Health Authorities: The Mental Health Act 1983*

GUIDANCE NOTE 2:      *GPs and the Mental Health Act*

GUIDANCE NOTE 3:      *Guidance on the Treatment of Anorexia Nervosa under the Mental Health Act 1983*

GUIDANCE NOTE 2/98:      *Scrutinising and Rectifying Statutory Forms for admission under the Mental Health Act*

GUIDANCE NOTE 1/99:      *Issues Surrounding Sections 17, 18 And 19 of the Mental Health Act 1983*

POSITION PAPER 1:      *Research and Detained Patients*

DISCUSSION PAPER 1:      *The Threshold for Admission and the Deteriorating Patient*

Practice Note 3: *Section 5(2) of the 1983 Mental Health Act and transfers and Practice Note 4: Section 17 of the Mental Health Act* have been withdrawn and replaced by Guidance Note 1/99.

## OTHER RELEVANT PUBLICATIONS

The following publications are available from The Stationary Office stockists:

*The Memorandum on the Mental Health Act 1983* (revised edition, 1998), priced £7.50.

*The Code of Practice on the Mental Health Act 1983* (revised edition, 1999), priced £7.50.

# INDEX